D1607439

TALES FROM KENTUCKY SHERIFFS

TALES FROM
KENTUCKY
SHERIFFS

William Lynwood Montell

THE UNIVERSITY PRESS OF KENTUCKY

Scholarly publisher for the Commonwealth,
serving Bellarmine University, Berea College, Centre
College of Kentucky, Eastern Kentucky University,
The Filson Historical Society, Georgetown College,
Kentucky Historical Society, Kentucky State University,
Morehead State University, Murray State University,
Northern Kentucky University, Transylvania University,
University of Kentucky, University of Louisville,
and Western Kentucky University.
All rights reserved.

Editorial and Sales Offices: The University Press of Kentucky
663 South Limestone Street, Lexington, Kentucky 40508-4008
www.kentuckypress.com

15 14 13 12 11   5 4 3 2 1

Library of Congress Cataloging-in-Publication Data

Montell, William Lynwood, 1931–
 Tales from Kentucky sheriffs / William Lynwood Montell.
   p. cm.
 ISBN 978-0-8131-3404-8 (hardcover : alk. paper) —
 ISBN 978-0-8131-3405-5 (ebook)
 1. Sheriffs—Kentucky—History. I. Title.
 HV7979.M66 2011
 363.28'209769—dc23
                           2011019570
This book is printed on acid-free paper meeting
the requirements of the American National Standard
for Permanence in Paper for Printed Library Materials.

Manufactured in the United States of America.

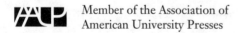 Member of the Association of
American University Presses

This book is dedicated to all sheriffs and former sheriffs across Kentucky whose fascinating, insightful stories made this book possible; and to my wife, Linda; her daughter and son-in-law, Lisa and Nick Atkins; my daughter and her husband, Monisa and Jack Wright; my son, Brad Montell, and his wife, Marla; and all of our grandchildren; also to Michael Ann Williams, head of the folk studies and anthropology department, and Drue Belcher, office associate, at Western Kentucky University.

CONTENTS

INTRODUCTION

Folklore is not the "falsehood of history," as it has been defined by a few academic professors and others in earlier times. In fact, it comprises the history of 99.99 percent of the world's population because it focuses on local culture, on people's lives and times, both past and present, as they are actually lived. As I indicated in my *Tales of Tennessee Lawyers*, "The same assertion is likewise true of oral history, which is both the method by which verbal information about the past and/or present is collected and recorded, and the body of knowledge that exists only in people's memories, which will be lost when they and other members of their generation have died. The body of knowledge about the past that is conveyed through oral history is different from the information typically contained in formal written documents. . . . Thus, orally communicated history can supplement written records by filling in the gaps in formal documents or providing an insider's perspective on momentous events."[1] As a folklorist and oral historian, I know that people everywhere build their lives in accordance with beliefs, customs, practices, and frequently heard stories. Much meaningful history can be written only after oral traditional accounts are adequately researched and documented, in much the same manner as formal sources. Oral history is becoming increasingly useful in conducting research on specific topics, especially those that focus on local life and culture. Thanks to books like this, a meaningful history of sheriffs and the culprits they apprehend is made available to professional, academic, and lay readers.

There are a few early published sources relative to certain facets of the history of Kentucky sheriffs. The first one I located is on file at the Kentucky Library, Western Kentucky University. It was compiled and published in Lexington by John Bradford in 1800. In the section relative to sheriffs it states: "Sheriffs shall be hereafter appointed in the following manner:—When the time of a sheriff for any county may be about to expire, the county court for the same . . . shall in the months of September, October, or November next preceding thereto, recommend to the governor two proper persons to fill the office, who are then justices of the county court; and who shall in such recommendation pay a just regard to seniority in office and a regular rotation. One of the persons so recommended shall be commissioned by the governor, and shall hold his office for two years if he so long behave well, and until a successor be duly qualified. . . . Every person accepting a sheriff's commission, shall in his county, enter into two bonds, with good and sufficient securities, payable to the governor for the time being."[2] Bradford's book goes on to describe the responsibilities of pioneer sheriffs.

Richard H. Stanton's book, published in 1871, offers practical advice to sheriffs, jailers, and coroners in Kentucky in brief sections within chapters, such as: "Who is eligible to the office," "How elected," "Term of office," "Elections, how contested," "Office, how vacated," "Sheriff's identification," "Sheriff's duties," "Place of birth and residence," "Executions," "Monetary responsibilities," "Sheriff's duties in regards to elections," "Arrests," "Bail," and "Conveying prisoners to county jail or penitentiary."[3]

When my books *Tales from Kentucky Lawyers* (2003), *Tales from Kentucky Doctors* (2008), and *Tales from Kentucky Funeral Homes* (2009), all published by the University Press of Kentucky, were in print, I felt it was time to begin a book project focusing on Kentucky sheriffs. Many people in the academic and public sector felt the same way, so they suggested that I interview sheriffs and former sheriffs throughout Kentucky. I contacted these law enforcement officers by telephone and e-mail, and many expressed a willingness to participate. I also attended portions of the annual statewide meeting of Kentucky sheriffs held September 14–18, 2009, in Bowling Green. I explained to potential interviewees that my academic interest lies in preserving the legacy of local life and times, and they became interested in contributing to the preservation of the history of their profession.

I did not attempt to shape the interviews, and thus the book, along lines of age, gender, or geographic location, although I did hope to focus on sheriffs and former sheriffs who were middle-aged or older and had served for several terms (such as Peanuts Gaines, twenty-eight years and still active, and Fuzzy Keesee, thirty-six years and still active), with the rationale that they would have a greater reservoir of memories from which to draw. To my pleasure, however, the younger sheriffs I interviewed also shared some great stories. Regardless of the counties in which they served, each of them had a wonderful diversity of stories to share reflecting the varying social and economic backgrounds fostered by local communities, families, and individuals.

The sheriffs and former sheriffs I interviewed for this book are as follows: Wayne Agent (Crittenden County), Mike Armstrong (Shelby County), Larry L. Bennett (Russell County), Patrick Boggs (Mason County), Charles L. Boston (Wayne County), Keith Cain (Daviess County), Joseph Conn (former sheriff of Wayne County), James Ralph Curry (Adair County), Qulin K. Escue (former sheriff of Grayson County), Jerry "Peanuts" Gaines (Warren County), Jerry "Slick" Gee (Monroe County), LeeRoy Hardin (former sheriff of Boyle County), Boston B. Hensley Jr. (Hart County), Barney Jones (former sheriff of Barren County), Charles E. "Fuzzy" Keesee (Pike County), Charles Lee "Chuck" Korzenborn (Kenton County), William D. Lewis (Lewis County), Glynn Mann (former sheriff of Clinton County), Carl E. Meece (former sheriff of Casey County), Kenneth Lee Morris (former sheriff of Butler County), James Pruitt (Cumberland County), Danny Rogers (Powell County), John E. Shipp (Taylor County), John "Tuffy" Snedegar (Bath County), W. D. "Billy" Stokes (Todd County), Harold E. Tingle (former sheriff of Shelby County), Danny R. Webb (Letcher County), William D. Witten (Johnson County), and Wayne "Tiny" Wright (Woodford County).

The stories included in this book fall within ten categories, all of which were chosen on the basis of the oral accounts provided by the sheriffs interviewed: the sheriffs' election to office, the behavior of people when arrested, mentally deprived people, law enforcement humor, illegal drugs, sheriffs' major problems and significant accomplishments, mistakes, stories about other sheriffs, dangerous or fatal events, and colleagues. The number of stories in each category ranges from few to many. Stories relating to arrested people's behavior, making and selling illegal products, and dangerous or fatal occurrences are the most numerous, thus providing evidence of the vital service sheriffs and other law enforcement personnel perform.

To gather the stories for this book I interviewed numerous sheriffs and former sheriffs. Before sitting down with them to record their stories, I mailed each potential storyteller a page of suggested topics. Approximately one week later I called or e-mailed the interviewees, asking for a convenient date and time for me to drive to their locale to meet with them. My invariable first question was phrased like this:

"Tell me why you decided to run for sheriff, then describe your efforts in seeking election for your first term." After their response to that question, I simply asked them to begin telling stories, choosing any topic that brought a story to their mind. Most of these sessions took from forty-five minutes to one and a half hours.

After each interview session I transcribed the contents of each cassette tape— typically a tedious task, as it takes approximately eight hours to transcribe one hour of tape. Transcription is notoriously subject to error, as sometimes the words spoken by the narrator are not clear. To ensure accuracy I sent a copy of each story to its narrator, asking him to proofread each account and make corrections, additions, and deletions as needed. Thus the stories herein are verbatim accounts provided by the narrators.

It is regrettable that no female sheriffs are represented in the book, but women sheriffs have been few in number across the years in Kentucky. Kathy Witt presently serves in Fayette County. The first woman in Kentucky to serve as a county sheriff was Lois Cole Roach, who was appointed on March 11, 1922, to the position by the county judge of Graves County after the untimely death of her husband, Sheriff John T. Roach. She was twenty-six years old. In the next general election, in the fall of 1923, Mrs. Roach ran against two other candidates for the two remaining years of the four-year term, winning the election by a majority vote of more than the other candidates' votes combined. She was a successful, devoted sheriff, serving with the aid of five deputies.[4]

Another interesting account relative to female sheriffs in Kentucky focuses on Pearl (Carter) Pace, native of Monroe County, Kentucky, and sister of U.S. senator Dr. Tim Lee Carter. In 1937 she became the first woman in Kentucky to be elected to a four-year term as sheriff, replacing her husband, Stanley Pace, who could not legally succeed himself as sheriff. Pearl came to be known as "Pistol-Packin' Pearl." After her tenure as sheriff she served on numerous state and national committees. She was active in the presidential election campaign of Dwight D. Eisenhower in 1952. In December 1953 President Eisenhower appointed her to the War Claims Commission, of which she became chair in December 1959, thereby becoming the second-highest-ranking woman in the Eisenhower administration. She resigned in early 1961 when John F. Kennedy became president. Pearl died January 14, 1970, at age seventy-four.[5]

While the bulk of information provided by sheriffs and former sheriffs is given in story format, many of these public service officers also talked about the way things were in earlier times relative to the way they are today. Many of these storytellers dislike the focus of the sheriff's job in present times, as they feel they have lost one of the aspects that made their jobs so worthwhile: personal contact with the members of the community they serve. The words of Lewis County sheriff William D. Lewis are insightful in reference to the way things are today:

> Law enforcement must seek a different paradigm to be effective. To become really effective, law enforcement must customize their services and retrain personnel to provide individual services, rather than one-size-fits-all. The greatest reward as being sheriff is having the freedom to make decisions to serve all citizens. I can do anything I want to, as long as it is [within] the parameters of the law. I will walk right up to the gray line, may even touch it, but will never step over it. The only boss I have are the voters of Lewis County.
>
> There are many activities I have initiated that take care of the public free of charge. For example:
>
> 1. I implemented a program of delivering prescription medication to elderly and disabled shut-ins that have no way, or difficulty, traveling to their pharmacy. The program works very simply by the person calling their pharmacy for the medication and method of payment (we do not handle money). Either the pharmacy or the individual contacts my office for delivery. There is no cost to my office because I have deputies on patrol anyway, and we pick up the medication and deliver it.
>
> 2. I purchased lockout kits for every officer. We unlock citizens' vehicles free of charge. Many times groceries, children, etc. are locked in vehicles. You name it, we've done it. . . . This is a great service to the public.
>
> 3. During inclement weather we transport items to the elderly, disabled, needy, or anyone that needs help. We've transported kerosene, firewood, groceries, medicine, and many other items to help people during these tough times.
>
> 4. I realize that you must have some organizational structure and some very broad policies, such as to go forward and do good. My experience has been that rigid policies are no good, and that thinking is good.
>
> 5. The position of sheriff is the only true grassroots law enforcement agency in the United States.

I want to express my admiration of and gratitude to the sheriffs and former sheriffs across Kentucky who took time from their job—one of the busiest of public sector jobs—to share their memorable stories of their years of public service. I have always known that the position of sheriff was important, but after interviewing these law enforcement heroes, I now truly appreciate their devotion to serving law-abiding local people and making staunch efforts to straighten up the lives of miscreants within their communities. All I want to say to the latter is: make your apologies as needed, get your problems sorted out, and reform your lifestyle so as to become a respected member of your community.

Notes

1. *Tales from Tennessee Lawyers* (Lexington: University Press of Kentucky, 2008), 5.

2. *The General Instructor; or, The Office, Duty, and Authority of Justices of the Peace, Sheriffs, Coroners, and Constables, in the State of Kentucky* (Lexington: John Bradford, 1800), 162–63.

3. *A Practical Treatise for the Use of Sheriffs, Jailors, and Coroners, in the State of Kentucky* (Cincinnati: Robert Clark, 1871), 3–5.

4. Personal information provided by former sheriff and high school teacher Lois Roach, when she was seventy-six years old. Information is on file as a vertical file clipping, Kentucky Library, Western Kentucky University, Bowling Green.

5. Biographical information on Mrs. Pace is a vertical file clipping at the Kentucky Library, Western Kentucky University, Bowling Green, initially provided by family members and Ruth Wooten, Burkesville, Kentucky, ca. 1992.

Chapter 1

BECOMING SHERIFF

In this chapter sheriffs explain how and why they made the decision to seek election to office. Some came from law enforcement backgrounds—having previously been deputies, state troopers, and the like—but others did not. Some had never considered such a career but were talked into it by friends and colleagues who believed they would do an excellent job. In one amusing case detailed below, a would-be sheriff's mom was asked her permission to allow her son to take on the dangerous position.

Many of the accounts below describe how the sheriff's job description has changed over the years, from a simpler time when training—if it was provided at all—was strictly on the job to today's more complicated and demanding requirements due to cultural, economic, technological, and other critical changes.

An unchanging theme over time, however, is the sheriffs' motivation to take on the job; many speak of their desire to serve, to be dedicated, devoted law enforcement officials for the betterment of their community.

SHERIFF PEANUTS

I was nicknamed Peanuts after my daddy. He was a young man when he worked for a Greek whose vocabulary couldn't say my daddy's name, which was Emery. He called Daddy Emey. So one day Daddy was eating peanuts, and this fellow nicknamed him Peanuts, and it stuck with him the rest of his life. When my brother came along, he was never a little Peanut, but when I come along I was a little Peanut. And on my daddy's tombstone is A. E. "Peanuts" Gaines.

I got elected as sheriff in 1977, when Jimmy Carter was president. And he really raised peanuts! So we used the "Peanut" thing all during my campaign. It used to be that you couldn't campaign within five hundred feet of polls here in Warren County. That means that you can't pass out cards or any kind of literature. So Mr. Higgins, who owns all these Minit Marts, called me one day and said, "Peanuts, I've got an idea for Election Day. I'm going to get you five hundred pounds of peanuts, and you can give them to people and ask them to drop them when going to the polls." At the time there were about fifty precincts, and five hundred pounds of peanuts in sacks would fill up a pickup truck's bed, and we took them and gave them to everybody in every precinct, and they would drop them as they went into the polls. They would look down, and there would be the peanuts on the floor. Well, it was about three elections before they caught me doing that!

We've used the peanut ever since then. We had a slogan back then that said, "It's Harvest Time; Pick Peanuts for Sheriff." Jack Witt painted me a big sign that had a drawing of a peanut man on it, and he wrote on there, "It's Harvest Time; Pick Peanuts for Sheriff." These days when I run for reelection, we write on there, "It's Harvest Time Again; Pick Peanuts for Sheriff." So we use the Peanut thing all through the campaign and on, and it's been very successful.

The other day, our new congressman, Brett Guthrie, was talking, and he said he ran into the vice president, Joe Biden. Biden asked Guthrie, "Do you know my buddy Peanuts?"

Brett said, "Yeah, we've been friends for about twenty-two years."

Well, one day last week, Brett was in a reception, and Hillary Clinton came by. He introduced himself, and she said, "Do you know my buddy Peanuts?" Of course, I knew her and Bill Clinton, and I've got a picture of all of us hanging here on the wall, where I've got a picture of me and many other notables taken across the years.

I got elected as sheriff in May 1977, then served until 1981 until I had to set out. I could not succeed myself as sheriff for four years. Then I came back and won again in 1985, and have been here ever since. So the Peanut thing and Peanut name has carried me on through the years.

When I go to some events, they just put Peanuts on my name tag. If I'm here in the office when the telephone rings, I'll pick up the telephone and say, "Sheriff's office." They'll say, "Is that you, Peanuts?" [*Laughter*]

I've run for many professional offices and have been elected. In one instance, I ran for board membership of the National Sheriffs' Association in Honolulu, Hawaii, and was elected. And I'm the first sheriff from Kentucky that was elected as president of the National Sheriffs' Association, which was a great honor. Sheriff John Aubrey of Louisville is now sergeant at arms, and will serve in this capacity as president in four more years.

I know sheriffs from many states, and they all know me as Peanuts.

Jerry "Peanuts" Gaines, Warren County, July 20, 2009

TAYLOR COUNTY SHERIFF

Back in 1995 I was getting ready to retire from the Kentucky State Police after twenty years of service in that capacity. Initially I had planned to go back to college and get my teacher's certificate in order to teach school. A few of my old classmates in high school said to me, "John, it wouldn't be a good idea for you to do that because of the way kids are now. Probably the first day, you would get mad and whip one of them. And if you did, you'd get fired!"

I was thinking about that when the county judge here in Taylor County, Fred Waddle, called and asked me if I'd be interested in having a job as sheriff. I said, "Why?"

He answered by mentioning Sonny Cave, who had been sheriff about a year and a half in a five-year term. He said, "Sonny is going to quit; he doesn't want to be sheriff anymore." So he asked me if I would consider it. Well, we talked about it two or three times, and he talked me into it. Little did I know that once I was appointed by him, I would also have to run a special election that year. I had never been in politics, because as a state policeman, we tried to stay out of politics. Well, I was nominated by the Democratic Party and ran against an ex-deputy.

I won the election by a good margin, and fifteen years later I'm still sheriff!

Before I ever thought about being a sheriff, I joined the United States Army and served in that capacity eight years, which was during the Vietnam War.

In 1975 I started as a cadet in order to become a state policeman, and served in that capacity until 1995. I was a road trooper in Elizabethtown, and from there I went to the governor's mansion and worked as a government security under John Y. Brown and Phyllis George for about three years. After that I went to the Columbia post and worked there until I retired.

Then I became a sheriff!

John E. Shipp, Taylor County, July 30, 2009

Campaign in Hart County

Like any campaign, there's a lot of things that happen. When people are running against you, they'll start making up tales that are not true. However, I'd been here so long in police work that the people knew what was true and what was not true.

I was a state trooper for twenty years, retired in 2002, then came to the sheriff's office after I retired. I was appointed as sheriff October 1, 2005, then ran for election, won, then became sheriff in 2007. It was a usual election, and I won.

Boston B. Hensley Jr., Hart County, July 30, 2009

Fuzzy's Career as Sheriff

"Fuzzy" is a nickname that was given to me by my father when I was approximately seven or eight years old. The reason for my nickname was that a gentleman lived near us in the community who was known as Fuzzy. He had a lot of bushy hair and a heavy beard, so I was afraid of him! When my mother and father would want me to come into the house if I was out playing, they'd say, "Here comes Fuzzy." Of course, I'd run to the house.

One morning I was getting ready for school, and I hadn't combed my hair. My father said, "Son, if you don't comb your hair this morning, I'm going to call you Fuzzy." And my nickname was born.

From then on, Fuzzy was the name that stayed with me, and I've always been proud of it since so many people can remember a nickname better than a given name. Such a nickname has been an advantage point in my political career.

When I was a young boy our family lived near a magistrate's office in Belfry, Kentucky. In those days the magistrates had judicial powers, and they tried a lot of misdemeanor cases since they were allowed to do so. You could always find deputy sheriffs and constables hanging around there on Saturdays because they had cases before the magistrates.

There was a young and very short constable who would carry a pistol on each hip, and I was quite frightened by him. When I would see that constable, it would scare me and I would run to the house. Actually, I spent most of my young years afraid of police officers. My brother once convinced me that if I ate a candy bar and threw the wrapper on the ground, the constable will pick me up and arrest me. That was enough to send me home numerous times with my pockets stuffed with candy bar wrappers. When my mother would ask me why I was doing it, I always had a simple reply. I would say, "Well, I'm afraid the constable will arrest me."

As I grew older my father thought he would like to be sheriff. He ran three, four, or five times, and always come in as close second, but never was elected. Then in 1957 he ran for sheriff here in Pike County and was elected that year as sheriff. He took office January 3, 1958.

At that time I had just exited the military service and moved to Louisville with the intention of going to law school. One night my father called and asked me if I would consider coming back and working for him in the sheriff's office. Since I hadn't started law school yet, I thought it would be a good opportunity, so I came back and worked for him. Oftentimes I would do clerical work in the tax department, and also worked on the road as deputy sheriff.

At the end of my father's term, which expired in 1961, people began to talk to me suggesting that I should run for sheriff. I never gave it a thought early on, but their suggestions made me start thinking that maybe I, too, would like to be sheriff and follow in my father's footsteps.

Since I did a lot of sheriff's work anyway at that time, I decided to run for office as sheriff. My father gave me the best piece of advice right before I filed. He said, "Be sure that you use the name Fuzzy," and I did. Sure enough, it proved to be a great idea.

There were six other candidates running for sheriff, including a former sheriff that my father succeeded. He ran again, because back then sheriffs could not succeed themselves. So I was elected as sheriff of Pike County that year. I thought the primary race was very close because there were so many good people running, and a couple of them had grown up in the Pond Creek area where I also grew up. I knew it would be a tough race, but I believe I won between six to eight hundred votes as a majority.

One of my opponents was a fine businessman, a very fine fellow and very well thought of. I ran as a Democrat, and he ran on the Republican ticket. On election night I really thought he had me beat. They had counted the votes and announced that I had been defeated [by] one hundred votes. But an attorney who was a friend of mine had been keeping tabs on the precinct and knew I had won by a little over a hundred votes. He informed everyone, "No, that's wrong. I've been keeping tabs. Fuzzy has won by a hundred and some votes."

This was the first year we had voting machines. There had been a minor mistake in tabulating the votes, and I had actually won by 107 votes! Well, the gentleman asked for a recount, and I didn't blame him since it was such a close vote.

During my first three terms I could not succeed myself, thus over a period of twenty-four years, I served twelve years in and twelve out, being reelected every four years. The next time I ran there were five candidates, and I was fortunate enough to win again. The same fellow I had beaten only by approximately 150 votes before ran again as well. But this time I beat him by about 3,500 votes.

In 1984 a Sheriff's Succession Bill was passed. The sheriff that was in at that time here in Pike County was in his second term, and he ran for reelection in 1985. I ran my fourth term in 1985 and was elected to take office January 1, 1986. I've been in succession since 1986.

One day this fine fellow came to me because he was getting close to running for election. He said, "Fuzzy, I just came in to tell you that I'm going to run for sheriff against you this time, so I want you to give me a few pointers." Unfortunately, he came in last of the five candidates. Anyway, he's deceased now and was a fine gentleman.

I've been fortunate enough to be serving my ninth term at this time. During those years I have seen many sad things happen to us, but I've also seen many, many funny, comical things happen as well.

Charles E. "Fuzzy" Keesee, Pike County, August 7, 2009

FROM DEPUTY TO SHERIFF

How I got started into a law profession is that I did a lot of custom work for people all over this county. In the late 1960s this fellow came to ask me if I would run for deputy sheriff with him running for the sheriff's office. So I told him, "Yeah."

So we ran for office, then got beat [by] about three hundred votes. Of course, we were running against the establishment, etc. So that passed on, then I got involved in another race. A neighbor was running for deputy on a ticket, so I went around and helped him campaign, then the county sort of laid dormant for several years. He got beat, but not by many votes.

We had a city policeman in Shelbyville who was not ready to retire, but he decided he wanted to run for sheriff. He came out here to this farm where we are right now, and he asked me if I would run for deputy sheriff with him. I said, "Yeah, I'll help you part-time." Actually, it ended up running full-time, but I continued farming and doing this and that. Then he won, but could not succeed himself after the fourth year. His name was Stanley Greenwell. His chief deputy was Tom Lincoln, and Tom asked me if I would stay on with him, and I said, "Yes, I'll stay." He was elected, and I was a deputy, and he later ran for president of the Kentucky Sheriffs' Association. The night he was elected as president, he had a heart attack and passed away. He was truly a good sheriff here in Shelby County, one of the best.

After that I ran as deputy for the next sheriff. Not long after that people got to pestering me, telling me I need to run for sheriff. Well, I got to thinking about it and said, "Well, I'll probably do it. I'll just take a shot at it maybe."

I really hadn't said I was going to run, and that caused an uproar, so on August 9, 1985, the sheriff fired me. But I just took that with a grain of salt, as I was still farming. But after that happened my blood got to boiling and I said, "Well, I'm going to run for sheriff. I'm going to do that." So the rest of it is history. I ran and won by a big number of votes, somewhere between a thousand and fourteen hundred votes.

Running for sheriff is political, so I ran as a Democrat and am still a Democrat. I ran for office again the next time, and beat the same fellow again. The next time I ran for sheriff, the Republicans were also running for office, but I beat him too.

I was sheriff for thirteen years, but all total I served for twenty years and seven months in public office.

Harold E. Tingle, Shelby County, August 14, 2009

Dream Come True

My name is Wayne Wright, but I'm known to everyone as Tiny. I am very fortunate that I am living my dream. Everyone wants to be able to say they are living their dream, and I am. I had always wanted to be the sheriff, and was elected in November 2006 and took office December 1, 2006.

I was appointed to finish the term of the previous sheriff, who retired. At this point in time, I have been in law enforcement for twenty-four years—ten years with the Versailles Police Department and fourteen years with the Woodford County Sheriff's Office in different capacities.

Wayne "Tiny" Wright, Woodford County, September 15, 2009

Successful Outcomes

I was born in the late 1930s in northern Kentucky and raised during the 1940s, '50s, and '60s, during a period of time when there was a lot of gambling, prostitution, crooked sheriffs, and other things. My mother was a Quaker, and my dad was a Prussian, so the Quaker part of me knew that something was wrong, and the Prussian wanted to kill somebody about it!

As I was growing up I could see all these activities going on all around me, and I didn't like it much. But there was a great mentor of mine, who was an honest cop in Ft. Mitchell, Kentucky, and his name was Russell Toole. As a kid I used to ride around with him. He was quite a mentor and had quite a law library. He was very well read. I admired him and thought he was the person to emulate.

I graduated from Beechwood High School in 1956 but didn't have a lot of money to go away and go to college. However, the University of Kentucky had a northern extension campus at Covington, where students could go at night. I took courses there for two years. After that I had to make up my mind what to do, whether to go to the University of Kentucky at Lexington or just quit.

I was talking to Russell Toole and told him I would be interested in law enforcement. Well, he said, "You don't want to be a cop around here, so let me introduce you to a special agent in the FBI, whose name is Robert Brooks, and they just started a co-op program." So, they interviewed me and told me they would send me to Washington, DC, where I would go to school at night, and work as a clerk in the Finger Print Bureau during the day. Then they told me that after I got my degree I would be a special agent.

Well, I hadn't said anything to my mother or father about this, but the agent came in one night with some papers I had to sign. My parents got all upset because I was going to leave the family business in order to be a cop. So I didn't do it. Then after forty-five years went by, and I was getting ready to retire, Senator Roeding, whom I had grown up with, and Steve Hensley, chief of police in Ft. Mitchell, said they wanted me to run for sheriff.

Well, a little lightbulb kind of went off in my head, and I had the idea of doing this many years ago, so I said, "Well, I'll give it a shot." Just by coincidence, I had been foreman of the grand jury, and when I'd get done signing the indictments I would go into court to see what was going on, and nobody knew me. I'd smell liquor on the bailiff's breath, and every once in awhile a fight would break out. I guess if it hadn't been for the local policeman, their criminal element would have just walked out onto the street.

So there were other things I didn't think were right, so I decided to run for sheriff. Well, I lost my first election by a narrow margin, but I then thought I'd just take this as an opportunity, so I studied sheriffs' statute books from Chief Hensley as much as I could. When the next election came up, the fellow that I did not beat during my first campaign retired, and they appointed the chief deputy for about three months. So I ran against him and won the 1998 election. I was sworn in January 4, 1999.

Before I was sworn in as sheriff, the local FBI agent got hold of me and asked me if I would get involved in a project with them. The sheriff I beat didn't like to do things like that with the FBI, so they said. So, that was just exactly what I had in mind, so after becoming sheriff, we formed a Three Unit Task Force, combined with Covington police and the Kenton County jail that assisted us.

We hit persons really hard when they were doing anything illegal on the east side of Covington for about a year. That was very effective, and they gave us an award they give once each year per state. We were the first unit in northern Kentucky to ever receive that award.

So that opened up a lot of doors for me. I'm the point of contact for members of the Secret Service contingency when they come into the greater Cincinnati airport. I have two men who are also sworn as U.S marshals, and one in the DEA, and I am presently in the FBI Joint Terrorism Task Force, and also a member of the U.S. Attorney's Anti-Terrorism Advisory Council.

I'm really proud of the way the office has moved forward, and we are the third of five sheriff's offices to be state accredited. The FBI sent me to their Law Enforcement Executive Development Session in 2002, and I graduated from that. They also sent me to the National Sheriffs' Institute in Longmont, Colorado.

I've been keeping up with my studies. I didn't get finished with going to school in 1958, so I'm still going!! It's been a very rewarding thing.

Charles Lee "Chuck" Korzenborn, Kenton County, September 17, 2009

TALKED INTO THE SHERIFF'S OFFICE

I worked for the state police for four years and was assigned to Monroe County. I really enjoyed it, and met a lot of fine people while I was there. At that same time I had people in Russell County say to me, "We want you to run for sheriff one of these days." And I thought, "Well, I wouldn't get but a few votes." As time went on, more and more people spoke up and encouraged me to run for sheriff. Finally, they talked me into it.

I filed, won, and am now in my fifth term. I was elected in 1989, took office January 1, 1990. People have really been good to me, so I plan to run for office again.

Larry L. Bennett, Russell County, September 18, 2009

SEVENTEEN YEARS ON THE JOB

Prior to being sheriff, I was magistrate in this district, which is Third District. When being magistrate, we had to approve the sheriff's budget, and I had access to how much money he was getting, what he used it for, and I just always thought I could do a better job for the people with what money they received. I just wanted to do something for the county, especially for young people. Thus I decided to run for sheriff. That was in 1981 when I ran. I won that election, and won the next four elections afterwards.

Prior to me becoming sheriff, my first tenure as sheriff was when we got the concession amendment passed which allowed us to run for more than one term. We got that amendment passed when I became sheriff and went to Frankfort. After that you could run as many times as you want to, so that's why I was able to stay in as long as I did. Before that was passed you could set out four years, then run again. But after that I could stay in as sheriff as long as I could be elected.

I wound up staying seventeen years as sheriff. I finally lost the next election, which was in 1999. I don't think I had done anything wrong; it was just because people want to see what the next guy is going to do. After I lost, I went back to work for the county in the road department. I then run for the judge's job, but didn't win. Right now I work for the City of Leitchfield.

Qulin K. Escue, Grayson County, September 22, 2009

DEDICATED SERVICE

To explain the rationale for wanting to become a sheriff, we'll probably have to go back to my childhood. I was born to two wonderful Christian parents, Laymond and Lottie Cain, both of which—but my dad in particular—instilled in me at an early age a strong desire to serve and give back to the community.

I served four years in the Marine Corps, and again this issue of service continued to be a strong motivation in all that I did. When I left the Marine Corps, I initially went into the family business. My dad was a self-employed truck driver who hauled agricultural lime to the farmers in and around the tristate area here. So I started working for him, and really thought I would take over the family business. However, after being in the Marine Corps and serving in Vietnam, I decided that my dad's type of work wasn't well suited for me. Thus I went to looking for something a bit more challenging, and began looking at the possibility of law enforcement as a career. When I came back from Vietnam, I took on a job that, at that time, was called a cross-country chaser (with the USMC). Basically, what we did was work with the military CID locating, apprehending, and transporting AWOL persons back to various military installations. So I had a little bit of experience of law enforcement by virtue of that job. And I enjoyed doing that type work.

When I came back home, I was wanting to do something that was more challenging and more engaged than being a truck driver. Let me make it clear that I'm not trying to lower the value of that profession, as my son is a truck driver. Something that my father taught me was that it doesn't matter what we choose to do in life, as long as we do it to the best of our ability.

I began to look at the possibility of a career in law enforcement; I was twenty-one years old at that time. I had less than a high school education, as I left high school during my senior year. What I decided to do was to join the Marine Corps, much to the chagrin of my mom and dad. They wanted me to stay in school, but I was seventeen years and thought I had a handle of what was going on, and was the master of my destiny. So I spent four years in the Marine Corps, thirteen months of which were in Vietnam.

Upon coming back home, one of the first things I recognized as needed, and with the assistance of the company commander in the Marine Corps, I obtained my GED. So I came out of the Marine Corps back in 1973. When I thought about getting involved in law enforcement, I took a day off from work and filed my application with the Kentucky State Police, the Owensboro City Police Department, and the Daviess County Sheriff's Department, all on the same day.

The process was a lot different then than what it is now, as you could do that pretty quickly back then. Well, I decided that the first one of those that chose to hire me, that's where I would go to work, at least temporarily. The first person to call me was the current sheriff, whose name was Charles "Boots" Norris. He knew my family. He called me and wanted to know if I was still interested in the job. That probably happened within a couple of weeks after I filed the application.

So I went down to his office to be interviewed, and after we got through talking, I walked out the door as a deputy sheriff! It is much different now, as things have changed from a job to a profession. Legislation was passed during Governor Patton's administration that was called the POPS Standards. That stands for Police Officer's Professional Standards.

My training as deputy sheriff consisted of Sheriff Boots Norris giving me a gun, a badge, and a used uniform from the lockup downstairs that had belonged to a previous deputy. The pants he gave me were about three inches too short, and I could barely fasten the shirt around me. Well, the next day I was patrolling the streets of Owensboro as a deputy sheriff with the Daviess County Sheriff's Department. In comparing the way we put people into service today, that's a scary situation to realize that's the way we put people on the street back then. But that's how it was done.

Back then I realized that although training wasn't required, but I went to training so that I could be well trained for the job. Basically, the first few years of my career I utilized my vacation days to find law enforcement schools and go to those schools myself. I paid tuition out of my own pocket for many of those schools.

A couple of years ago there were some federal funds through the Department of Criminal Justice called the Law Enforcement Assistance Administration. That was a funding mechanism wherein they provided the money for law enforcement officers that wanted to go to college. Well, I was already taking advantage of some of my GI bill, that was helping me pay costs at some of those schools. So for the next eight years I worked as deputy sheriff during the day, then went to school at night at Kentucky Wesleyan College and Western Kentucky University and obtained a bachelor's degree while working.

After being deputy for a couple of years working uniform patrol, I was assigned to a joint narcotics task force that consisted of law enforcement officers from the sheriff's office and the Owensboro Police Department. I worked on that task force for six or seven years and the funding for that dried up, so I was reassigned back to general investigation. In that job I worked general criminal investigation in plain clothes.

Thus I spent my entire career in narcotics, general investigation, eventually taking over as chief of the investigative unit, which actually involved only two of us. So I worked exclusively in criminal investigation and narcotics right up until a fellow by the name of John Bouiver was elected as sheriff here in the early eighties. I became his chief deputy and actually worked in a dual capacity in the office, as chief deputy and chief of criminal investigations.

During all that time my primary responsibility and love for my job was generally in the area of investigation. I liked working a case from its inception and initial call, and putting pieces of the puzzle together, and eventually locate, apprehend, and successfully prosecute a guilty party. I began to feel very successful at doing that, and worked in that capacity up to about twelve years ago when Bouiver decided to retire and not run again. By that time I'd been with the department more than twenty-five years, so I decided that I would be a good sheriff.

I filed for the office of sheriff because I knew a little bit about the political system, having worked in it for many years. I wasn't really engaged in politics, because my job was chasing bad guys. I went ahead and ran for sheriff, and became the first sheriff in the recorded history of Daviess County that ran unopposed in this county in both the primary and general elections. Nobody filed against me, so I considered that an extreme compliment. I won the election handily, but after my first term of service the sheriff that retired decided that he wanted to come back as sheriff. So he ran against me that year, and it was a rather controversial election, but the voters of Daviess County liked what they had seen in me, and I was able to beat him about three to one, which is a pretty handy margin.

In my third election no one filed against me, so I ran unopposed again. At present we are nearing the end of my third term, and I'll be running again next year. I read one time where a person said, "There can be no victory without battle." I'm here to tell you, I've run elections in both ways, and I can tell you that victory is just as sweet in one as it is in the other, and it's a whole lot cheaper when you don't have opposition.

I'll tell you one thing about an election that keeps an individual humble. There is always a contingent of people out there willing to tell you what you are doing wrong. [*Laughter*] And just to be honest, I'm not so sure that's a bad thing, because when we run unopposed repeatedly I think it is good for people to bring to our attention our weaknesses so that we can push ourselves to improve things. I try to keep that in mind when I have opposition.

I've had a wonderful career because I've been with this department for thirty-six years in April 2010. My department has grown considerably since I started, but a small department has both its pros and cons. In a small department there is not as significant a chance for advancement as in large departments, but you have a more familylike atmosphere, and people get to know each other on a by-name basis, which I think is important. Too, it's imperative that we are able to establish rapport with the community we serve as an entity they can trust, place their confidence in, and that they know will be there when help is needed. I take that charge very seriously, and I like to think that's why I ran for sheriff without opposition.

Although I've had opportunities to go to other agencies, such as United States Marshal Service, United States Secret Service, and I was approached numerous times requesting my application for the FBI, and I also passed up a job with the North Carolina Bureau of Investigation. A number of years ago I was offered a lateral move over to the Owensboro City Police Department as a ranking supervisor in their detective bureau, but I passed it and all those other jobs up. I turned all of those job offers down because I really believed God had a place for Keith Cain, and I think it's right here at this sheriff's desk. My job has been good to me, it's been a great career. One time I heard somebody say, "Anybody can make a living, but few people can make a difference." So it's much more than just a paycheck; it's about making a positive difference in the lives of the people whom we serve.

In terms of my future as a sheriff, I don't plan to continue for as long as I can be reelected. As I have already said, I got my bachelor's degree in about eight years, and then I was very fortunate back in 1989 to attend the National FBI Academy in Quantico, Virginia. It's very difficult to get in that, and I was very honored to be accepted by the academy back in 1989. So I went to the National FBI Academy for three months, and by virtue of having done so, when I left there I had somewhere between six to nine hours of college credit with the University of Virginia. When I came back to Owensboro, I thought about already having those hours toward a master's degree, so I said to myself, "It's a shame to waste those credit hours." Thus I went back to night school, and after four more years I graduated with a master's degree in criminal justice from Kentucky Wesleyan College. Since I now have a master's degree, that's not bad for a high school dropout.

Along about that time, I began thinking there was something else I could give back to law enforcement, and that I'm not going to be around here forever. I believe very strongly that for those of us that have been in this profession for an extended period of time, is important to train others to take our place. Every one of those men and women that work for me should be provided with the training, the opportunity, and the resources to where they could advance in the law enforcement field, whether it's in this office or somewhere else. So I began to teach classes in law enforcement, and for about the past twenty years I've taught in the law enforcement curriculum in Owensboro Community and Technical College. I also do a lot of instruction for the Kentucky State Police, the Owensboro City Police Department, and a host of law enforcement agencies throughout the country. Teaching law enforcement is probably my second love. I'm a practitioner first, but I love to pass that knowledge along to others. A lot of my students across the years are now in various types of service in law enforcement agencies throughout this country.

One of my law enforcement students graduated and went on to work for the Kentucky State Police for about five years. After that he went on to work for the FBI, and is now serving as an FBI agent down in Austin, Texas. To this day he calls me when he is working cases to ask me my advice on them. To me that is a tremendous honor.

Like everyone, I want to leave a legacy. The first is that I want people to remember me as a good Christian individual. And my second preference is to be remembered as a dedicated, devoted law enforcement officer who was a public servant, and also to be remembered as a teacher and mentor. Those are [the] kind of adjectives I want people to use when I leave here to go to be with the good Lord.

Let me also say that if there are any credits to be given to me for the accomplishments that I've made in life and in this profession, much of that credit goes to my father, Laymond Cain, who was my lifetime mentor. He always said to me, "If you're going to do something, give it 150 percent of your effort. Don't be marginal in anything you do." My mother also was very precious. So, to use the old traditional adage,

"When you leave this life, it's not what you take with you, it's what you leave behind."

Keith Cain, Daviess County, October 1, 2009

BUTLER COUNTY SHERIFF

I was a deputy sheriff from 1976 to 1979, got out of law enforcement for awhile, then ran for and was elected magistrate of the Fifth District in Butler County in 1986. I had it in the back of mind to run for sheriff someday, and several people approached me and asked me if I would consider running. So I decided to run, and ran against an incumbent. It was a close race, but I won that pretty close vote.

Butler County is a Republican county, but both of us ran as Republicans. I won, but I had a Democrat opponent that fall. However, I won that race also. That was in 1989, but I took office in January1990. My subsequent terms were all back-to-back due to the law passed by the state legislature in 1984. I had an opponent every time, but after my first race I never had a close race after that. For the second race I had two opponents, and I almost doubled the vote on them.

The first sheriff I worked for was Wallace Dockery, who was a real nice guy and had a lot of common sense. He always told me, "Now, if you do your job you will make some people mad, but if you don't do your job the right way, you won't get reelected either." Anyway, I went on and served as sheriff for seventeen years.

We had one odd year during that time. The state legislature was looking at a way to save money, so they were trying to get it so we'd have a cycle every four years in which there would not be an election in the state of Kentucky. They said that would save the counties, plus the state, a lot of money. As a result of that the governor, sheriffs, and all local officials had to change that to a five-year term for that one time only.

I served as sheriff from 1990 through December 31, 2006. I decided to leave the sheriff's office for two or three reasons. One was I was not receiving enough funding, and did not have enough help. At that time they'd cut me back to two deputies. Second, I was working too many hours, and was not as young as I used to be. Third, I hardly got any vacations and still worked a lot of hours, thus was on call all the time due to the lack of deputies.

I did run for judge, but failed to win that election.

Kenneth Lee Morris, Butler County, October 11, 2009

Shelby County Sheriff

My father worked in this office back in the late 1960s and early 1970s. I reckon that as a child the size I was back then, you always look up to your father. But being in the type of law enforcement he was in, I always had in the back of my mind that was something I wanted to do. However, during my school years in Shelbyville and my years at the University of Kentucky, I never seemed to get myself in this position. Well, in 1989, I was asked to be a part of a campaign for which another sheriff was running. We were very fortunate—got elected and did very well. I was very fortunate in that I was able to become chief deputy in January 1990. Actually, I was the second man in charge. Back at that time there were only six of us working here as deputies, and the sheriff.

Back in those days you worked maybe sixty to eighty hours per week, but you only got paid for forty. That went on for several years, and probably wasn't the best thing for my finances, but I really loved what I did. You can just say that we fell in line with everything, and moved right along. So, when I had the opportunity to run for sheriff, there was no doubt about my running.

When I ran for sheriff there were a lot more than six employees here. I was still the chief deputy, and everybody knew that I was running for sheriff. To me, that was one of the better days of my life, other than my family. I was fortunate to have won that election for sheriff in November 2002, and took office in January 2003. So that's the way I got started in being a sheriff, and doing the best job possible in this position.

I ran for reelection four years ago, and was fortunate enough not to have any opposition. That is not typical for those who are running for some sort of public office.

I was thirty-two years old when I started to work in this capacity. Once we got going, we moved on. I'm sure we haven't pleased some people, but I'm also sure there are lots of people pleased with the way we have done things.

Mike Armstrong, Shelby County, November 6, 2009

Casey County Sheriff

On Thanksgiving Day, November 1968, my mother was killed by a drunk driver. After that happened I ran and was elected as constable in 1969. After I had been constable for three or four months, the sheriff asked me to work full-time as deputy for the sheriff's department. After serving four years as deputy, I ran for sheriff as a replacement for Sheriff Overstreet, who couldn't run again for sheriff at that point in time. I won the race and received the biggest majority of votes that anyone had ever received in becoming a sheriff.

I worked very hard in my job as sheriff, doing the best I could. I worked endless hours because there wasn't such a thing as a forty-hour shift, or an eighty-hour shift. I had only one road deputy, and I think Casey County has 368 square miles all total. We were devoted to doing the best work possible for county residents.

I retired as sheriff in January 1994.

Carl E. Meece, Casey County, November 12, 2009

WORKING FOR THE PEOPLE

Before I became sheriff here in Bath County, I ran dozer equipment and farmed. I owned my own dozer equipment, a backhoe. Later on I became a city police officer and served in that capacity for almost thirteen years. I enjoyed working for the people back then, and I still do. I told my wife what I wanted to do, and she said, "Well, do whatever you want to do, but I wouldn't want you to. It's dangerous." [*Laughter*]

I like to be around people all the time, and I like doing them favors. That's why I ran for sheriff. I was appointed as sheriff two years ago, then in 2008 I ran for sheriff and won the election.

I have only one deputy, but another that is part-time. When I go out on a call sometimes I don't get back home until about twenty hours later.

Here in Bath County constables don't get paid. If they did, they could serve papers and do things like that. So when I get way behind things that need to be done, I help to serve papers in order to get caught up.

John "Tuffy" Snedegar, Bath County, December 11, 2009

BARREN COUNTY SHERIFF

I was born on a farm, grew up on a farm, and worked in an industry for ten years. I always enjoyed a farm life, but at the same time I felt like I wanted to do some type of public service. Thus, being a sheriff would be a respected decision, especially from a law enforcement category. I wanted to get into that type work, so I worked as a deputy sheriff for four years in Barren County, 1984–1988.

The existing sheriff at that time decided he wasn't going to run for sheriff again, so I ran for sheriff in 1989, was elected in November 1989, then took over as sheriff on January 1, 1990. I was successful in four campaigns, one of which was a five-year term, so I wound up being sheriff for a total of seventeen years. I chose to not run again in 2006, so one of my deputies ran for sheriff, was elected, and took over the office in 2007.

I have been retired since then, and have missed being involved in public service, and this sort of thing. I've had considerable encouragement to run for county judge executive, and am presently running for that office, which will be voted on in 2010. If that works out, I will take office January 1, 2011.

Barney Jones, Barren County, December 21, 2009

Career in Law Enforcement

Right before I got into the sheriff's office, I had worked in construction for a telephone company and doing things such as setting telephone poles, burying telephone lines, etc. My mother-in-law got a job as a clerk here in Junction City, and they needed a police officer. So she asked me to come down here to be a police officer, and that was back in 1987. Well, just for a joke, I went down there just to see what would happen. After I went down there and applied, they had a council meeting just two or three days later. Lo and behold, they hired me that night as a police officer! I had no training, so I didn't know anything about the law. So when they hired me, they didn't send me to school but put me in a cruiser three days later and I rode around one night with the chief, and then turned me loose.

So there I was out there doing on-the-job training, and had an injury wreck. Of course, we have all these numbers, such as 1046 (injury accident), 1045 (noninjury accident). Well, when they gave me a 1046, it was just right down the road here from my present store. I took off down there, worked it by myself, but didn't have a clue what I was doing. However, I actually did work it by myself. That was probably the best training I ever had before I went to the academy at Eastern Kentucky University in Richmond. I was scared to death, but back then it was okay to do something like that. Right now you couldn't do that, no way, no how. But I went on like that without training for about eighteen months before I went through the academy in 1989.

After I spent ten weeks in the academy I worked over here as deputy until January 16, 1990. The older sheriff didn't run again, but one of his deputies, Carl Luttrell, who had been deputy since 1971, ran for office. He was elected, as nobody ran against him. Soon after that he had a guy to quit in order to be employed as bailiff. So Carl came and asked me if I wanted a job in his office. I told him yes, so I went to work for the sheriff's office, January 16, 1990, as a deputy. I worked there for thirteen years, and he stepped down and didn't run again. So he appointed me to fill out a little bit of his term.

When I was appointed we had a little controversy in the office. I had guys that were above me who wanted to run for the sheriff's office, but they didn't want to keep me and two or three other guys. They called in one guy and he said, "Well, I'm going to run; are you with me?"

This guy said, "Well, what about LeeRoy, and what about these other guys?"

He said, "Well, we don't want them. We're just going to run, and we'd like to have you on board."

Well, actually, I hadn't made up my mind yet whether or not to run for office. I didn't know if I could win it or not. So he looked at the deputy that was on the inside, and said, "Well, if LeeRoy runs, I'll beat him, because I ain't worried about LeeRoy."

When he come out and told me that, I decided right then to run for office, so I went straight across the hall and gave them $50 in order to file and run for sheriff.

There were about five of us in the race in 2002, but fortunately I won the primary, then went on and was elected during fall 2003. Actually, we won the election pretty good. I was a nervous wreck the first time I ran, and actually spent about $15,000 to run, and didn't know if I would win or not. Well, when the primary votes were counted, I had thirty-two hundred votes, and the next guy had nine hundred votes. Another guy had six hundred, and the other guy that didn't want to keep me got only five hundred votes, as did another deputy.

I ran two terms successfully, and won them with a pretty good margin. But I stepped down January 1, 2010, as things became too political for me. I'm not a politician, but I am a people person. I like working for the people, and that's who I worked for. What's wrong with the country right now is that if you elect these certain persons into office, they think that everything in there belongs to them, but it doesn't. The way I see it, everything in the office belongs to the people out there, so I decided to not put up with the stress that is involved now. I stepped out of the office January 1, 2010. People are trying to get me to run again, but I am not going to do it.

LeeRoy Hardin, Boyle County, January 11, 2010

ADAIR COUNTY SHERIFF

Back in 1985, John Ballou and Bobby Willis came to me and asked me if I would be interested in running with them for the Adair County sheriff's office. At that time I worked for a Charter Market owned by Super Test Oil Company and was there for about thirteen years. I then bought a country grocery store here in Adair County on Clay Ridge where I lived.

John and Bobby came out there one day and wanted to know if I would run for deputy with them. I told them to give me about three days to make up my mind. I did, as I had always thought I might want to get into law enforcement. That was in January 1985, when I was thirty-nine years old. I turned forty on March 3. I told them I would run. We did win the election. Ballou had two opponents in the primary and one in the general election, and we won both races. I served as deputy under him for four years, and then Bobby Willis ran for sheriff, and he won. I served four years under him as a deputy, and then I ran for sheriff in 1993.

I was elected, and was forty-nine years old at the time. My service began in January 1994. I stayed in office for seventeen years, but then decided not to seek reelection. We were short on help then, as I had only two or three deputies. So things were pretty hard on me. I was working anywhere from twelve to fifteen hours a day, so I decided I was just going to quit. Well, I let some people talk me into signing up to run again, and I did. I lost that race to a Republican opponent, and I am a Republican. Adair County hadn't had a Democrat sheriff for about fifty years, so I guess my opponent thought he had it won since he had beat me. Well, the Democrat opponent came in and beat him in the general election, and served as sheriff for four years.

I left the sheriff's office in 2002 and went home, but decided to run again in 2006. I beat both of the same guys. One was sheriff at that time, and he was the one that beat me. So I took office again in 2007, but I plan on retiring at the end of this term in 2010.

All total, I will have served thirteen years as sheriff, and eight years as deputy, for a total of twenty-one years.

I must say that I have enjoyed it, but have had times when I wished I wasn't sheriff. However, most of the time I did enjoy working with people, and we've done a lot of drug busts.

James Ralph Curry, Adair County, January 11, 2010

INDIVIDUAL INITIATIVE

Prior to becoming sheriff of Lewis County in January 1999, my law enforcement background was twenty-five years with the Kentucky State Police, a highly structured organization. There is a policy for almost every activity conducted by the KSP. Due to these policies, the public receives basically a standard product of law enforcement. Such rigid policies restrict common sense and initiative of the individual officer. When policies require an officer not to think on his own and tell him/her to only go from Point A to Point B and to Point C, it is counterproductive. The complex field of law enforcement requires today's officer to think much differently so as to provide custom-made services to the public. Officers should make decisions on their own to solve the problem presented to them, rather than relying on rigid policies. The officer should have the authority to go from Point A to Point C to Point Z—whatever it takes, within legal parameters.

William D. Lewis, Lewis County, January 13, 2010

CLINTON COUNTY SHERIFF

When I decided to run for sheriff, I was retired as city mail carrier. In doing the mail deliveries, I walked up to thirteen miles each day for ten or twelve years, then was finally able to get a Jeep. When I retired from mail service after thirty years and twenty-eight days, my cohorts started begging me to run for sheriff. Ira Lee Dicken, who was a mail carrier but is deceased, asked me on and on and on, but I wasn't thinking about running for sheriff because I was retired, and I had also been in the wrecking business/junk business and I was going to work on that. But they kept on and on, so I decided I would file.

When I filed I started campaigning, and I had little catchy phrases like "For you and your county, so think about it. If your child was out at night and didn't show up by 3:00 a.m., what would you do?" Then I said, "Call Glynn Mann; think about it."

I had little mottos like that. My campaign just went on from there, and the former sheriff had passed away, and J. T. Butler was running in his place. I didn't know whether or not I would win because he got a lot of sympathy votes, but I won the race and started serving as sheriff in January 1989.

I enjoyed being sheriff a whole lot of the time, but it got pretty dangerous. I hadn't been in there but a very short time until we had three killings, and a young fellow was killed in an accident out on Highway 90, and I had a lot of other problems when I first went into the sheriff's office, and our chief of police got run over and killed.

Glynn Mann, Clinton County, February 8, 2010

Mom's Permission Solicited

My first campaign to be elected as sheriff took place several years ago. I was a deputy to start with, but I don't even recall why I became a deputy. There was an old gentleman by the name of Hershel Henninger who was hunting a deputy. Well, I was home one day and he came by and asked me if I would be interested. I said, "Well, I don't know, I never have thought about it." And I really hadn't thought about that.

He and I talked awhile, and I think I asked my wife if I could serve as deputy. Anyway, we both decided I could, but Henninger decided he'd have to ask my mother before he'd let me come to work as a deputy. Well, after we talked, he left and went to my mother's house and talked with her. Evidently, she told him that I could, so he came back and hired me as a deputy sheriff. That was in 1975.

Hershel Henninger had been a state policeman and retired, then he was elected as sheriff, so that's how I became interested in being a deputy and sheriff. He and my mom were relatives. Anyway, you didn't have to go to school, so I didn't know anything about the law. Well, after his term was over he asked me to run. So I ran for sheriff but was defeated. I ran for jailer and magistrate, but was never really interested in winning a race, because the drugs and things were so bad. However, I quit work for one year and spent my time campaigning to be elected as sheriff, and I was elected as a Democrat in a Republican county.

Charles L. Boston, Wayne County, February 13, 2010

FROM STATE TROOPER TO SHERIFF

When I came home from Vietnam I applied for the Kentucky State Police, and I was accepted as a trooper in late 1971, then graduated from the Kentucky State Police Academy in Frankfort, January 1972. After completing my academy training, they sent me to the Hazard Post, which is my home area. The Hazard Post includes Perry, Knott, Letcher, Breathitt, and Leslie counties. At the Hazard Post they didn't want to send me back to Letcher County because that was where I was from and I knew everybody. That makes it hard on a police officer trying to deal with people we were raised with. So they sent me to Knott County, where I served as a trooper. It took awhile before they accepted me as a police officer because there were two older state troopers there, and here comes this young trooper to also serve in there!

My training officer at the academy worked with me for about three weeks, then told the captain that I was ready to go. It took me awhile before the people accepted me. They'd call the jailer to report crimes, because they didn't want to make long-distance calls to Perry County. At the jail they had a radio and used it to call the trooper. Sometimes when I was working they'd call and say, "Is Trooper Turner working?"

They'd say, "No, but Trooper Webb is."

The caller would then say, "Na-a-ah," then hang up. [*Laughter*]

It took awhile before they would even let me come and work their cases. In the late 1980s we had several big murder cases, one of which prompted the book *Dark and Bloody Ground* to be written by Darcy O'Brian. It is based on the murder of Dr. Acker's daughter in 1985. She was home from college, and these guys who posed as FBI agents got in the house and killed her, and thought they also killed the doctor, then ran away with almost $2 million that he had locked in a safe. I served as detective-lieutenant in charge of the operation.

I served thirty years as a state trooper, 1971–2001, and served in various important capacities during those years. I retired in October 2001, and the sheriff's filing date for the 2003 term began the next day. After I filed for sheriff I'd tell everybody that after I retired from the state police, my IQ shot up to two hundred and I decided I wanted to be sheriff!

I began running for sheriff on qualifications that I had been a state police officer for thirty years, six years of which I had served as captain. I attended Eastern Kentucky State University and received a BS degree in police administration. When I began campaigning for election as sheriff, on the first day I went out the first thing I'd hear from people was "You can't win the sheriff's race because you're a trooper." Believe it or not, every state trooper that had ever run for sheriff before I did got beat. I'd go back home and tell my wife, "They're using against me what I thought I could look forward to."

I knew a lot of people due to my career, so I just got in my pickup truck and started going around from door to door. I'd go to every event I could so as to talk to people. I think that after they got to know me, they'd think, "Well, he's not just a state trooper, he's really a person—a person that cares about what goes on in this county."

So I won by a pretty good margin, and then won for my second term. I'm now in the fourth year of my second term, and I'm currently running for sheriff again.

Danny R. Webb, Letcher County, February 27, 2010

Campaigning in Monroe County

When I was in the first grade in school, a good friend of mine was Max Anderson, and when I put crème oil in my hair, my hair was so greasy he started calling me Slick, and every since then I have always been called Slick.

After I grew up, I really decided to run for sheriff based on my previous twenty-four years of experience as a Tompkinsville police officer, then I served as assistant commonwealth detective under commonwealth attorney Fred Capps, who was murdered a few years ago. So in 1998 I decided it was my time to be elected as sheriff. I ran on the basis that I was honest and served the people of Monroe County regardless of race. I filed in November 1997, then began campaigning during the main primary in 1998. So my wife and I started going together from door to door. She's a schoolteacher, so when she had time she'd go with me, and we went about every night except Sundays. We tried to cover all portions of the county, going from door to door, meeting and talking with the people, explaining what my intentions were in being sheriff. I always told people I wanted to try to do something about our drug problems, update the sheriff's department, add more deputies on the streets to do more patrolling.

I covered the county pretty good while campaigning for the May primary. We went to every kind of monthly and yearly group activities, including benefits, anywhere in the county. Actually, I ran against seven people, and I won. I ran against eighteen people in three primaries, and I have not been beat. I ran against two independent contestants and got three thousand votes. The closest one to me was the chief of police at that time, and he got seventeen hundred votes, while the second one got about five hundred votes. I firmly believe that my interest in serving countywide residents is what got me elected for three terms.

I didn't go door-to-door campaigning for my second term. I just mainly began hitting high places, such as going to all the big events we have here in Monroe County, including all the high schools' and middle schools' social and sports events. . . .

This is my thirty-sixth year in law enforcement, so I am retiring December 31, 2010.

Jerry "Slick" Gee, Monroe County, March 18, 2010

Dangerous Campaigning

There were several reasons why I wanted to run for sheriff. Of course, Stanton is a small town, but being sheriff is good pay. The county has a good retirement plan, but another good reason as to why I ran for sheriff is that I wanted to see if I could help improve the communities here in Powell County.

When I started campaigning that gave me a good chance to get out and meet the people. While doing that, I actually ran into people I was related to but didn't really know it. People on my mother's side were actually living here, but I didn't know it. You get out and meet everybody, and you talk to a lot of people. Well, sometimes you'll have good days and sometimes bad days, when you are campaigning. But campaigning was very interesting. I'm not a political person, so I just try to treat everybody like I want to be treated.

I won my first campaign, and that was the first time I ever ran for anything. Actually, I thought I wouldn't win, but I was elected and was kind of surprised that I did win. Actually, I won the race by a pretty good margin, and have been sheriff since January 2007. Before that I was a police officer for seventeen years.

I vividly remember one event that happened while I was out campaigning. I went to a dead-end road, and there was a trailer setting up there. I went to the front door and knocked on the door, and suddenly dogs started barking, barking, and barking. So this guy comes to the door and opened it by cracking it open about one inch. I told him who

I was and that I was running for the sheriff's office, and that if he could help me I would appreciate it. He said, "Okay," then took my card. Well, those dogs were just barking and raising Cain.

I thanked him, then said, "I'll see you later, and have a good day." Then I began walking back to my pickup truck. Well, those dogs had never stopped barking. They just kept on barking. All of a sudden I heard dogs barking out behind that man's trailer, then I looked back and here comes a dog from behind that trailer and was running after me. So I took off running and just barely got into the back of my pickup truck to keep that dog from biting me. I don't know whether he let the dog out on purpose, or if it just got out to chase me.

People here in this Democratic county know that I'm a Republican, but they tell me they vote for the person, not the political party. Of course, I'm not political; I'm just here to do my job.

Danny Rogers, Powell County, March 27, 2010

Chapter 2

ARRESTED PEOPLE'S BEHAVIOR

Perhaps one of the most dangerous aspects of a sheriff's job involves apprehending suspects and taking them into custody. As the stories in this chapter show, the behavior of people being arrested is unpredictable. Escape attempts are common; herein we read of officers' attempts to overtake fleeing offenders, both in vehicles and on foot. Descriptions of foot chases are often interestingly indicative of backcountry life and times, as in these stories sheriffs, deputies, and even FBI agents pursue runaways through the woods—with a sheriff in one case finding himself up a tree in the line of duty. Physical resistance to arrest is another common reaction, and several exciting stories herein describe suspects fighting back—often with firearms, sometimes with fists.

Some of the sheriffs' stories about arrests are wildly funny. The storytellers describe Keystone Kops–like scenes, as in the case of the deputy who accidentally maced himself or the sheriff who caught his man by almost tripping over him in a cornfield. The offenders' actions can be equally humorous: several somehow end up naked, one hides in a clothes dryer, and one is eager to reach the jail in time for supper.

Highlighted in several stories is the psychological acuity sheriffs display in successfully defusing potentially perilous situations. Sheriffs' negotiating skills persuade armed suspects to calm down; one amiably provides a cigarette to an agitated man as they talk, while another helpfully procures a bottle of whiskey. One sheriff reaches out to help juvenile offenders turn their lives around with the inspiring words of a country music song.

EVERYTHING THAT CAN GO WRONG WILL

This is a funny story I'd like to share. In my first term as sheriff, about

1980, a football player was on LSD and he stole a Seal Test milk truck and they caught him coming down the interstate going northbound in a southbound lane. We stopped him, then found his mind was blown.

We were taking him to Western State Hospital in Hopkinsville. There is a square here in the middle of Bowling Green, and we got him out. People would go over there in the summertime and eat lunch, have a concert in the park every Wednesday.

All this fellow had on was a T-shirt and blue jeans. He was barefooted. In his mind he was a football player, and he was six foot, four or five inches tall, and weighed about 280 to 300 pounds. He was a monster!

There was a screen between the deputies and this fellow. They couldn't get to him, and he couldn't get to them. Well, they started around the square in the officer's car, and this fellow started kicking with his feet, and he kicked the left window out. When they got around to the other side of the square, they said, "He kicked that window out."

He started out of the vehicle, and he went out headfirst but his blue jeans caught, and he flipped out and the jeans pulled out around his ankles. He was completely naked! There used to be a Charles Department Store there, but it's gone now. It went from Tenth Street to the square. Well, me and one of the deputies was running through there, and when we crossed the street people were looking at us running. When we got up there, this fellow was kicking like a chicken. Everybody was looking at him, and who he was. One of my deputies had gone out with his Mace can, and he maced the other deputy who was holding that fellow. Mace would spray about ten, twelve feet, and hit you like tear gas. It would blind you temporarily. You just couldn't stand it.

Anyway, the deputy then turned around and accidentally maced himself. He was walking along, and this fellow was laying on the ground just a-kicking, his naked body exposed to the world.

So I jumped on top of him, and two or three more. People had gathered around, and we had him covered by then. Well, this fellow got me by the right hand and had it in his mouth. He was biting down on my hand, but I kept saying, "Don't you do it. Don't you do it."

They sprayed him in the eye and he let go, so I got my hand up real quick. In the meantime, they sedated him and put him in an ambulance. That was so funny that something like that happened.

Jerry "Peanuts" Gaines, Warren County, July 20, 2009

DRAMEDY IN THE CREEK BED

One of the first things that took place after I became sheriff was kind of serious, and humorous, too. I was home in bed one night about 3:00 one morning when the Campbellsville city police started chasing a car. The chase ended up out on Kentucky 289, just less than a half mile from my house. They called me to come and help them. Evidently, the guy, who was approximately twenty-two or twenty-three years old, had wrecked and jumped out of his car. So when the city police ran up to get him, he started shooting at them. So they called me.

I had a tracking dog, and I'd gotten a drug dog that also tracked. So we had him out there, and I followed the dog and its handler down through the woods where the guy had run. As we were going down through there, suddenly a shot rang out and I could see where it was coming from. The guy that was shooting was in a creek bed shooting at us.

We worked our way over toward him and found him sitting in a creek bed. As soon as we got up to him, he took a gun and pointed it toward himself. Of course, all the other officers got there, too, and surrounded the creek bank where he was located.

I started talking with him and we got him calmed down a bit. Then he wanted a cigarette, so I got one and pitched it down to him, then I sat down on the bank, which was probably four feet above him. While I was trying to calm him down the other officers were covering me.

What was funny is that the drug dog we had was not attack trained, but I trained with the dog, and I had trained jointly with the other handler I had gone to school with. The dog was so upset, and was trying to get to the guy. He thought the man in the creek was going to hurt me, so the handler had to lay down on the dog to keep it from doing anything.

Anyway, I was talking with the fellow in the creek, and he would bring up the gun and then laugh. Well, he wanted to talk with his sister, so I thought that maybe that would help get him to come out. So we relayed and got another officer to go find his sister and bring her out there.

That was going on for an hour or so, but just as soon as his sister got there, the two of them started arguing and made things worse. I thought, "I've got to do something. I don't want to shoot the fellow." I knew he didn't want to kill himself, so when he was distracted and looking at his sister and hollering and yelling, I dove off the bank headfirst right at him. In my head, I said, "When I dive I'm going to grab the gun and then subdue him."

When I dove I missed the gun. I said, "Oh, shoot." I'd hit him just enough to knock him over, and he was kind of disoriented. I reached out and covered that gun with my hand, and jerked it and held it up. When that happened, another guy jumped off and grabbed the gun, so we got it!

About two weeks later that fellow came to me and apologized, then said, "I'm sure glad you tackled me." [*Laughter*]

In serious things, you've got to fight them, even with a little humor in it, too.

John E. Shipp, Taylor County, July 30, 2009

NEVER LET YOUR GUARD DOWN

There's humor and tragedy in police work at all times. I encountered this one guy that lived in Bald Hollow, located between Taylor County and Larue County. Well, every time I'd get him, I'd have to fight him. It was always, we had a fight.

I got a call on two drunks one night out in a car, and I was out on Highway 210 here coming to Campbellsville looking for them. Well, here comes this one guy I always had a fight with. He was walking down the road, drunk. So I stopped and got him, and as I was trying to arrest him, the two fellows I was looking for went by. Well, instead of searching him—and it wasn't that cold, but he had a big navy peacoat on—I threw him in the car, then took off looking for the other two, and got them stopped. I arrested them, then put all three in the car, but had only one set of handcuffs. Back then that's all they issued to officers. So I put the handcuffs on the drunk, but should have put it on the other guy. Back then you had a choice: either a screen or no screen in the car, since they didn't have enough money to put a screen in all police cars. So I was a tough guy and didn't have a screen.

We were coming back to town, and for some reason I kept watching this guy that I had always arrested. Almost to Hodgenville, I saw him squirming around in a weird way, so I asked him, "What are you doing?"

I looked around, and he was under that peacoat pulling out a big old long gun. I thought, "Oh, shoot, what am I going to do?" As he raised up, I hit the brakes. We were right by the old fairgrounds in

Hodgenville. I slammed on the brakes, and luckily I didn't have a screen. As I reached over, he was bringing that gun up to shoot me. I grabbed his revolver, then grabbed the cylinder and held it. He was sitting there trying to pull the trigger! At that time, I hit him in the nose pretty hard and got the gun away from him.

After I got him in the police station, I got to cussing with another guy, put the handcuffs on him and took him down to the police station. That's probably the only time in my whole career that I ever hit a guy that was cuffed. He come off with a comment, and I hauled off and hit him again!

No matter how routine your job is, you've got to follow precautions, and usually the guys you arrest all the time are the ones that are going to hurt you eventually. You get relaxed because you know who they are, then they come up with something new.

John E. Shipp, Taylor County, July 30, 2009

Hungry Prisoner

I arrested a notorious guy here one night. We had to fight, or he'd give us a lot of trouble. We got a call telling us he was out on a certain road causing trouble. I didn't want to go because some nights you just don't feel like fighting. But I did go out there and saw him setting on the side of the road. So I whipped around and pulled up, then started to get out of the car. Well, he jumped up and started running to the car, and I said, "Oh, my gosh."

Well, he run up to the back door of the car and jumped in. He yelled, "Hurry up."

I said, "What are you talking about?"

He said, "Hurry up. Doggone, it's almost suppertime and I'm going to miss it at the jail." [*Laughter*]

Sometimes you expect trouble, but don't get it.

John E. Shipp, Taylor County, July 30, 2009

Fast Cop

There was a fellow that walks around town here in Campbellsville. He was in the Vietnam War. We had a standoff with him out here in the county one night before he got as bad as he is now. He was out in the woods and had all kinds of guns on him.

He was supposedly out in the woods, so we had the house surrounded. Well, he came walking into the house, and the ones closest to him jumped up and told him to stop.

He didn't stop. He took off running back down through the woods. But dumb me took off running after him. I knew I was fast in track years ago, but didn't know I was now. I ended up being right behind him, and everybody else was coming up behind me, and he stopped and turned around and got a rifle and started bringing it up. I ran on down and said, "Don't; let's talk this out."

So he stopped, and we stood there quite a while, talking. But the bad thing is that someone had brought the dog. We had canines back then. The handler was behind me, and the dog was real close to my butt. I always wondered what would have happened if that dog had lurched and bit me. But after about forty minutes we talked him out of his gun, and he came on in. We took all of his guns away.

That fellow walks around town here now, just mumbling to himself. His ex-wife handles his affairs, but he lives by himself. He hasn't bothered anyone so far.

John E. Shipp, Taylor County, July 30, 2009

Wrong State

I was headed east here one afternoon, going toward Lebanon, and there was a lot of traffic in front of me. I kept seeing dust coming up, and wondered, "What in the world is that?" I was getting around the traffic, and when I got up there I saw an old car off on the shoulder of the road. The driver was driving in the gravel. I was able to finally get them to stop, and there were two old Tennessee men in it, and the car had Tennessee plates on it.

I walked up, and both of them were as drunk as everything. I got their IDs, and the driver was sitting there. I said to him, "Sir, have you been drinking?"

He said, "Oh, yeah."

I said, "Where are you going?"

He said, "I'm going down here to ———."

I didn't recognize the name of the place he was talking about. I said, "I don't know where that is."

"Well, it's down right beside this place," he said.

I said, "Do you know where you are?"

He said, "Well, yeah."

He named the place, and I said, "What state is that in?"

"What do you mean, what state? It's Tennessee."

I said, "Sir, you're not in Tennessee. You're up in the middle of Kentucky."

About that time, he took his hand and backhanded the passenger and hit him, then said, "Dad blame you, Fred, I told you we should have turned left back there."

Well, I like to have died. [*Laughter*] It was so funny, I hated to arrest them. No problem, but they were so drunk they didn't know what state they were in.

John E. Shipp, Taylor County, July 30, 2009

DEALING WITH BULLIES

What I learned from years past is that when you go to a new county, as I did in Hardin County, you go out and find the bullies of the county and find out who they are. Then you go to them, and if you had to arrest them, you'd do it. Unfortunately, the first bullies I met was when I had two of them in my car, together. I had to chase them through western Hardin County. All the troopers that were out were trying to find us. I got them stopped, but the way I talked to the bullies caused them to get right in the cruiser. As a matter of fact, I was out searching their car, and one of them stuck his head out and said, "Hey, there, calling you on the radio." They already knew my unit number!

I didn't have a bit of problem with them there. Other units started, "We'll meet you at the jail."

So I took the two guys and went to the jail, got them inside and within two minutes they had a terrible fight in there with all the other troopers. A lot of it depends on how you talk to them, but usually if you had to get in, I was prepared to try it. But if you take care of the bullies first, then the word got out that you didn't take crap. That means you're a nice fellow, but you said what you meant.

John E. Shipp, Taylor County, July 30, 2009

EARNING RESPECT

When some new guys and I first went to Raywick, Marion County, I told them that we've got to establish ourselves, and we did. Years ago, one of the old bartenders over there came in when I was first running for sheriff. When he got there, he gave me a check to help in my campaign. I said, "Jimmy, I've put you in jail, I've closed your bar down by the ABC [Alcoholic Beverage Control] for a month at a time. Why are you giving me money?"

He said, "Well, John, you know the troopers before you would tell us they're going to do something, and they never did. So that's why we kept doing what we did. But when you come, you told us you were going to do something, and you did it. If you'd tell me you were going to break my damn arm, you broke my arm. And we understood that, and we knew where we stood. Now, we might not have got along all these years, but I respected you. And if you want to be sheriff here, I want to contribute this money to you."

The things you do that you think no one sees, there's people watching.

I arrested a fellow one afternoon who was giving me a lot of crap, and I finally got him in the car and he looked at me and said, "You get my damn hat and give it to me."

I said, "This cap?" and he said, "Yeah."

I said, "Okay," then threw it out in the weeds! There wasn't a soul around.

A few years later I was right here in town and was eating one day. This guy spoke up and asked me, "Aren't you John Shipp?"

I said, "Yes, sir."

Then he told me the story about him watching me arrest that fellow. He said, "You had a terrible time with him, but you did it. It was funny when he told you to get his damn hat, and you picked it up and threw it over the fence."

Little things that you do, people see it and think about it.

John E. Shipp, Taylor County, July 30, 2009

SHERIFF JIM BEAM

Off Kentucky Highway 1107 at Lively Lane in Thelma, Johnson County, this man and his wife were fighting. She called 911 stating that her husband had a bomb and was going to blow their house up. We responded, and saw him with gunpowder on the floor. The state police arrived to assist us, and the man then stated that he would come out if I gave him a drink of whiskey, because he had run out.

I obtained a bottle of whiskey, and the fellow then came out of the house. He was subdued and placed in the back of the sheriff's car. I went back to speak with him, and he said I needed to keep my promise and give him a drink of whiskey. I obliged him by giving him a drink prior to his being taken to the detention center.

William D. Witten, Johnson County, August 7, 2009

High and Dry

Perry Parrish, a probation parole officer here in Cumberland County, and I went to look for this lady on whom he had a warrant. We tried to find her several times, but couldn't find her. We went to where she lived, and we asked her husband, who was a paraplegic and couldn't move much, if she was around. He kind of nodded his head to say that she was. We went on sort of looking for her, and we searched everywhere in the house.

We turned around and started into the basement and looked it over good, then looked around a few minutes, and then we started out of the basement. Perry happened to turn around look, then saw something in the dryer. So, we ran over there and looked, and the lady was up in this dryer. We started to turn the "on" button on to see if it would work. But we didn't try to do that. We tried to get her out of the dryer, but she was hard to get out of that dryer.

I don't know how she got in it, but she was hiding in the dryer. She said that she had been hiding in the dryer both times we had been up there looking for her. After that, when I go looking for somebody, I look in the dryer! [*Laughter*]

She had been caught for drug use several times, but was a very nice lady. She just got caught up on drugs, and she got out on probation. However, she missed a time or two to come see Perry, so he had to get a warrant for her and that's why we went looking for her.

In order to get into the dryer, she had just taken a shower and was kindly wet, and by being wet she got into the dryer but did not have any clothes on.

She and I still have a big kick about what happened. When she comes in, I look at her and start grinning, then she points her finger at me and says, "Don't say nothing." [*Laughter*]

James Pruitt, Cumberland County, August 10, 2009

PLAYING POSSUM

One night I took a female prisoner from Shelby County to the Franklin County jail because we couldn't put them in ours. About halfway to Frankfort, I thought she had died, so I had to get out of the vehicle to see what was wrong with her. I touched her.

You know, when you put your hands on somebody, especially some lady, she can do anything. Well, I was talking on that radio, telling that this lady had done passed out. I was talking to them so they'd know what I was doing. Anyway, I got her to the jail in Frankfort.

When I had touched her, that wasn't anything violent, but it was just something you have to watch. She really didn't do anything to let me know she was alive. I just jumped back in the car and drove about a hundred miles per hour, as I was about ten miles from the jail.

When I got her to the jail she kind of came to, so I knew she was alive!

Harold E. Tingle, Shelby County, August 14, 2009

NAKED PRISONER

One time I was going to Louisville, and this female prisoner who was sitting in the back seat took all her clothes off. As that happened, I was talking on the phone to get another car. There was a deputy who pulled up just as I got to the hospital, because I talked on that phone all the time.

I don't know why she took her clothes off, but I don't think she was trying to be sexual. But by golly, maybe she was, because she'd get up in the windows as those truckers passed by! Now, that was something else!

As sheriff, I've had some interesting experiences. There's a lot of that kind of stuff that happens.

Harold E. Tingle, Shelby County, August 14, 2009

THE STING

Since we had all these outstanding warrants to serve, one of the things we got involved in when I had a connection with the U.S. marshals was to go into a joint venture. In December 2000, we set up a sting. A U.S. marshal, myself, my chief deputy, one circuit court judge, and one of my trustworthy clerks, Lisa Gutsmann, were the only people that knew about this operation because it had to be pretty secret. We created what we called the Kentucky State Tax Reclamation Agency. We had my clerk to send out about five hundred notices to various felons who were wanted on serious crimes in Kenton County or federal violations.

The statement told them that they had monies coming back for overpaid taxes, ranging anywhere from $500 to $2,000 or $3,000. Most of these people never worked or earned a penny in Kentucky, but we knew they would want to get some money. We gave them a call number. I had the clerk to sign off sick, then I told everybody she was in the hospital for something. Well, she took appointments at her home on a special phone. We told her to space the calls out to about fifteen minutes apart. This went on for a period of weeks. Just before we were getting ready for these people to come in, I'd informed people in the county system, and had all my deputies to meet me at the last minute. I told them they had to come, no matter what their occasions were, such as being opening day of deer season. Some of them weren't too happy. I also called local agencies, as I needed some perimeter protection. A lot of these people were kind of dangerous, so we needed to step up security.

We were supposed to start getting appointments about 9:00. I had my briefing by 7:00, and by 7:30 or 8:00 the first one was knocking on the door of a special office we had set up on a vacant floor in the county building. It turned out he was wanted on a federal murder warrant.

That started things, and everybody was tickled to death that they were in on it then. We went on until well into the afternoon, and by that time we had served eighty-nine warrants. That was pretty interesting, and also there was a rather humorous twist to it. Some of the people asked us if we would let them use their check for their bond. They believed that sting right up to the point where we were slamming the door on them!

That was a very exciting thing to do. We cleared up a bunch of warrants, both federal and local, and that gave us a good reputation again. We'd just started to build up our reputation from being a do-nothing office to being an active office. Our office is now the second busiest in the state. We now have more than fifty thousand papers that come out of the court system. We go all over the country, to California and any place across the country, to pick up people that have been picked up for major crime convictions. On rare occasions we also got someone from Canada.

Charles Lee "Chuck" Korzenborn, Kenton County, September 17, 2009

Dumb Luck

I had several chases. Our third work shift was from midnight until 8:00 a.m.

This story is an intuition, or just what can be called "dumb luck." You have this feeling about running a license plate, and it turns out to be a stolen plate. One morning about 1:00 or 2:00, I was just coming to the office to do something. I turned down Sutton Street in Maysville and saw a car that caught my eye. It was an old Bronco or old Blazer, and the driver slowly crossed in front of me, then stopped at the stop sign. I read the license plate, and it came back stolen. It was the fire chief's vehicle from Vanceburg, Lewis County.

I turned around and found him three streets over on Limestone Street. As soon as I turned the lights on, he put the car in park, then jumped out and took off running. Well, I throw my car in park, but left the keys in the ignition. I think about that constantly, wondering why I left the keys in the car. Anyway, I chased him down the street about one quarter of a mile, radioing and running at the same time. There wasn't much traffic in Maysville at this time of day, so it just so happens that the man crossed Third Street by Simon Kenton Bridge, and here comes another officer and he almost clips him.

No contact was made, and I was far enough back that I didn't get hit, but I could still see the suspect. I didn't have to catch him, because the other officer did catch him in an alley right next to the bridge. After the prisoner got out of jail on bond or something, it wasn't a week until he wrecked a stolen car in West Virginia. He was put back in prison, and he served the rest of his prison time.

Patrick Boggs, Mason County, September 25, 2009

Foot-chasing Sheriff

I'm known by others in the Mason County Police Department for the chases in which I become involved. I get in the foot chases! One local reporter gave me the name Feet. Truth of the matter is, if somebody outruns me, it's because they had too big of a head start.

I was bailiff when I first got in the sheriff's office. The city of Maysville is very historic, and has several walking tours that take place throughout any given day. We were in our old courthouse that was made of several old sandstone stairs. Security is lax, as we've never had metal detectors or anything like that in our courthouses. This was when the public defenders would take the inmates back into the courtroom and do their discussing relative to their cases.

One day when I was bailiff, the public defender and his client Stephen Collier, who was on a felony charge in circuit court—back then, they didn't have shackles on, no handcuffs, etc., they just all walked in wearing their orange jumpsuits—Collier and the public defender were meeting in the back of the room. Well, at that time, I guess I was young and didn't know what to wear for shoes. I was wearing cowboy boots, not the best running shoes! That day, something in my mind had me watching him in particular while court was going on. Well, sure enough, when he got to the back he sat down, and all of a sudden he bolted out through two swinging doors, then out the front door.

Well, there were probably six or seven large sandstone stairs from top to bottom. I bolted through the doors and literally jumped to hit the bottom step, and that was it! I wasn't hurt, so I stayed on my feet. There was a walking tour going by the building at the same time I had pulled my gun out and was screaming at him to stop. He ran on and went behind the bank, which was probably three quarters of a mile, but I finally caught him.

One of the local businessmen was leading the tour I mentioned, and they were yelling at me to let me know which way he was going. It was embarrassing, but as soon as I crossed behind the bank, and there were trees everywhere, I tripped over a tree root and fell flat on my face. My gun goes sliding toward the fellow I was chasing, but he was still running. He didn't know the gun was there.

That was embarrassing because all the people in the tour were watching what took place. I got wounds that day from that. I chased him a quarter of a mile, and was really out of breath. A couple of civilians were walking by, so they helped me out by sitting on the man I was chasing until I got my breath and could handcuff him.

Patrick Boggs, Mason County, September 15, 2009

RACE TO THE CORNFIELD

Early in my career I ran with a pistol in my hand when chasing somebody. But later on I tripped and fell, so I didn't do it anymore. As sheriff, I was at our local Germantown Fair, where we always do the security details. One time, there at the fair, I didn't know why this boy was running. My sergeant and one of my deputies and I were out there working. I was talking to my sergeant when the deputy hollers out that he is chasing this seventeen years old juvenile due to something the young fellow had done. Anyway, when the deputy yelled out for us, I immediately took off running.

Well, I passed the deputy running full force about two hundred feet from where I first heard him call. I kept on going, and we watched the fellow run up the hill. That was the longest foot chase I was ever in. It was well over a mile.

I don't know why people ran from me. I don't know whether I look like I just can't run or what, but they do.

Anyway, that young man ran straight down across the parking lot. There were no lights in the parking lot, so you couldn't see anything and I was just running in the direction that I thought he was running. There was a cornfield at the time on Kentucky Highway 10, and corn was everywhere. Well, he ran into that corn patch and it scared the crap out of me. I was still running full force as fast as I could, and I almost tripped over him. He was lying down in the corn, so he was caught.

I guess I had at least a half dozen more running events, trying to catch the person that needed to be arrested.

Patrick Boggs, Mason County, September 15, 2009

REACHING OUT TO JUVENILES

I think this is my best story of all times, and it brings tears to my eyes when I tell it. I'm a Christian, but I do wrong, just like everybody else. When I haul juveniles to detention centers, I liked to try to let them know that I'm a person. Most of the time, I'm not the reason they're going to juvenile detention, but I have them under control in my police vehicle for two hours if they have to go to detention, one hour to Bowling Green and one hour back.

Most of these juveniles are from fourteen to eighteen years old. Some of them go on up to age nineteen. I feel like it's a duty of mine to get something in there that will stick in their minds. My favorite country music singer of all time is George Jones, and I'm his biggest fan that ever was. Back in the late 1990s George Jones sang a song that had the words, "Nobody is perfect; we are all flesh and blood," and it went on to say, "The only thing different in sinners and saints, is one is forgiven and the other one ain't."

What is the difference between sinners and saints? We are all sinners. How can we obtain that status we want to obtain, and it will help us throughout this lifetime more than anything in the world, but we've got to ask for it.

So I took it on myself to establish the same thing, unless this person was a repeat offender. In my vehicle, I have a CD player which has that particular CD readily available.

I will communicate with the juveniles in my vehicle, stop and buy them a hamburger or whatever on the way. I let them know I'm their friend and that I'm just transporting them, but I let them also know they are going to have to turn their life around. I always play that George Jones song, and if I happen to be in a squad car that doesn't have a CD player, I'll sing part of the song to them. After I tell them, "The only thing different in sinners and saints, is that one is forgiven and the other one ain't," I'll say, "How do you think that that person got forgiven?" Or, "Why do you think one don't get forgiven? It's all the same answer, so tell me: what do you think?"

I'll let them ponder about that for a long time. Sometimes from Russellville to Auburn, or from Elkton to Russellville; it just depends on when I think I can get their attention.

Not long after being in office, I was walking down the hallway to the courtroom entrance, and I saw this boy I hauled as a juvenile a year or two back. He had been doing well and wasn't in trouble again, and when he looked at me, he said, "Mr. Billy, I still know what the difference is."

I was all stressed out, worried about this and worried about that; I had to take juveniles here, and got calls waiting here, and a state policeman was mad at me, or this person was mad at me, so I was trying to get my job done and everything. I said to the juvenile who had just spoken to me, "What in the world are you talking about, son?"

He said, "I know what the difference is."

I said, "What do you mean?"

Then he said, "I know what the difference is between sinners and saints. I still remember. One is forgiven and the other one ain't."

When he said that I cried in the courtroom. And two other juveniles told me the same thing on the soccer field the other night. They are doing good, doing a lot better.

I feel good about that. It's a spiritual blessing.

W. D. "Billy" Stokes, Todd County, September 17, 2009

CAR WRECKS

Probably one of the first things that happened to me during my first term in office was when four teenage boys stole a Mustang car in Bowling Green. They ran two roadblocks over there, then contacted my office and asked me to try to catch them, because they were coming to Caneyville here in Grayson County.

So I set up a roadblock in Caneyville, and I had my brother-in-law with me. My roadblock was set up to where they could get around me if they wanted to, because by law they had to have an escape route. The town marshal of Caneyville was with us, and we seen the Mustang coming, but they stopped at the top of the hill. So the town marshal decided he would go up there and catch them before they started over the hill. Well, they ran him off the road, then proceeded on towards me. Well, myself and my brother-in-law were setting in the car, and he looked at me and said, "They're not going to stop." So as we exited the car, they hit my cruiser, which was the sheriff's car. I was so close to my cruiser when they hit it, the fender turned around and tapped my britches' leg as I was jumping over a road ditch.

Well, they totaled my sheriff's car and started bailing out of their car. At that time I fired two or three shots up into the air. That caught two of them and I made them lie down on the ground, but the other two got away from me. Meanwhile, the yard that I set my roadblock up in was an ex-sheriff's sister that lived there. She called the police department in Leitchfield and told them that they had better get somebody down there, that I had shot a couple of guys. She saw them lying on the ground and thought I had shot them.

The story gets worse than that. The two boys that got away went across the road, and we caught one of them in the basement of a house over there. By that time some state policemen had come down there and were trying to help us. They caught one in the basement of the house, but the other proceeded on to Otis Bryant's feed mill and got in one of their feed trucks and headed to Butler County.

A trooper was following him, and the town marshal was following the trooper. They got down there on a dusty back road in Butler County, and the feed truck they were chasing stopped, and then the trooper stopped. But when the trooper started to get out, there was so much dust. He heard the town marshal coming with his siren on, so he gets back in his car to tell the marshal they were stopped, but before he could tell him they were stopped, the town marshal ran into the trooper's car and drove him into the feed truck. They sent the trooper to the hospital in Bowling Green to take some stitches in his head.

We probably tore up three or four vehicles that day, just trying to catch those boys from Bowling Green that had stole that Mustang. Those boys were all eighteen or nineteen years old, thus were all adults. Because of what they did, they were charged here in Grayson County, and they were charged in Bowling Green for auto theft. I don't know what all we had them charged with here, but after they got finished with their charges here, we sent them back to Bowling Green. I'm sure that whatever they got in Bowling Green, we just let our term run concurrent with it.

But I never did get paid for my sheriff's car. I lost my cruiser.

Qulin K. Escue, Grayson County, September 22, 2009

COMEDY OF ERRORS

One of the funny stories is about this guy that should have got away. This guy was trying to extort money, and at the time I didn't know who he was. He was trying to extort money from this lady at the Citizens Bank in Leitchfield. He had written her a note and threatened her that if she didn't have so much money somewhere at a certain time and place, something was going to happen to her.

This fellow at the bank and I called the FBI to get them involved in what was to happen. We also called the state police. We all worked together on it. Bottles was the head FBI agent who was out of Louisville at that time, I think. We had an office set up at the Boy Scout camp command post, close to where the money drop-off was going to be. I went over and got the FBI set up in there so they could hear us talking.

The police chief at that time was in an airplane, and he was up in the air with the Kentucky State Police, I think. Bottles got hold of the state police up in the air, and I could hear them flying up and down the road.

We put the money where it was supposed to be. Actually, the time of the drop was just right at dark, maybe dusty dark. So my job was to drive the van and drop the FBI agent and the state police off near the point where the boy was going to pick up the money. Well, I drove the van over toward Rough River Lake and was going to let the officers out then, but there was a car not very far behind me. So I drive on through, turn around, and start back. I remember distinctly that there was a black FBI agent and maybe two white FBI agents. They had on their alligator shoes and their suits. But as I turned around and started back, about the time I started to let them out, there was a car that drove up behind me. So everybody had to get out fast. The back door flew open on the van, and the FBI agents jumped out of the back of the van right into a ditch that was half full of water. I mean water was just going everywhere.

Buford Stafford was the state police detective. He was sitting beside me, and FBI agent Bottles was sitting next to the door. Well, Bottles opens the door, jumps out, not thinking that the trooper sitting in the middle was going to get out, too. So when Bottles gets out, that detective also started to get out. Well, Bottles slams the truck door on the detective's head who was also trying to get out.

Well, we finally got them all out, got them set. I went on back to the command post, and Bottles, Buford Stafford, and the state police went over in the woods. Just as soon as they got there, the agent started hollering, "There's somebody in the woods! I think they are after us!"

What they had done, this guy had a bunch of Holstein steers over there, and those steers got after those FBI agents and was running them through the woods!

Well, it was almost time for the guy to come to pick the money up. Bottles, who was head of the FBI, had on some night-vision goggles . . . and he was telling Buford Stafford how good he could see with night-vision goggles.

About that time there was a car coming over the hill, and Bottles looked at that car. Well, those night-vision goggles just took those headlights in and it blinded him. He couldn't see nothing. Well, about that time the guy stopped to get the money, but Bottles couldn't see. Buford said, "He's there to get the money!"

Well, Bottles took off running, but he got hung up in a barbwire fence. He couldn't get over the fence with those night-vision goggles on. So Stafford, the state trooper, went down there and apprehended the guy when he stopped to get the money.

So by all means the guy should have got the money and got away, by the way the story went! But the guy is dead now, and I don't remember his name. He was captured by the feds and served time.

Qulin K. Escue, Grayson County, September 22, 2009

Smart Thief

This story has been printed in *USA Today*. I'll not read it, but I know the story from heart because I'm involved in it.

I believe this was in 1985 when I got a call at 8:00 or 9:00 one night. I was told that some farmers had caught a guy trying to steal their cattle. They honestly tried to kill him. They shot the tires out on the trailer; they shot the truck; they shot the truck all to pieces.

This guy's name was Roger Allen Marlow, probably in his sixties, and he was from Arkansas. After catching and interviewing him and picking up some evidence, I picked up an atlas that he had in the seat of his truck. He had that truck fixed up so he could turn out every light on it. The brake lights wouldn't come on or anything.

After getting his atlas and looking through it I noticed that he had Xs marked on different spots on the interstate, different states. I think it wound up being seven states. When I got to interviewing him, he wouldn't tell me a whole lot, so I called the Western Cattleman's Association in some state out west, probably in Oklahoma. I told them what I had found, that I'd found his atlas and that he had different Xs. What he would do was drive the interstates, and when he would see fields of cattle, he'd mark the location by the mile marker with an X. He would put those cattle up, then come back after dark and get them. There were seven states in which he had stolen cattle. He worked alone. He told me he broke his own golden rule; he never messed with farmers' cattle that were calving—that is, getting ready to have baby calves—because he knew the farmer would be watching.

It so happened that these cows were getting ready to calve, and the farmers were watching. When they'd come to check on them and saw they were all there, instead of calling us, they just stood there and waited for him to come back. I mean, they tried to kill him. Well, I got the FBI involved. We had a local agent here that I worked real close with, and he worked with us here, and connected out-of-state for us.

Roger Allen Marlow was a notorious cattle thief. He was an old rodeo hand. As a matter of fact, he tried to sell me his saddle before they extradited him back out west. I wish I had bought it, just for a keepsake! A lot of times he would put a baby calf in his trailer, and that's how he would get those cows in there. Then he would take them all back to his local ranch in Arkansas. If they had any ear tags or markers, he would take them off, keep the cattle for awhile, then run them through the stock pen.

After learning more about Roger Marlow, I learned that he had served five years in the pen out in Oklahoma. His job was taking care of the cattle. So when he got out of the pen, he went back and stole all their cattle! That's the truth.

I talked to one of the guys out there, and he said that Marlow was so smart he stole a bunch of cattle out west one night, and was stopped by a highway patrol officer because he had no taillight. When the highway patrol let him go, he was smart enough to know that on the next day they were going to know those cattle were missing, and that trooper was going to remember stopping him. So when that trooper let him go, he took those cattle back, puts them back in the field and fixes the fence.

He was probably one of the finest thieves I ever run on to. But they said he had stolen thousands of head of cattle. He made a lot of money, because cattle prices were high at that time.

He served his time, and when I heard from him after the story came out in *USA Today*, he was foreman for a construction crew out in Arkansas.

Qulin K. Escue, Grayson County, September 22, 2009

COMPOUNDING THE CRIME

One of the first arrests I made took place when I got a call about this drunkard over in the Grancer area. I went over there and proceeded to arrest him. I think a domestic problem was involved. I cuffed him and put him in the back seat. At that time I had not installed a cage in the back of my cruiser. I walked back up to talk to this lady to see if everybody was alright, and while I was doing this I heard my car start up. Well, he had got the handcuffs around in front of him so he could drive the car, and he was trying to drive off with my cruiser. He was stealing it. He never did get out of the drive with the car, but he was trying to.

By golly, I had to go back down there and capture him the second time. I said a lot of things to him, but I'll not repeat what I said! Just let me say that I wasn't too happy with him. But I didn't beat up on him. That's something that I don't do, and I refuse to let my deputies beat up the prisoner. Once you have handcuffed them, you keep your hands off of them.

As a penalty, that fellow got a few days in jail. I charged him with A.I., but I don't think I charged him with trying to steal the cruiser. He didn't work, didn't have any money, so he just stayed in jail for a couple of weeks.

Kenneth Lee Morris, Butler County, October 11, 2009

THE DEPUTY AND THE DOG

Back in 1991 my deputy Terry Fugate wanted to start a K-9 program and get a K-9 unit, which we did. This person had a German shepherd dog named Gil.

Well, we got a call from people down in the Riverside area telling us about a guy that was in a building down there, that he had a warrant on him but wouldn't come out. Terry and I went down there and found out this fellow had a two by four, and when the deputy got up there he was going to hit him on the head with it. Of course, Terry was a pretty good negotiator. He took Gil up just to the top of the steps, then gave Gil a command to attack. Of course, he was holding Gil back, but Gil's feet and teeth just popped. Terry said to that fellow, "I'm going to turn this dog loose if you don't drop that club. And if it hits this dog, I'm going to be terribly upset. If he don't get you, I will."

After that was said, that guy threw the club down and came down. The deputy arrested him, and that was all of it. But that could have been another serious situation.

Kenneth Lee Morris, Butler County, October 11, 2009

LACK OF COMPREHENSION

There was a fellow here in the community I had known for a long time, but he is now deceased. He was a gentleman who had a few little issues in things, and later in his life he was convicted of some kind of sexual assault on one of his children or a grandchild. I can't remember exactly. Anyway, we had transported him to the state penitentiary in LaGrange.

He was so very, very destroyed about the whole thing. We were taking him to LaGrange and were trying to explain to him some of the programs you must complete before you can be released from the pen. He kept telling us that he wasn't going to take them, and we kept trying to explain to him that you've got to take them because you have no choice. We told him that if you get there and don't want to take them, they will just let you sit there and you'll have to serve for twenty-five years.

I kept trying to tell him that he won't make it through twenty-five years due to his age. He probably had only about ten years left due to the fact he was an older gentleman.

That's not a funny story, but it's just one of those things a lot of people whom we take to the pen don't really understand what they're headed to. In this particular situation, I don't think he ever came out of the pen there in LaGrange. He was sent there, but I don't think he ever got out. We tried to convince him to take that program, but he never took it. He kept saying, "I didn't do anything."

We run into a lot of people who probably don't understand exactly what's happening.

Mike Armstrong, Shelby County, November 6, 2009

EMBARRASSING ESCAPE

This is an unusual situation. I worked a case once on several checks being passed around in this county and in other counties in this area. I had worked myself hard on that case and put a lot of time in while doing it. Finally, I had zeroed in on an individual that lived in Henry County.

You always want to do things right, and not do things that will embarrass you. So I contacted a trooper from that county, and we got together one night and went out to a residence there in Henry County and found the house was full of people. We started interviewing these people. What we were looking for was this guy who had forged a lot of checks when buying different items.

After an hour or so we finally convinced the people there in that house to talk to us. And after another several minutes we finally convinced somebody there in the house, and he told us who in the house was the guy we were looking for. So, as a result of that, we ended up making an arrest. After making the arrest, I had the proper things searched, handcuffed him, and all that. I actually used the trooper's cuffs to put on this guy. The trooper's cuffs were hinge cuffs that did not have a chain in between them. So when you put them on, they are totally locked.

I had worked this case for several weeks, and felt really good in doing the right thing. This trooper and I were taking the guy down to my vehicle, and it was a brand-new cruiser I had just gotten. I put the guy in the back seat, shut the door, got his hands cuffed behind his back, closed the sliding window, and slammed the door shut. I decided that I would go back to the house, but mistakenly left my keys in the car.

I went back up to the house to talk to some people. The trooper followed me back, and he was standing in the door watching me, and also looking back down toward the cruiser. Well, after we were there at the house for a couple of minutes, the trooper was watching me more than he was watching the car, which is the way it should be since we had that guy locked up in the car and was not going anywhere.

Well, when I came out the door and started toward my car, I saw the light inside the car was turned on, and then I see the passenger's door on the far side open. By golly, when I get to the car, there is nobody in the car! This little guy had taken his feet and got them out from under him, then opened the sliding window, crawled out through that hole, got in the front seat, and was gone, with our hinge cuffs!

Of course, you have to call other police officers, so every officer in Henry County that had a red light or a blue light came to this residence, and here I stand over there in Henry County, and me and this trooper let this guy get away from us. We never found this guy until several months later, and he was in Alabama. We never found him that night because we never caught up with him, but when we did get him back to Kentucky from Alabama, he explained to me just how he did it.

He said, "You know, you guys let me in that vehicle and then you walked back up there to that house. So I got my cuffs out from under me, and I remember that I was setting back there in that seat, so I just thought I would try to kick something out. So I kicked one time on that little old screen, and that door you had shut popped open." (It was a new door and it just didn't latch when I shut it.) "Well, I slid that thing open, crawled right out of there, took off, and I was gone."

He broke his wrist while trying to get the cuffs, but he got them off somehow, and he just ran away on his feet. Here I was in another county, and I was totally lost over there, so I had to sit there and be embarrassed because I knew a lot of guys working there. Every one of them got to riding me a little, and they also got on the trooper from that county. I think he had to pay for the cuffs!

Anyway, when the authorities caught him in Alabama, they sent him back up here. I think he wound up spending some time in prison because of all those checks he forged, and also for being charged by us for escape.

Mike Armstrong, Shelby County, November 6, 2009

CHASING BANK ROBBERS

In the early stages of my career these fellows robbed the First National Bank in Russell Springs. The morning that happened I was out sowing grass up at a little store located about four miles from here. A guy came running in and said, "They're robbing the bank!"

Two fellows by the name of Herbert Crenshaw [pseudonym] and Felton Estes [pseudonym] were the robbers. I knew both of them. I later got with Sheriff Wendell Wilson, who was an awfully good friend of mine. We were together when they called on the radio to tell us that there was a gentleman down at the Dunnville iron bridge wanting to see me.

We were on Torch Ridge in Russell County at that time, and we immediately went to the Dunnville iron bridge. This fellow told me, "Carl, right there's the car they were in when they robbed the bank." The car had an Ohio license plate on it. Well, they headed down Riffe Creek and were going too fast, which resulted in knocking the bottom out of their car. They lost all their oil, and the car was setting just barely down in the edge of Adair County by an old store building. They had headed up Barnetts Creek, but someone had seen them go into the woods running away.

We followed them into the woods. I didn't have my own gun at that time, but a state detective or state police had loaned me his gun. When we went into the woods after them, we tracked them several miles, and each time they would stop and rest. One of them would take a stick and make a little hole in the ground, and made it real uniform. Everywhere they would stop, Felton would get nervous and would take that stick and make the hole look like a top, a cone, that you can spin.

We were chasing them toward Clementsville, located in south-western Casey County, and we heard some dogs barking while we were down in this hollow. So we split up, with Wendell walking up one branch of the hollow, and I walked up the other. I got up there in the edge of a field and climbed a big hickory tree. When I got up in the tree I saw Herbert Crenshaw and Felton Estes going down the branch right toward Wendell.

I skinned down that tree and took off over the hill toward them just as fast as I could go, but in the meantime they were walking right toward the Russell County sheriff. They were coming up the branch, and he was coming down. But they had got up there and the dogs started barking, so they turned and went back down into the hollow. In doing that they walked up on Wendell, and he drew his gun. Well, Herbert took off up the branch, and Felton had a gun stuck in his belt. He went for his gun, and Wendell fired a warning shot, but he got a little closer than he meant to and he shot right between Felton's feet.

Herbert came running up the branch right toward me. I got behind a big beech tree there, and when Herbert came by I tackled him. I put my finger in the back of his head and told him if he tried to get loose, I would blow his head off. I took my belt off and tied his hands behind his back with the belt. He had had a bunch of tattoos taken off. Well, I got him pretty bloody when I tied that belt on him where he had had those scabs that resulted when he had those tattoos taken off.

Two shots had been fired, but Wendell hollered at me twice, and I'd hollered at him twice, but we must have been hollering at the same time because neither of us heard the other one. So I took Herbert and started down the branch to check on Wendell, and we met each other. Wendell was coming up the branch with Felton. I told Wendell that it looked like there were some people in that field located quarter of a mile from us. So we headed to the place where those cruisers and cars were parked upon that ridge. We were still in the edge of Adair County, but we got up there and the FBI was there. I remember the FBI taking Herbert's and Felton's pants loose and dropped their pants down around their knees. They did that in order to keep them from running.

Well, Herbert had most of the money, and he had a suede jacket on that he had cut and crammed it full of that money, mainly $100 bills. They had cleaned out the vault at the bank. However, I think just about all of the money was recovered, except somewhere around $1,700 or $1,900.

That event was the starting of my career, and I think I was working as constable at that time. That happened in 1970, before I became a deputy for Ray Overstreet.

Herbert and Felton were both tried in federal court in Bowling Green and were both sentenced to the federal penitentiary for, I think, twenty-five years.

Carl E. Meece, Casey County, November 12, 2009

TREATING THE DOG

I was out about 3:30 a.m. on Highway 80 at the Russell-Casey County line. These robbers had broken into the Jamestown Bank and were going to try to cut into the vault. Well, they were on foot and running. I called the bank and asked if they wanted me to come help them, and if they wanted me to call Sam Catron and ask him to bring his dog. Sam was probably the best friend I ever had.

He immediately got his dog, and here he comes. We started tracking the thieves down toward the Jamestown Marina. The dog was doing that, too. While we were down there looking for them, we found several patches of marijuana down there below Jamestown. The chasers were about 100 to 150 yards behind this one bank robber, but I was closer to him than anybody else. He was running across this field that was grown up with bushes and everything. Well, while we were hunting for him, we came up on this marijuana.

The robber we were chasing came up through there, and he had a brown jersey in his hand. One of the troopers hollered at me and said, "Carl, get down out of the line of fire! I'm going to take him out!"

I yelled back, "Don't shoot, I'm going to catch him!" Of course, I loved to run. I stayed in good shape by doing it. So I ran him down, ran up on his back. That took place during the spring of the year, when fescue was really growing. He looked just like you had striped him with green paint on his face. That happened as he went scooting down through there.

Anyway, I had his arm up behind his back and was holding him, then here comes Sam Catron. I'll never forget what he said, which was, "Carl, let me treat my dog. Don't let this fellow up; just let me treat my dog."

I looked up and I've never seen such a head on a dog in my life, and that dog looked like he was going to eat us both up. He smelled that guy, and just as soon as he smelled my prisoner, that dog was satisfied.

I think those robbers pled guilty. I don't think I've ever had to go to court on them.

Carl E. Meece, Casey County, November 12, 2009

TRUSTWORTHY CRIMINAL

One of the mistakes I made that could have really turned into something bad on my part, but it turned out good! One Monday morning about 3:00 a.m., or a little after, I had been out all weekend. I was still out, so I thought I would wait until I got calls on Monday morning, since calls would come in about thievery, or something. After I had taken care of all calls that had come in, I'd come home and take a shower, clean up, then go back to work.

A car pulled out from a business place there in Liberty, Kennedy's Supply. Kennedy was an older fellow and a pretty good friend of mine. I didn't know the driver, so I got behind him and followed him and his companion. His car had Indiana plates. I had a plastic seat cover, and I would use it to write down notes and things, especially license numbers. If I thought these was going to be problems, I always wrote down a little note to primarily use for 1047, which is what we used in order to run license checks.

So I wrote that Indiana license number down on my seat cover, and I followed that fellow in his car up Hustonville Street, and he never did make a bobble, so I had no reason to pull him over.

The dispatcher called me a few minutes before 6:00 and told me that Jargo Kennedy had been robbed. Of course, I had that license number, so I ran it, and it came back to a Calvin Jessie Snyder [pseudonym], Edinburgh, Indiana. (That's where a lot of our roughs and toughs went.) Well, they had stolen four or five cases of knives and knife cases, and some guns.

I called the state police in Columbia, gave them the guy's name and a description of the car, and asked them to call the state police in Edinburgh. I didn't know who the other person was, but at that time in the state of Indiana, when they'd stop a car and make an arrest, they'd inventory the car. They don't search it, but call it an inventory because they had been sued one time. Anyway, they had left some valuables in the car and alongside the road.

It wasn't any time until they called back down at my office and said they had two subjects stopped, whose names were Calvin Snyder and Buster Evans [pseudonyms], and that they had also recovered a bunch of knives and some other stuff that had been stolen out of the store. Before I could get to the judge and get a warrant, they called me back to tell me that both of those fellows had waived extradition, confessed to everything, and was ready to come to Kentucky to be tried. I went ahead and got my warrant and went up there to get them and bring them back to Casey County. Naturally, they both pled guilty.

Well, Buster Evans was a tough one, but was a nice-looking young man. He stayed in the pen so much and worked out, and was a real hoss. He whipped the Casey County attorney, H. Marr Garner. He had also been commonwealth attorney and was a state representative. He could have been anything he wanted to be, but he wouldn't stand success; he would destroy himself.

What happened is that Buster got out of prison and had promised Marr he would whip him, and he did. I mean, he gave him a bad one over there in the Liberty Grill. But I had arrested Buster several times, and he's always been super nice to me. I was also good to him, too. I just had to put him in jail when I'd catch him out there drunk and violating the law.

As I said, he pled guilty, and when it came time for me to take him to the penitentiary, I had to take him to Eddyville because he was more than a three-time loser. LaGrange wouldn't accept prisoners if they had been there three times. I went over to Eddyville to pick him up one morning, and he said, "Carl, I hate to ask this of you, but my wife and children want to follow us to Eddyville to the penitentiary. Would you care for them following us?"

I said, "Well, I don't reckon it matters."

We got about halfway down to Eddyville, and I was getting hungry, so I pulled into a restaurant and his family pulled in beside me. We all went inside and ate, and I paid for everybody's dinner. Then we came back out and headed on to Eddyville. There is still water on each side of the road near Eddyville, but there is still some dirt showing where you can pull off before you get to high water. We were going down through there, and they were still behind us.

I don't know why I trusted Buster, but I did and had always been good to him. He said to me, "Carl, I won't feel hard at you if you say no, but would you pull over and let them pull up beside us, and just let me say good-bye to my family?"

So I just pulled over at that pull-off, and his wife pulled in behind me. I don't know what made me do it, but I was dead wrong to pull over for her and her brothers, all of whom were very mean.

I was talking to the circuit judge about that the other day, and he said, "I doubt if they'd have done anything with you if he would have escaped since he was in your custody."

Anyway, I pulled over there, and they pulled in behind me. I said, "Buster, you've got fifteen minutes, and I would appreciate it if there will be no physical contact while you are visiting with your family for fifteen minutes. I'll be back to pick you up in fifteen minutes."

I drove off and went down to a little curve, then turned around and drove back. That was the longest fifteen minutes I ever spent, because everything that could happen was running through my head. I expected to go down there and see him swimming one way or another, trying to get away from me, but when I pulled up, he was standing there beside the car talking to his sister and all her brothers. Then he got in the car with me and had big tears rolling down his cheeks. He was very appreciative of me putting that kind of confidence in him by letting him visit his family. So we loaded up, and I took him on down to the penitentiary but didn't see or hear from him anymore for about three years.

Carl E. Meece, Casey County, November 12, 2009

Fight Avoided

One morning about 3:00 I got a call from just off U.S. 127 about a mile. There was a little lane that went out to this Cannon family home, and they had throwed a beer bottle, or someone had, and hit this woman's car. She was coming in from work about 2:30 or 2:45 p.m. She called me, and I jumped into my pants and shirt and away I went.

I hardly ever carried a gun because I had back trouble. Usually, when we had court, I would dress up in uniform, and I'd have my gun and stuff with me. Anyway, that night I didn't have a gun, but went rushing out of here and got up there and pulled in behind this big rock. After I got there I knew I was in trouble, or thought I was. This Randolph guy was there, and you had to fight him every time you arrested him; everybody did.

I got out of the car and here he comes. He was wanting to fight, but was not going to jail. He took a pop at me, and I hit him hard and finally addled him pretty good and then snaked him to the car and put him in the back seat. I drove back up there, and a guy by the name of Merle Foster [pseudonym] was there. He's been in the penitentiary many times and jailed in Indianapolis. Anyway, he and I had had a fight the Sunday before this took place, and I had his arm twisted up behind him out there on Bartle Lane, and was trying to make him give up. Finally he did give up, and his face was all scratched up by the fine gravel where I'd been scooting him in that gravel. He was a great big guy, and was very dangerous.

He said, "Carl Meece, you have to kill me this time. I told you I'd never go to jail if you are against it, so you are going to have to kill me tonight."

I said, "Now, Merle, we've already had two or three fights. You might not go to jail, but one of us will go somewhere."

He said, "I'm not going to jail. You're going to have to beat me to death."

Buster Evans [pseudonym] was in the crowd, and was leaning up against that big rock that was probably twenty feet high. He was leaning kind of back in the shadow, then stepped down and said, "Merle Foster, Carl Meece ain't going to have to whip you tonight. I told you when you hit that woman's car with that beer bottle we would all wind up in jail. Now you're going to jail. My three brother-in-laws are going to jail, and I'm going to jail, and anybody that wants to fight has got to whip me first."

They all loaded up and we had a happy ole time going to Liberty.

Carl E. Meece, Casey County, November 12, 2009

THE BARTLEY FAMILY

One of the funnier stories is about the Bartley [pseudonym] family that lived in Dunnville. They were getting drunk at all times, and of course we would have to put them in jail. They would fight among themselves, but they all liked me. I put them in jail when needed. Poor ole Alvey was arrested fifty-one times one year, and I arrested him forty some times of the fifty-one.

They called me Duck. Top Bartley wrote songs about me. They called him Top. Morton Bartley also wrote a song about us. Dr. Tommy Bartley's wife has got all the songs they wrote.

One night they called me to Dunnville about the Bartleys. So I went down there and arrested Andy, whose real name was Randolph. I also arrested Top Bartley, the guy that wrote and sang all the songs. He caused fights many times, but he was in the crowd. And Roy Bartley's wife was in the crowd, as well as Charles Bartley. There were four of them, and all were in Gate trucks. Well, I arrested two of them for drunk driving, then I pulled their trucks down there in the ball yard after I put them in my car. They were one right behind the other, and I passed them and arrested all four of them.

They didn't have any harm in themselves, but they just liked to get drunk. Anyway, on my way down there, I saw this old white Oldsmobile car setting there beside the road, and this guy was stretched out across the car. I thought, "Well, I'll check him out when I come back."

I got all the Bartleys loaded up, pulled the trucks down there in the ball park, and as we were coming up through there, I saw this white Oldsmobile that had Illinois plates. I pulled up and had my lights on him and pecked on the window to wake him up. He roused up and I opened the door and asked him to get out, and he did. He was six foot and two inches and weighed 380 pounds. (Back then they had your physical on your license plate, and that was several years ago.)

So, David and Doug Johnson were brothers, and David was later elected over me when we ran for judge. They stopped and asked me if I needed any help, and I said, "No, fellows, I don't need any help. I've got four prisoners there in my car that will help me if I need any help."

I always put somebody I didn't know in the right rear seat if I was expecting trouble. I never did use a screen. Anyway, I put him in the right rear seat, and was going up Old Walnut Hill Road. Well, Top Bartley reached around the seat and gouged me in the ribs. Naturally I looked up, and could see that this big guy had a knife out that was about ten inches long, handle and all. When I saw that, I just pulled over but didn't even have a gun. However, earlier on I had arrested a guy from Russell County and I then took a .25 automatic off of him. I still had it in my pocket, but I took the shell out of the barrel, and there were five shells in the clip.

So I remembered having that gun when I got out of the car. But by the time I had stopped the car, Top had reached up there and got hold of the car door and quickly got out of the car. I began trying to persuade him to get back in the car, but couldn't do anything with him. Well, the only time I fired Bill Wilson's gun that I had with me was when I meant to shoot once under Top's feet, but I shot twice. In other words, I pulled two off instead of one.

Top then said to me, "You cowardly son of a bitch, you wouldn't even shoot a chicken."

I said, "No, but I'll bite your big bottom all night," then stuck my gun back in my pocket!

After that we started fighting, and R. C. Weddle called the sheriff's office and said to the dispatcher, "Mr. Hugle, we've got the worst fight going on out here that ever was. I've never heard such hollering, and there's been some shooting and I don't know what all is going on. We need some law out here."

Mr. Hugle said, "Well, Carl Meece left Dunnville just a few minutes ago with the Bartley family. He ought to be coming through there just about any time."

Well, I was the one needing the help. I was the one fighting this guy, but I failed to crawl out of the car. See, it all happened so quick, and we fought all the way from R. C. Weddle's grocery down to the church. Top would take those big swings, and I was going under him trying to take the wind out of him so I could clip that jaw, and boy, I finally got him. I knocked him down, and boy, he hit the ground like a ton of brick. His head sounded like a pumpkin when it hit the ground. He was just laying there on the ground, and would go, "Grooh, grooh," and just jerk. Well, that scared me.

I went into a helpful mode, and by golly the Bartleys were there cheering me on. They were cheering me, and Top was calling the fight! Then, after I knocked the guy out, and we were probably a hundred yards from my car.

That was another mistake I made and, of course, I was scared. We didn't have handhelds back then, and I was holding this guy up because there was blood coming from his nose, one of his eyes, and I was scared, and I had arrested him for drunk driving. I was afraid he was going to die. I told Hade to run up there and get my cruiser.

He went up there and gets in my cruiser, then calls the sheriff's office and said, "This is Hade Bartley. I am helping the little duck-legged sheriff arrest a guy weighing a ton." Then he dropped my mike down in the steering wheel, turned the siren and blue lights on, and here he comes. He got so close to that big fellow that I believe if I hadn't jerked the big man over a little bit, Hade would have run over his foot.

We like to have never got the fellow loaded. We were all loading him, so we just rolled him up and finally got him in what was just a two-wheel car. It took a long time, but we finally got him in the back seat, and then I put the other three up in the front seat with me, and told Top to hold his head up so he won't get strangled on all that blood.

With Top holding that big fellow's head up, we took off for Liberty, but hadn't got to the foot of Walnut Hill when Top just turned him loose and started shadow boxing and causing that fight again. I could hear voices on the radio trying to call me, but Hade had dropped my radio down in the steering wheel, and he pulled my mike out of the radio. I could hear them talking, but I couldn't talk back to them.

They sent Charlie Moore, a city policeman in Liberty, to come look for me. I was driving through there real fast and had my blue lights on. Charlie said, "Mr. Wesley, I see him coming, but there ain't no way I can catch him. He's flying, so I don't know where he is going."

Mr. Hugle said, "Why, the crazy thing probably had to whip some of them down there and take them to the hospital."

So that's where I was going. We got him over there to the hospital, but we couldn't get him out of the car. I mean, we got him out but got him wedged. We had the front seat scooted all the way up, but he was so big we got him wedged between the seat and that post. I made one final effort to get his hips loose, and when I did that belt broke, but that cleared him and he fell out on that concrete and bounced like a rubber ball.

There were two men working at the hospital, and one of them, Bob Clements, took the stretchers and turned them up sideways, then took them up against that big fellow. Then I went around, a couple of us, but didn't realize I was hurt as bad as I was. We got hold of that man, but Bob and the other guy turned the stretchers back over, and we held onto the man and finally got him on the stretcher. Then we got him into the hospital. Well, he had five patches on his head, not tape or anything, and I couldn't figure out what those patches were.

The registered nurse on duty checked him out, and he came around after a little bit. The nurse told us, "The blood on that man's head just came from some contusions where he had hit that blacktop, but that ain't nothing. Them other cuts he's got on his head are more dangerous than what you've done to him."

At that time, the Pulaski County sheriff was Gilmore Phelps, and he had heard me calling Columbia to get them to run a check on him in Chicago. Gilmore said, "Carl, how many of you did it take to take him?"

I said, "It took me and four more."

He said, "Well, me and John Henry Johnson and Trooper Wesley just about had to beat that thing [fat man] to death two or three nights ago. We had the awfulest time with him that ever was. Has he still got that bandage on his head?" [*Laughter*]

The next morning, they brought him over from jail and the judge was going to take a plea from him. That man said, "I want to talk to that little sheriff [Meece] before I make a plea."

They sent for me, and I went over there to talk to him. He was really apologizing to me. Of course, I was pleased to see him up and healthy looking.

The judge fined him pretty heavy and gave him six months in jail. Probation was provided, but he was never back in Casey County again. He wasn't ever going to come back to Casey County!

I went in and talked to the judge about Hade Bartley, and said, "Judge, I just don't feel right. We lock the Bartleys up all the time. It would be alright with me if we'd just forget about Hade Bartley. There is a whole bunch of them Bartleys, and they really helped me last night. It's going to be impossible for me to get them charged with DUI, and then me sending him after my cruiser, and he drove it a hundred yards.

The judge just smiled and said, "They'll all plead guilty and there won't be nothing said about it." And they did plead guilty, but I never did serve the bench warrant on Hade. I just couldn't do it.

Carl E. Meece, Casey County, November 12, 2009

BEAUTIFUL DRUNK DRIVERS

Back around 1994 there was an officer out working with me, and it had snowed a lot of snow, and it was also very cold. What happened took place just a little bit after midnight. We had received a call from an adjoining county telling us that a vehicle was coming up the highway, and the people in it were intoxicated. The motorist that called was driving behind them, and he said they were driving all over the road, even though we had a lot of snow.

The vehicle actually came into town, so the other officer with me got in behind them, turned his blue lights on, and got them pulled over. I pulled in behind him to assist him a little bit, to see what was going on. He walks up to the car, and the persons in it were two young ladies, and boy, they were really intoxicated. They actually were crying as we walked up because they were scared. Evidently, they were so intoxicated that they got on the wrong road to go home, so they ended up here in our town. They were definitely lost.

The other officer had asked the lady that was driving to get out of the car. Well, she said that she wasn't going to get out! He asked her several other times, telling her she needed to get out of the car. Finally she got out of the car, but couldn't stand up. Actually, neither of them could stand up because they were scared.

They were really beautiful little girls, really pretty. We put them in the back of the officer's cruiser, and were walking back to their car when I just happened to ask him, "Do you think this is a bad time to ask for a date?" I wasn't married at the time.

He started laughing and said, "Yeah, this is probably a bad time, so you'd better not do that."

Anyway, we took care of them, took them to jail and got it all worked out.

Wayne Agent, Crittenden County, November 3, 2009

TOPLESS FEMALE ROADBLOCK

I've spent quite a time dealing with some women whom I arrested. When you arrest a woman and bring them in to jail, you have to report the mileage to go pick them up, then return. Otherwise, persons [in the court system] will think you are out there doing something else. A woman is really the worst thing you can arrest. We are not questioned about going to pick up a man, but we are questioned if we go pick up a woman. They not only question the number of miles, but they also ask how long you were there.

When you arrest a woman, they can give you a good cussing, but I'll not mention the words they may say. [*Laughter*] They do indeed get hostile, even though they are guilty of doing whatever reason I go to pick them up.

I'll even tell about this woman that tried to flirt with me several times. This happened a right smart time back, but she came through a roadblock. I motioned her on through, checked her, then said, "You can go on."

Here she comes back through again, and this time she had her top off, and her body was exposed all the way down to her waistline. I said, "You get on out of here. I don't want to see nothing like that."

All she said was, "Don't you want to meet me somewhere?"

I said, "Nope, nope."

Some women are tough. They'll try anything!

John "Tuffy" Snedegar, Bath County, December 11, 2009

A FIGHT EVERY TIME

I had another fellow that every time I was involved in arresting him, also with every other police officer I ever talked to, you had to fight him. He was not going to give up peacefully. He was always going to fight you. He was just a little wiry kind of a guy, and he had to have a fight. It was just that simple.

I got a bunch of warrants on him, and I received some information he was held up in an old house out in the county that was just a shack. He was in the house but had not been staying there, just moving in and out. I got some information that he was there by himself, so I went by myself again. When I got there early that morning, he was still in bed. I went into the house, got to the bedroom where he was located before he realized I was even there. He had no way to get out except through the door in which I was standing. The windows were barricaded up. It was dark in there, so I opened the door and that put some light into the room. I told him I had a warrant on him. He got up and was putting his clothes on. When he started to put on his shoes I saw him pulling those shoestrings pretty tight, so I knew he was going to try to do something.

When I started toward him he hit one of those old windows that had metal over the top of it, but it didn't bust down. It just partly went down. So he and I were fighting in the window area there, part of our bodies on the inside of the house and part of us on the outside. Ultimately, we wound up on the outside of the house standing on an old porch.

Like I said, he never did win a fight. Anyway, he did a pretty job on me by tearing my clothes off. I finally took him on to jail and went on up there to my office, and someone said, "What happened to you?"

I said, "Oh, I had a little problem out here. I had to go back to get my badge." He had torn the badge off my shirt, tore my buttons off, and so on.

They said, "Where is he?"

I said, "Well, he's in jail. Where do you think he is?"

Anyway, I went back out there and picked up some of my clothing, and I think I lost a flashlight out there on the back porch.

That was a rather interesting experience.

Barney Jones, Barren County, December 21, 2009

ALL IN THE FAMILY

Back in the 1970s there used to be a lot of cattle rustling around here in Boyle County. They caught the guys that did that, and they spent a lot of time in prison. Stealing cattle used to be bad here. After they stole them they'd take them to some other place where they could sell them. A lot of that took place in the 1970s and early 1980s.

Usually, when something like that happens, it's not the local people that do it. The thieves are from other counties, even from other states. However, we've got one or two knuckleheads around here that you deal with. You start out dealing with their dads and their grandkids. It's just like a vicious cycle, and you start dealing with the whole family. Dads learned it; their sons learned it, and his sons done it. When you go out on calls, it's normally the same people time in and time out. There are certain individuals that I'll bet I've been on calls dealing with them at least two hundred times. They never care to learn about stopping.

LeeRoy Hardin, Boyle County, January 11, 2001

Unusual DUI Arrest

On May 22, 2001, my office received a call telling us that a male was extremely intoxicated on Kentucky Highway 3311, Montgomery Road, in Garrison. The male suspect was driving a riding lawn mower pulling a small wagon. A woman was riding on the small wagon. The operator of the riding lawn mower is a middle-aged town drunk in the area. The woman riding on the wagon was the drunk's wife, and they were engaged in an argument. Prior to the deputy's arrival, the drunk man pulled the towing pin from the wagon's tongue, causing the wagon and wife to run off the road over an embankment into a creek. The deputy arrived and the operator of the lawn mower was arrested for DUI.

Well, on June 10, 2002, I received a call on the same middle-aged drunk operating a riding lawn mower on Kentucky 10 near Garrison. I arrived on the scene and turned on my emergency equipment, and the drunk attempted to flee at approximately ten miles per hour. He finally stopped and I exited my cruiser, but when I did that he took off again on the lawn mower. I ran on foot and knocked him off the lawn mower and arrested him for DUI.

William D. Lewis, Lewis County, January 13, 2010

Interstate Arrest

On January 4, 2001, I initiated an investigation regarding a series of thefts that had been conducted by a Lewis County man. He had recently got out of prison in Ohio. A boat, Jet Ski, and numerous other items had been stolen from a storage building near Cincinnati, Ohio. Following numerous leads, I discovered he had brought the items to Lewis County and had burned a boat that had been stolen. The man then had gone to Maysville, Kentucky, rented a truck where he had gone to an equipment rental and loaded the stolen items in the truck, then left the state.

Intercepting communications, I learned he was traveling to, and had arrived in, Arizona, where he took a plane to Hawaii.

A few weeks later I learned his girlfriend in Lewis County was going to travel to Hawaii to meet him. I forwarded warrants and photographs to the authorities in Hawaii with information regarding the flight his girlfriend would be on.

When the plane landed in Hawaii, authorities arrested the man when he met his girlfriend at the airport. The man was extradited to Lewis County where he was convicted, and also convicted in the other respective jurisdictions.

William D. Lewis, Lewis County, January 13, 2010

Arrests Change Behavior

When you capture someone and put them in handcuffs, their behavior changes right then. They just start cursing and things like that. I've had some who kicked the windows out in the back of my cruiser, and do just about everything.

We arrested this one guy who was about twenty-five years old, and what he had done wasn't really anything major. It was domestic, and due to the law we had to do our job. So we told him what we're doing, and then arrested him and put him in handcuffs. We had not used handcuffs on him before because he was pretty cool. But once we told him he was under arrest and was under handcuffs, he began telling us that we were the most awful people on the face of the earth. I mean, he started cursing us and he used every bad word he knew.

Well, we put him in the back seat. Since that happened several years ago, we didn't seat-belt him. He just kept hitting his head against the window, and we'd open the door to talk with him. Well, the last time we had him, he laid down in that seat and kicked that window in the back of the cruiser plumb out.

So I guess putting him in the back seat of the cruiser just tore him up and caused him to go ballistic. Of course, when that happened we had to shackle him and everything, because he was kicking and doing other awful things.

After all that happened, we'd see him and he'd speak like we were good buddies. There are several others who act like that when they are arrested. Of course, they'd curse you, but I'd just let it go. I never really had any bad problems with people. I treat them the way I want to be treated, and when you do that you get along with them afterwards.

Danny Rogers, Powell County, March 27, 2010

GRATEFUL SPEEDER

I was actually running radar up on Mountain Parkway back when I was a city police officer. There was a deputy with me and we had stopped this girl for speeding. I could tell she was nervous when we went up to her vehicle; she was just shaking. I got her driver's license, but she didn't have any warrants, etc. Actually, she was running about twenty-five miles an hour over the speed limit. I explained to her that she could lose some points off her driver's license. I said, "I know you are nervous. You are just torn all to pieces."

Normally, people don't act the way she did, but she was just extremely nervous. So I said, "I'm not going to write you a ticket." Well, right there on the side of the parkway she grabbed me and kissed and hugged me right there, and there was traffic flying by. My deputy was standing there, but you'd think she acted like somebody had given her a million dollars!

She was really happy, and what she did to me was really funny. I mean it was a big squeeze.

Danny Rogers, Powell County, March 27, 2010

STRIPPER SHOWS THANKS

This is something that happened in the presence of four officers in Stanton. An officer had stopped this lady, who actually was a street stripper from Lexington. I'm not the one that stopped her, but I was in the back of the vehicle. She was wearing something skimpy, but really nothing. The officer was going to write her a ticket but he didn't. She wanted to thank him, but she just jerked off her clothes right there in front of God and everybody right there on the side of the road.

As she stood there in the presence of all of us, she said, "Thank you, thank you for not writing me a ticket." I guess she considered taking off her clothes as a payment to all of us!

Danny Rogers, Powell County, March 27, 20010

Chapter 3

MENTALLY DEPRIVED PEOPLE

The stories herein describe sheriffs' encounters with mentally incompetent people who found themselves on the wrong side of the law. We read of a man who entered someone else's home, thinking it was his own; a fellow who shot and killed a deputy sheriff; a woman who threatened to cut off a deputy sheriff's head. In one tragic story in a different vein, a young autistic girl accidentally drowned.

Wrong House

There's a private hospital in Nashville that is kind of like Western State in Hopkinsville. One night a fellow in there got out. Well, a doctor had left his key in his car, and this mentally instable fellow got in the doctor's car and drove up 31W, and he got down here in Rich Pond, Warren County. A farmer [and] his wife had gone to bed upstairs in their house.

We don't know if this fellow unlocked the door, or if it was unlocked, but he went to the door at the house and went in. He turned on the TV, and was watching it as he sat there with a big cowboy hat on. The farmer's wife said to her husband, "You left the TV on."

He said, "No, I didn't," then picked up his gun and went downstairs, and there this old boy sat. He thought he was home, so when the farmer asked, "How are you doing?" the fellow said, "Yes, sir."

So the farmer called us and we went down there to Rich Pond.

To make a long story short, this fellow got out of the hospital. And everything just clicked in his favor. He thought he was home because he had seen the night-light. He wasn't no trouble to arrest. We brought him back and put him in jail. His mama and daddy came over here and got him in an ambulance they were driving from Nashville. They had bought a brand-new Mercedes.

This fellow they had come to pick up still had on that big cowboy hat. He said something to his daddy, then his mama just slapped him right up on his head. I got tickled at what she did. She rang his bell!

So many things go on that are funny when you arrest someone.

Jerry "Peanuts" Gaines, Warren County, July 20, 2009

Mentally Deprived Killer

This fellow has been incarcerated in a mental institution for several years, and they bring him back once a year to evaluate him. He has talked to us about hearing voices that tell him to kill people, and he actually did kill two people. He told us all about it. One of those killings happened here in Hart County, and that's the reason he's up there in the institution.

I don't know who would have arrested him, but he's never been tried for that offence. But the sheriff's office has to go pick him up every year, and he gets evaluated.

Boston B. Hensley Jr. and Deputy James Veluzat,
Hart County, July 30, 2009

Deputy Killed

On May 15, 1979, I had a deputy killed in a line of duty. His name was Earl Smith, and he was a fine gentleman. He had received a complaint about a person in his neighborhood that had a very bad reputation, and had already been arrested by Deputy Smith. This man had been shooting a pistol in his neighborhood, so a neighbor obtained a warrant for this person.

Deputy Smith had a couple of other deputy sheriffs to go with him to the mobile home this fellow lived in. Deputy Smith told the other two deputies to go to the front door of the mobile home, and he'd go to the back door and try to ease in and get him. This way the two deputies at the front door would keep him occupied at the front door.

In the meantime, the fellow left his living room in the mobile home and walked back through the hallway. The two deputies at the front door didn't see him do that. So when Deputy Smith tried to open the back door, he found that it was locked. So evidently the person they were trying to get heard him and shot five rounds through the window of the door with a fully loaded .38 revolver, and hit my deputy with three rounds in the head area, and he was killed instantly.

I got there on the scene shortly afterwards, and that was a very, very sad time for us. It certainly hurt our department, as he was a good officer, and worked for several years.

The person that shot my deputy was declared incompetent to stand trial, thus was sent to the mental institution in Lexington. I'm quite sure he's deceased now.

After a few months in the mental facility, unbeknownst to me they sent him back to a nursing home in the community that he had lived in. The family of the deputy sheriff that was killed also lived in the same community. When I heard about it, I sent a couple of deputies over to bring him out of the nursing home since I still had two warrants against him.

The management people at the nursing home didn't want us to take him, but knowing what he had done they did bring him out and put him in the detention center. When the mental facility in Lexington heard about that, it upset them very much. One of the supervisors even called me and said, "Now, Sheriff, we're going to sue you. You don't have any right to serve that warrant."

I said, "Yes, I do. It's a murder warrant, and he's never been tried or convicted on this warrant for murder. The warrant is still active."

"Well, we're going to sue you. After all, that's where his family lives," the supervisor replied.

"Yes, but that's where the victim's family also lives, and we will not let him stay here," I firmly stated.

Of course, they took him back. I don't know whatever happened to him. I think they sent him to some place up in Indiana.

Charles E. "Fuzzy" Keesee, Pike County, August 7, 2009

TRAGIC DEATH

I recall a little autistic girl whose closest friend was her dog. Everywhere the girl went the dog followed. I think the dog was an Irish setter, and its name was Red.

The girl had wandered outside the house, and the dog showed back up at the house without her. As a result there was a massive search to look for the girl. When I went out I noticed that the dog's feet were wet and muddy when it had come into the house. It was a dry summer day, and the dog's feet should not have been wet. So my attention was drawn to a pond located within walking distance. When we drug the pond, we found the girl's body. Apparently she had just wandered in and drowned.

This wasn't a criminal event at all; it was just a tragic, tragic accident. I can always remember the daddy, who significantly loved his little girl as only a father can do. I don't recall the reason, but his attention had been diverted and his little girl wandered out of the house. She wasn't allowed to wander out, she just went out on her own.

She was five or six years old, and was autistic. I can remember how much her daddy cried. Tears were just running down his cheek, and all he could say was "Why? Why? Why?" The futility in my not being able to answer that question has always haunted me.

Keith Cain, Daviess County, October 1, 2009

MACE THREAT

One morning at 2:00 I went out by myself, as I had no backup back then. I had a mental warrant to take this guy to Bowling Green to the sixth floor for evaluation, then probably transport him over to Western State in Hopkinsville. I didn't know the guy, as it was up next to the Warren County line.

To get to this guy's house I went to the address they had given me, and this guy was walking back and forth on his front porch, and it was 2:00 in the morning. I called his name, and he turned around and said, "Yes."

I said, "Come off the porch, as I need to talk to you for a few minutes." I didn't tell him I had a warrant.

He shook his fist, then said, "You're going to have to take me."

I thought, "This isn't going to be good," because you don't need to put a gun on a guy that's crazy. Well, at that time we'd just started carrying pepper Mace, so I pulled my pepper Mace out, and just about the time I started to release some of it, he turned with his back toward me, then threw his hands up and said, "I give."

Come to find out, he'd been maced before, so he didn't want any Mace. Anyway, I cuffed him, took him up there in Bowling Green and they evaluated him and sent him on to Western State.

Kenneth Lee Morris, Butler County, October 11, 2009

SHERIFF'S EXPERIENCES

It was always an interesting situation to deal with the mentally ill people. That's another job that law enforcement people have to deal with, especially the sheriff's department, in order to transport mentally ill people. Back several years ago, we could pick people up and lodge them in the county jail, even though they were potentially mentally ill. When Bereton Jones was governor, he signed an executive order stating that you could no longer house mentally ill people in a county jail.

I agree with that, but at the same time it created a lot of problems from the law enforcement standpoint about getting those people anywhere they could be evaluated and assigned to a facility, not something you could wait until tomorrow to transport them. You've got to do it right then. LifeSkills [a crisis services organization] was involved, and from an evaluation standpoint in getting all paperwork together, it could take six to eight hours to get everything prepared in order to eventually transport one of these individuals to Western State Hospital.

However, anybody that has a mental problem has got to be handled differently from the normal prison individual. I remember some situations dealing with mentally ill people. When we were transporting females, we always had a female guard with us. I didn't have anybody to go with me one day, and I knew I was going to have to transport this lady. I took my wife with me, and we hadn't much more than got this lady loaded up and headed to Western State Hospital when I looked back through my rearview mirror and saw this lady in the back seat taking all of her clothes off. I told my wife, "You need to start doing something with her back there."

My wife started talking to her and told her to put her clothes back on, and she did.

That was just another incident like that. I had other situations such as the time I got a call from a neighbor who said, "I've got this woman who is naked running through my front yard."

We went out there and discovered that this lady had mental problems, and that another lady had gone out there and wrapped her up in a bed sheet, and she was clothed in that bed sheet when we got there. We took her and got her evaluated, then took her to Western State Hospital.

During my twenty-one years in law enforcement, I got two black eyes, both of which were caused by someone mentally ill. Normally, handling those people is a lot different from the way you handle a normal prisoner. We don't want to hurt anybody, but you have got to subdue them. In one instance, this fellow was in the backyard, and he had done thrown all the dishes out of the kitchen into the backyard. One of the deputies and I went out there to get him. We had to corral him out in his backyard, and the deputy didn't have a good enough hold of that fellow's arm when we grabbed him, and that fellow come around and hit me, and I got a black eye out of that deal.

In reference to mentally ill male and female persons, I found out the two things they will be talking about basically are the Bible and sex. Those are the two chief things they're going to be talking about. What they say about sex is typically not relevant to them; they just make comments along those lines. But if it's a man doing the talking, they may be talking about their wife or girlfriend. Women talk about men, about themselves, other women, and the Bible.

Barney Jones, Barren County, December 21, 2009

Veteran with Alzheimer's

About ten years ago there was this older gentleman that was a veteran of World War II, and he had held himself up in his house there with his wife. He wouldn't let her leave, and I think he was in the beginning stages of Alzheimer's. It had already got dark that evening, and the state police had the initial call, and they had been negotiating with him for a good while.

I went on down there to his house, located close to the lake, and they were talking back and forth with him on the bullhorn. He was screaming and yelling back at them. I hollered at him and told him I was there on the scene and needed to talk to him. He didn't want to talk with me, nor anybody. But he had an open phone line, and a dispatcher had talked to him over the phone. Of course, they already had their SWAT team there, and it soon got close to midnight.

I called the dispatcher and told him, "You tell him that I'll be glad to come up there and talk to him if he'll just come out on the porch and talk."

Well, I relayed my message, and we could hear him raving at that point. The dispatcher come back in a few minutes and told me what the old man said, then went to say, "Sheriff, I don't believe he is going to vote for you at the next election." [*Laughter*]

I said, "Okay, we tried!"

They kept talking to him, and there was a big open porch on the back of his house. They had that SWAT team right up there close to it, and they finally talked with him on the phone and told him that they would come up there and talk to him if he would just go out on that back porch. They told him that they wouldn't get too close to him, that they just wanted to talk to him about this and that. They told him, "We're still out here in the road now, and are one hundred yards away from you." But that SWAT team was located within a very few feet of him.

Well, the minute he opened that back door, that SWAT team made the worst noise you've ever heard. There were about six of them on top of him, and we finally got that situation handled.

Barney Jones, Barren County, December 21, 2009

DECAPITATION THREAT

If you get a telephone call about a mentally disturbed person, you have to go and check to see this and that. Down here on Frisby Road, this one-arm man was keeping elderly people. You know, government pays you to keep them. He called one night, and me and another deputy, Skyler Denney, went down there.

When we got there, this little old lady was standing in a room there at the elderly people's house, and she had her hands shut up. She knew me, so I talked to her and said, "We're here to get you some help."

She said, "If you come close to me, I'm going to cut your head off."

I said, "Now, you wouldn't want to do me that way, because you wouldn't have nobody to whistle at you," or something like that.

She was really serious, but I couldn't see what she had in her hand. I knew it wasn't a big knife, so I just started easing over toward her. Well, here she comes with her hand drawn back. I caught her hand and found a cigarette lighter in her hand. Once I got that away from her, she just quieted right down.

We brought her to Monticello, and she was taken to Eastern State in Richmond, and she stayed about two months.

Joseph Conn, Wayne County, February 13, 2010

MENTALLY ILL BROTHERS

Up on Cole Bank was this man who had three boys, and the oldest one had a set of twins. At one time all three of the boys were in Eastern

State. They had drugged and then went crazy. Well, one of them ran off and was coming home when a social worker picked him up at Burnside, then let him out here at the shopping center in Monticello, then came and told us what happened.

We went up there to the shopping center but couldn't find him. The next morning it was snowing, but we went up there and run him through the woods. Well, his daddy came in that morning and was hit right in the face by a skull rock that his son threw at him. We ran him for two miles through the woods, finally caught him. Well, we and the police chief were way down on the back side of the hill when we caught him, and I told him to lay down. When I told him to, he did lay down on the ground on the back side of the hill when I caught him. I said to the police, "You all go get the car and meet me down in the holler."

The prisoner said, "I ain't walking. You'll have to pack me."

I had handcuffed him, so I said, "No, you are going to walk." Then I went over and took my pocketknife, cut me a stick about the size of my thumb that was about three feet long. I waved it at him and said, "Do you see this?"

He looked up; then I said, "If you don't want me to lie on you like ugly, you get up and head down the holler."

Well, right down the holler he went. As we were taking him back, his twin brother ran off. Well, we caught him and sent him back, then the other brother came in. They had discharged him, and he was working out in the strip mine, doing good, and was living up there in a house he had built. We got a call one night telling us he had gone off again.

We went up there and saw he had torn the house down and knocked the lights out. We walked in with a flashlight and saw him standing right in the middle of the floor, and a baseball bat was standing right against the wall. I said to him, "We've got to go to town to get you some help."

We started moving real slow, and I said to him, "You are not going to get that ball bat. You might as well head for the car. You're not going to make it. Now, believe me."

He got up, then they took him to Eastern State, and he ran off again. That's when he stole a truck here in Wayne County and drove it to Alaska. That was the last time I ever seen him.

It's really pitiful about mentally bad people. They think everybody is their enemy and they think everybody is going to harm them regardless of how you have dealt with them before.

Joseph Conn, Wayne County, February 13, 2010

HOSES AND HIGH HEELS

When I was working as a deputy for Sheriff Joe Conn, we got a call telling us that this lady had gone crazy, or gone off mentally. So we got in Joe's car and went to the residence to pick up this lady and take her to the doctor, or whatever needed to be done. When we got there she was out in the yard and was holding a water hose. She was wearing high-heel shoes! So we began talking to her and found out she had no intention of leaving to go with us. She said she was going to stay at home.

Well, the water hose was our first problem because she began squirting water on us. I think she had been watering flowers before we got there, but we finally got it away from her after we had spent some time. We started to put her in the car with those high-heel shoes on, but she kicked us with her high-heel shoes! If you've never been kicked with them, like in the stomach, you've not been kicked. It's a very painful way to go.

Considering all I've ever done, I guess that's the most interesting event I ever had. It wasn't fun having water squirted on us!

Charles L. Boston, Wayne County, February 13, 2010

FALSIFYING MENTAL ILLNESS

This is about something that happened recently, just at the end of my second term as sheriff. At least once a week this guy would holler "Suicide." He'd go to the hospital and threaten to kill somebody, so it was our responsibility to take him to Bowling Green to LifeSkills and have him evaluated. When we took a person there they either sent them back home or they sent them on to Western State in Hopkinsville.

This went on forever. When we were taking him down there or picking him up at LifeSkills, he never did do anything he threatened to do. He never sliced his wrists; he just said he was going to. So one Saturday I was off and was asked to be at a funeral. I said I'd go, so I got my car washed and had plenty of time for the funeral. Me and a couple of deputies were sitting here in the office talking when we got a call on the suicide hotline in Bowling Green. The person on the phone said, "Would you please go out here and check this guy out? He's boring us to death. He's called us about fifteen times."

Well, we started out there and it was two or three miles from my office. I was driving down a side road and saw this man sitting over here in a field. He had his hand up, so I waved at him. When I waved the deputy that was riding with me giggled a little but I didn't pay much attention to it. But when I turned to go to the guy's trailer where we were headed, I hit a mud hole. Well, that made me mad because I'd just washed my car for the funeral. Anyway, I'd already decided what I was going to do when I got there, so I went in. I knew this was a hoax, so I go on in and he was sitting on a couch. He had taken a shower, had shaved, was all dressed up, and had his suitcase packed. He was waiting for us to come pick him up. I asked him, "What's your problem?"

He said, "I just don't want to live no more."

So I said this just to say it: "Why don't you go ahead and take care of your needs? If you don't, you will bore us to death."

He said, "I tried to last night."

I said, "Well, what did you do?"

He said, "I took forty Xanies and drank two pints of whiskey."

I said, "I don't believe you, because if you did that you wouldn't have been able to get out of bed this morning and take no shower, or do anything. Are you a bright OD?" I then said, "I'll tell you what, I'm just tired of this old crap." When I said that, I pulled my I-38 pistol out and said, "Here, go ahead and kill yourself and be done with it, and everybody will be happy. You'll be happy, and you won't be boring us to death."

"Oh, no, no, no, I don't want that."

Then I said, "I'll tell you what; I'll just do it for you." Of course, I'd already unloaded it, but I pointed it at him. My deputy didn't know what I was doing, so he ran out the door. Well, that guy I pointed my pistol at jumped up and grabbed his suitcase and ran to the door, saying to me, "You're one crazy son of a bitch."

That happened five or six years ago, and that guy has not called me since then! That put a stop to him, but we have this kind of thing two or three times a month. There were a couple of people that sliced their wrists a little. They may be doing that in hopes of drawing a check, or attention, or what. Most of the people who do things like that may be acting crazy enough in hopes of getting a check. That's what I think it all really boils down to.

Over the years there have been some serious people we took to LifeSkills because they were crazy. So they received mental treatment there. However, the majority of people we take down there are just pulling a joke. They just want attention, or are wanting a check, or a monetary increase on the checks they are drawing. What they do is ridiculous, but it wears us out.

Jerry "Slick" Gee, Monroe County, March 18, 2010

DOOR SCREWED SHUT

This is about a woman who was close to being mentally retarded. I got this domestic call one time from someone located ten or twelve miles east of Stanton. I pulled up to the residence and went to the door. Well, this guy was standing inside knocking on the door and I said, "Well, let me in."

He said, "I can't."

I said, "Why?"

He said, "She screwed the door shut." [*Laughter*]

So she had screwed the door shut and closed the windows so he couldn't get out.

I asked him, "Where is she?"

He said, "She's in the bathroom."

I said, "Well, get out of the way," and then I kicked the front in and then stepped inside. I had my gun out when I got inside. She was in the bedroom and was standing back there by the bed with a knife in her hand. We had never had any trouble out of this lady, so I told her, "Drop the knife," and said that to her several times.

She began to walk toward me, and I said, "No, don't you do that. You need to drop that knife."

By then I knew she wasn't going to hurt me, or nobody. But she still had that knife in her hand. By the way, she had sores on her arms and on her face. I don't know what had caused that problem, but she still wouldn't drop that knife. What I did at that time was to take my pepper spray out, and boy, that stuff hurts. I said, "Look, I'm going to tell you one more time to drop that knife."

She didn't drop that knife, so I just sprayed her with that pepper spray and filled her full of that spray. Well, the spray got in her sores and it eat her up. She started hollering and screaming and going berserk. So I had to take her down and cuff her, and that spray was eating her up. I took her out and put her in my car and then got to looking under the mattress in her room. She had nine screwdrivers and pieces of steel, all of which were laying right under that mattress on her side of the bed.

But she never did say she screwed the door and windows shut. However, her husband never could get out of the house.

That was kind of funny, but he was scared to death. I did arrest the woman for an assault degree, and since she had that knife I arrested her for wanton endangerment. We worked it out later. She wasn't going to hurt anyone, but that was a situation in which Tasers would have come in handy, rather than a gun. So in that case I could have shot her with a Taser rather than with a weapon if she had come after me with that knife.

Danny Rogers, Powell County, March 27, 2010

Chapter 4

LAW ENFORCEMENT HUMOR

Humor features in virtually every aspect of life, and the arena of law enforcement is no exception. And that is all to the good—humor often helps sheriffs, deputies, and even guilty persons deal with difficult, frightening, and sometimes dangerous situations. Further, the humor of a story can provide valuable insight into the life and times the narrative depicts.

The amusing vignettes in this chapter feature as subjects criminals (such as the notorious tomato bandit), victims (including the mother who asked the sheriff to arrest her six-year-old son), and law enforcement personnel (who sometimes relieve the tension of their challenging job by playing pranks on one another).

BLACKGARDIN'

Back when people used to cuss, they called it "blackgardin'."

One day we went out here in Warren County along the old Greenville Road, and we saw this old lady that had snuff coming out both sides of her mouth. She'd called the law about what her son had been doing. She said, "That GD SOB has been blackgardin'."

Actually, she said the real words, thus was doing more cussing than he was!

We laugh at things like that because they are funny. And we run into things like that over the years, and they are funny. Of course, you can't laugh at the people, but what they do would make a TV series!

Jerry "Peanuts" Gaines, Warren County, July 20, 2009

MOTHER'S WEIRD REQUEST

One of the funniest things took place when I was running for sheriff. I was trying to work and campaign at the same time; trying to please everybody. After all these years, I realize you can't please everyone.

I got a call at the police station, so I came in and answered the phone and there was some woman who was calling. She said, "I want you to come out here and get my son."

I asked her, "How old is your son?"

She said, "He's six."

I said, "Why do you want me to come get him?"

She said, "I'm trying to get him ready for Bible school, and he won't put on his good shoes."

I said, "That's what you're calling me for, lady?"

She said, "Yes, I want you out here now."

I said, "Ma'am, when I come out there, I'm going to arrest you. If you can't get your six-year-old son to put his shoes on you've got problems, so I'm going to take you."

She said, "Never mind," and hung up. Evidently, she didn't need me! [*Laughter*]

John E. Shipp, Taylor County, July 30, 2009

PRANKING SHERIFFS

The Larue County sheriff and I used to play tricks on each other. Another officer and I would get that sheriff to talking, like when he pulled up to us in his car one night. As soon as we got him to talking, I kept the other officer distracted and went around. The blue light on a police car had little catches, and you'd just pull them and the plastic cover on the blue light would come off, leaving the clear lights.

We took that sheriff's blue light catches off one night while he was still in his car. Then we went to this other officer's house. A few minutes later this sheriff came up and had a bat in his hand. He said, "I'm going to get you SOBs."

He said he'd gone out and stopped a car and flipped his lights on, and it looked like daylight! After he got out and looked, he knew what had happened, and he'd come after us!

John E. Shipp, Taylor County, July 30, 2009

Illiterate Officers

I have known police officers that had the power of arrest and everything, but couldn't write their own names. They would take somebody along with them who would write the ticket and sign it, then the officer would make an X.

[One officer] stopped somebody one day and he handed him the book to fill out the ticket, because he couldn't write. So this fellow put the officer's name in the ticket!

And I've known a police officer that supposedly stopped a man and asked him for his driver's license. This guy handed him his driver's license, then the officer asked him, "Where are you from?"

That fellow said, "I'm from Illinois."

The officer said, "Don't you be lying to me; I see this Chicago address." [*Laughter*]

Boston B. Hensley Jr. and Deputy James Veluzat,
Hart County, July 30, 2009

Whiskey on Duty

I know another story about a police officer and it's a true story because it was told to me by the police officer in Munfordville. He's dead now, but he would enjoy my telling this. What happened is, the mayor got to looking for him one morning and couldn't find him. Then he saw the officer's car setting down here by the courthouse with its blue lights on behind a tractor-trailer truck. He opened the door on the tractor-trailer truck.

What had happened, the officer had stopped this truck driver for drunken driving. Some way or another, the officer liked whiskey, too, so he sat down up in the cab with the driver and they drank until they both passed out. [*Laughter*]

That's a true story.

Deputy James Veluzat, Hart County, July 30, 2009

Shooting on Duty

We had one officer, but I'll not identify the department in which he was working. He had a fellow run away from him out at Kessinger, so he just pulled his weapon out and fired a shot. Actually, he didn't really know whether he was shooting at him or wasn't shooting at him.

Anyway, that officer was on the witness stand, and the defense attorney had him up there. The defense attorney asked him, "Didn't you shoot at my client going down the road?"

The officer said, "Well, he's setting there, ain't he?"

That fellow who was running away is still living! I always thought that was funny.

It is said the officer did nick that fellow's ear when he shot at him. You're not supposed to shoot at people, or fire warning shots.

Boston B. Hensley Jr., Hart County, July 30, 2009

JUDGE'S GOOD ADVICE

My dad had a first cousin who was a circuit judge, Judge Keesee, and he had a very good sense of humor. Back in the late 1950s and early 1960s, if a person came up with a venereal disease and failed to go in for treatment, a doctor at the health department obtained a warrant for the person. Then we would arrest them and put the person in jail.

I was the sheriff at this time, and on this particular day the judge asked me to sit on the bench with him and be his bailiff. We were in this trial, and here came this young jailer, who was probably in his second term. When he came through the door, he was all excited and came up to the judge's bench and began pecking on it.

"Sheriff, tell him to be quiet! He's disturbing the court," Judge Keesee whispered while nudging me.

The jailer rapped on the desk again, then I said, "Jailer, the judge says you're disturbing the court."

"But I've got to talk to him; I've got to talk to him! Fuzzy, I've got to talk to him," the young jailer said.

Finally the judge heard him, then leaned down behind me and whispered, "Jailer, what is it, son? What is it?"

"Don't you know I've got a woman that's got an ole bad disease, and what must I do with her?" the jailer said.

"For God's sake, son, stay away from her." [*Laughter*]

Charles E. "Fuzzy" Keesee, Pike County, August 7, 2009

MENTAL PATIENT OUTSMARTS THE JUDGE

A circuit judge told me one day that he needed to go to Lexington, Kentucky, to see a friend of his. As it came up, I had a mental petition on a person that I had to take to the mental facility in Lexington.

"I don't have any cases tomorrow, so I'd like to go with you," the judge replied. On our way to Lexington he and I talked about a lot of things, and the mental patient sat in the back seat of the car quietly. He was very quiet and never said anything the entire trip.

When we got to Lexington the judge knew what building his lawyer friend was in, but didn't know just where it was located. "Son, I don't know where the building is," the judge told me.

I noticed a couple of blocks down the street a police officer was directing traffic. I stopped and the police officer told me exactly where the building was located and how to get there. I drove on down another block or two and realized I still wasn't sure about the directions. "By the way, Judge, are we supposed to turn here?" I asked the judge.

He said, "Son, I don't know; I wasn't listening."

Then the mental patient told me exactly what the police officer said and how to get there. And I did! I followed the directions of the mental patient to find the building.

"I'll tell you what, son," the judge said. "I don't believe I'll go to the mental institution with you. They're liable to keep us both!"

Charles E. "Fuzzy" Keesee, Pike County, August 7, 2009

TOMATO BANDIT

We had an unusual thing to happen to us. We have two courthouses here in Pike County. One of these is in the north end of the county at Belfry, or what we call Pond Creek. There we have a sheriff's office, county clerk's office, trial commissioner's office, social services offices, as well as a senior citizens' office.

A lady that lived up near Belfry called up to our office there, and the clerk answered the phone. The lady who was calling was very excited, and said, "Honey, there's a man here in my garden stealing all of my tomatoes."

Although they were laughing about it, the clerk dispatched one of our deputies to the area to check on the tomato bandit. He thought it was just a joke, but when he got there, there really was a man in this garden with a bag taking this lady's tomatoes.

The bandit saw the deputy pull up in his car, so he took off running up this big hill. The deputy jokingly called back on his telephone to report back to the office. "Well, I'm going after the bandit, and I've tracked him because he's dropping his tomatoes. I've chased him to the second flat of the hill, and he's lost all his tomatoes, so I lost track of him. The tomato bandit has escaped." [*Laughter*]

Charles E. "Fuzzy" Keesee, Pike County, August 7, 2009

UNUSUAL POTTY PLACEMENT

We had knowledge of this elderly man who was a bootlegger, selling mostly moonshine. Evidently, he was a pretty good maker of moonshine liquor. We decided early one morning to raid him, due to some complaints coming into the office about him.

After obtaining a search warrant we proceeded to his residence to see if we could search this fellow. When we got there, for some reason the front door was left open and we didn't have to knock or anything. We walked on in and could tell that the lady of the house was fixing breakfast.

We went on into the kitchen where the woman was standing at the stove cooking. We looked over in the corner and there set her husband. Of all things, he was using a little pot he had there for the bathroom! He was sitting on that potty, and was doing his bowel movement business right there in the kitchen, as his wife cooked breakfast!

We had a warrant for him, so we arrested him. He was just laughing. He didn't mind.

You'd be surprised at some of the things we run into as we perform the duties of a sheriff.

Charles E. "Fuzzy" Keesee, Pike County, August 7, 2009

GOODY'S GOOD

When I was born my grandma nicknamed me Goody, and that stuck with me for a long, long time. Every once in awhile one of my brothers or sisters will tell somebody about that name; then they look at me and say, "Hey, Goody, how are you?"

I'll say, "I'm fine and that's the reason my grandma named me Goody—because I'm good!" I carry right on with that name, and we have a good time with it.

James Pruitt, Cumberland County, August 10, 2009

Snake Repeatedly Killed

We killed a snake one time in Monroe County. We were in Humvees and they were going to put that snake in a box right behind the seat in which I was sitting. Well, I didn't ride there. I got in another Humvee, and we came out over there in Monroe County.

This snake wasn't dead, so we pushed the lid up over the box, and this guy that was in a Humvee jumped out of it and he was going down the road and ran into a pallet mill over there where they were sawing pallets. We all jumped out and started shooting that snake again, and killed it two or three times that day!

James Pruitt, Cumberland County, August 10, 2009

Let's Use Your Car

We've got this gentleman out in Guthrie Chapel area who really gets drunk sometimes, and when he gets drunk he lays down in the middle of the road, and just lays there. So we get quite a few calls on him.

I went out there one night, and when I got there he was lying there in the middle of the road. I turned the lights and things on, so that hopefully nobody would run over him, or me either.

My other deputy comes out there, and I started to put this fellow in my car. When that happened I smelled something really bad, so I said to the deputy, "Let's put him in your car."

So we put the fellow in the deputy's car and they drove off. Down the road the deputy radioed back and said, "I owe you one big time."

What happened is that the gentleman had messed all over himself in the back seat of the car, in the floorboard, and everything.

He told me that he owed me one big time, so I'm still watching out for it today!

James Pruitt, Cumberland County, August 10, 2009

One Big Hog

People joke us a lot about this. I was driving along 3108 Highway one night, and Terry Grider and this other gentleman were after this big old hog. And I've never seen a hog like that. We were trying to get it out of the road so it wouldn't run over somebody, so I turned on my emergency lights and got out to help them.

Well, that big hog tears up a fence, and there was a lady coming down the road in a car, and she just kept coming even though my lights were on. That hog hit the front end of that car and busted the grill out and rolled the hood up on her car. She said, "I'm going home. I can't believe I got hit by a hog."

I said, "Ma'am, that's more hog than I've ever seen. I've never seen one like it."

Well, we chased that hog that night for about four hours, then the hog hit a tractor and knocked it backwards, and it knocked Terry Grider in a ditch lane. That hog knocked the tractor back about a foot, I'd say.

We had an awful time that night. Of course, everybody has laughed at us. But now I've got a little hoglike thing in the front office that a lady that works here gave me. On the back of that little handmade hog are the words "Catch me if you can."

People make a big deal out of that hog story.

James Pruitt, Cumberland County, August 10, 2009

"Car" Is a Bicycle

One time when I first got elected I had this call about 10:45 p.m. about a wreck of the Clay Lick Hill, located on Highway 90 West. My deputy went there and saw a man sitting on the side of the road. The man had been scratched up and was bleeding. We asked him if he needed an ambulance, and he said, "No." He went on to tell us that a truck ran him off the road and he went over the bank.

We looked for his car and could never find it. We asked him about his car and he stated that he was not in a car, but was on a bicycle. I sat down beside him and started to laugh.

James Pruitt, Cumberland County, August 10, 2009

Talkative Sheriff

When I was in school the one disciplinary problem I had was that I talked too much in class. And I can remember the report cards very well. My mother would be looking at it and said, "Chuckie reads and talks in class too much."

Well, I finally got a job where I was encouraged to talk, and all this stuff has been boiling out! So I've got to watch myself so that I don't talk too much!

Charles Lee "Chuck" Korzenborn, Kenton County, September 17, 2009

STOP THE CHICKENS

We were having a capital murder case relevant to a murder that took place before I became sheriff. They were having the trial in 1990 and it went on for several days. It was a murder for hire, and the accused did wind up getting the death sentence. I later took him to the Eddyville Penitentiary to death row.

Back during the trial, the case had been given to the jury, and they were deliberating. That took place most of the day, and it was going on into the night. The judge wanted to stay to see if they could reach a verdict.

It was about dark, and this elderly lady, Mrs. Lawless, was on the jury. She was around eighty years old at the time. I was the sheriff, and part of my duties was to guard the jury. She pecked on the door, and I had to see what she wanted in order to relate it to the judge. When I opened the door she said, "My son is out in front of the courthouse waiting for me." She could not drive, so her son, who was in his sixties, was waiting for her. She went on to say, "Would you go out there and tell my son to go home and stop the chickens up so the fox won't get them?"

I told Judge Eddy Loveless what she wanted, and he said, "Well, go outside and tell her son to stop the chickens up from the foxes." [*Laughter*]

Eddy told me he was thinking about writing a book, and if he did he would include that story.

Larry L. Bennett, Russell County, September 18, 2009

NONDRIVING DRIVER

My two deputies received a call from someone who told about drunk drivers going up and down the road there at the Jabez community. They were very intoxicated and were weaving along the road. So my two deputies, Charles Mann and Ron Ooten, I think it was, went to Jabez and located the vehicle they had been called about. Sure enough, the vehicle was driving all over the road. So they stopped the vehicle and arrested the individual for driving while intoxicated. They put him in the back of their cruiser and started to the Jamestown jail.

Well, they came up on another car and it was also being driven all over the road, just weaving. So they stopped that car, with the prisoner in the back seat. When they stopped this other car, it was another person who was driving intoxicated. So they arrest him for driving under the influence and put him in the back seat with the other prisoner.

The two deputies were listening to the two prisoners talking on the way to jail. One prisoner asked the other prisoner, "What did they get us for?"

The other one said, "DUI, driving while intoxicated."

The other prisoner said, "Well, I wasn't driving, *you* were."

But the deputies got them out of two different cars! [*Laughter*]

Larry L. Bennett, Russell County, September 18, 2009

GOD ACCEPTS SHERIFFS

One Saturday morning I went into my office, and I was the only one there. I was sitting there, and this man and woman come into the office and said, "We want to get married today."

I said, "Okay, you need to go over to the clerk's office and get your license."

They said, "No, you don't understand; we want you to perform the wedding."

I said, "I don't have any authority to marry anybody."

They said, "Well, we've thought it over, and both of us draws a check, and if we get married one of us will lose our check. We've thought about it, and we believe if you would perform the ceremony, God would accept it." [*Laughter*]

I said, "I can't serve you."

Larry L. Bennett, Russell County, September 18, 2009

AND *TWICE* IN A BUGGY

This guy was ninety-seven years old, still driving himself around. In fact, it was during the tax time when my office was really busy. There's a lot of people in paying their taxes. Most usually they are lined up in the hallway. So the office was full. Well, this elderly gentleman came into the office and I asked him, "You are ninety-seven years old and you still drive yourself around and are able to get out and pay your bills. What is your secret?"

He said, "Don't take any medicine."

I said, "Well, that sounds pretty good."

Of course, everybody's ears were listening to what he said. He talked pretty loud anyway. Well, he started to tell me a story. He said, "Let me tell you a story about Granny. She was a hundred years old when all her kids and grandchildren and everything were gathered around giving her a hundredth birthday party. One of her nieces came over and said, 'Granny, you are a hundred years old, and you've never been bedridden.'

"Granny replied, 'Oh, honey, I've been bedridden thousands of times, and *twice* in a buggy.'"

Well, everybody was listening to him, and that tickled them to death, and that's the way I learned not to ask people questions!

Larry L. Bennett, Russell County, September 18, 2009

DOG DOODY ON DUTY

My father is actually the political mind in the family. He was mayor of Maysville for several years, and was also a city commissioner. He's got twenty-six years in public service. He's always been big on law enforcement, and his influence got me involved in law enforcement. He always comes down to my office, now that I'm sheriff, wanting to be involved in law enforcement. I still get my adrenal rushes, and I still get the excitement of the job. I love my job every day. It's not a job, because I love it so much. I guess I take for granted things that are everyday in law enforcement, but he still wants to learn something, or do something, about law enforcement, and being involved in it. Well, he got his chance one day.

I was sheriff at the time, and was on duty. My office was adjacent to the new courthouse. If I made it to my front door, I could usually see somebody coming out of the courthouse. A juvenile takes bolting out of court and goes running up Sutton Street hill, a very steep hill. He went running away that way, but I ran down the block and then up an alley trying to cut him off. However, he'd already made it down and across, but I ended up catching him up on Fifth Street. He had come down through a yard and crossed over fences, and I go in just behind him.

Well, it just so happened that my father was coming up Fourth Street, where I crossed over. He sees me running and he knew he had to get involved. So he heads back down to a family member of mine that lives on the corner of Fourth and Limestone Street because that's the way we were going. He had no clue what was happening, but he carries a weapon (CCDW; carrying concealed deadly weapon, a legal permit) everywhere he goes. He'd help any law enforcement officer, especially me.

So I'm hopping fences after this kid, and was just two houses from my family member's house. Well, my father was coming toward me and he sees me hop this fence, and I fall flat on my face right into a pile of dog sh——. [*Laughter*] When I jumped that fence that's what I landed in! I had it all over my clothes and everywhere.

I got up and started hopping the fence, and I told him where to go. He runs down between this family member's house and the house next door, then held this guy at gunpoint until I got there.

Patrick Boggs, Mason County, September 15, 2009

Clueless Constable

We had this constable at Clarkson, Kentucky, and I was told this story about him by the town marshal. This constable was a retired old railroad man, but you could run for constable, so he did and was elected.

He pulled these boys over one night up there and was sitting there talking to them. He looked at their license tags, and could tell they were from Illinois. He asked them, "Where are you boys from?"

They said, "Chicago."

He said, "Well, don't you lie to me. I see *Illinois* tags on that car." [*Laughter*]

He was serious. He wanted to do the best job he could. I remember one time when I was working a wreck, and he was plumb out of his district. He drove right down there where I was located, and he pulled right up behind me. When we got ready to leave, he was hung up. I had to get a wrecker down there to pull him out so I could get out!

Qulin K. Escue, Grayson County, September 22, 2009

Crossing the County Line

Back in the days before cell phones, some twenty-five years ago, I went with a Kentucky police officer one night, and it was really cold. We had received a call telling us about an abandoned vehicle near the Daviess-Ohio county line. And it was an anonymous call that had been called in. So we went out, and sure enough there was a vehicle out there, and we checked it and learned it was a stolen vehicle.

This was way up in the wee hours of the morning and neither of us wanted to complete the required paperwork on the stolen vehicle. We looked and saw that we were within a few yards of the county line. Since we knew it was an anonymous call, we just took the car out of gear and pushed it over into Ohio County! Then we called and indicated that the car was in Ohio County, and that they should notify the Ohio County authorities so we wouldn't have to work the case. We made that call anonymously, so they didn't know who we were.

So we just waited for the Ohio County unit to respond and were watching them. A couple of deputies that had responded got out and looked around until they saw where the vehicle was. You could imagine our chagrin when they looked around a little, got into the stolen vehicle, put it in neutral, and pushed it back into Daviess County!

Sure enough, within minutes we got a radio dispatch telling about a stolen car in Daviess County. That showed they were thinking the same thing we were thinking.

We said, "Well, what the heck," so we went ahead and worked the call ourselves.

That's a true story.

Keith Cain, Daviess County, October 1, 2009

ZINGERS

There have been many lighthearted moments during my career. For example, as a young uniformed patrol officer, I stopped an elderly motorist whom I knew had recently had his operator's license revoked. Upon approaching his vehicle, I asked, "Mr.——, where is your license?"

His immediate retort was, "Don't tell me you guys have lost them already."

I once stopped a driver for disregarding a flashing red light. Upon advising the obvious "alcohol-impaired" driver as to why I stopped him, then gesturing to the distant flashing red light, he studied it for a moment, then confidently replied, "But officer, I must've went through it when it was flashing 'off.'"

There was a rambunctious young attorney who defended his client's right to refer to me as a "son of a bitch." Well, that landed him in the old Quarterly Court, charged with disorderly conduct.

"Your Honor," the barrister argued, "Deputy Cain is an officer of the law, and as such, should have a thick countenance, thus not be upset with such utterings." After saying that, he foolishly continued, "Why, I myself have been called the very same thing, and it didn't bother me a bit."

The judge nodded his agreement when I replied, "Yes, Your Honor, but with Mr. ——, it is much more applicable!"

Keith Cain, Daviess County, October 1, 2009

Polecat to the Rescue

I remember this older trooper, Curtis Wood, breaking in a young trooper, Tommy Smith, who is soon going to be a chief deputy in Warren County. They arrested an ole boy known as Mater Head, who probably takes a bath once a year when he has to. They arrested him for DUI, and on the way in to jail they ran over a polecat. The young trooper said to the old trooper, "I used to hate polecats, but thank God for this one today." [*Laughter*]

Kenneth Lee Morris, Butler County, October 11, 2009

Lack of Communication

This occurred when I was chief deputy. We had a very energetic deputy here who wanted to get into things, and he was a real good fellow. He had had some issues, and the sheriff reprimanded him a little bit. Anyway, a probation warrant was issued and I had been working on it. This deputy was going to help me get in this man's apartment, because I'd received word that he had some dope in his apartment.

I had taken the warrant and talked about it to this deputy. Well, in about four hours I got a call from this deputy and probation officer. They were in another community here in Shelby County. The deputy said, "You need to come down here. I'm in so-and-so's apartment, but he's not here." He was talking about the guy for whom I had the warrant.

I said, "What?" We went through that process. I told him to stand still and that I was coming down there.

I went down to where they were, and he said to me, "I took that warrant, and me and the probation officer thought we would just come on down here and get it."

Of course, I dealt with that, knowing he shouldn't have done all of what he did. He went on to say, "I talked with the neighbor, and the neighbor told me that he was here in the apartment."

Well, I was already upset, bothered by the way this whole thing had occurred. So I started backtracking by going over to the neighbor's house to find out all that happened relative to the story he was telling. When I got to the neighbor's house, a very friendly young lady of Hispanic descent came to the door. I asked her, "Do you know who lives next door to you?"

She said, "Yeah," and then I asked, "Was he here today?"

Again she said, "Yeah."

I asked her, "Did the deputy sheriff talk to you about this, and did you explain everything to him?"

She goes, "Yeah."

After about four or five of her "yeah's," I looked at her and asked, "Is your name Mike Armstrong?"

She said, "Yeah."

I turned to my deputy and said, "She can't even speak English. She just said 'Yeah' to anything. I'm Mike Armstrong, but when I asked her if she was Mike Armstrong, she said, 'Yeah.'"

My deputy said, "I asked her those questions and she said, 'Yeah.'"

It all boiled down to the fact that she couldn't even speak to him, but she was trying to make me and the deputy think that she was a legal resident of Kentucky. I turned to the deputy and said, "She can't even speak English, and you are relying on what she is telling you!"

After I asked her if her name was Mike Armstrong, I realized that she didn't even know what I was saying to her!

Mike Armstrong, Shelby County, November 6, 2009

Luck Runs Out

The state police and my office had a complaint from out in the county one snowy night. I didn't go out there, but my deputy and state police did go. I think the trooper was actually chasing this guy who wasn't going too fast but wouldn't stop. He was drunk and just wouldn't stop. Well, they got on a little side road up through there, and the trooper's car ran off into a ditch. The next thing you know, the deputy's car was also off in a ditch. So all the police officers were stuck.

The guy they were chasing wasn't stuck, so he gets over in a field over there and lets his truck spin. The reason he was spinning in the field is that he was indicating with some hand gestures as what he thought about the police! After making the signs, he pulls out into the road, drives by them really fast, then takes off because he was free to go!

He was gone for a few minutes, and there the officers were, still stuck. They couldn't get out of the mud, but they hear this fellow's truck coming up to them again. Well, it wasn't good enough that he could leave and get away from them after he had done all this, he drives back up through there, and the next thing that happens is he also gets stuck!

So, by golly, they end up capturing him anyway! [*Laughter*] He had initially left and could have gone anywhere he wanted to go, but he decided to come back and take his chances again. But he got stuck and it was all over.

Mike Armstrong, Shelby County, November 6, 2009

TWO FOR ONE

I had one guy I arrested due to a domestic dispute, and I told his wife, "You are going to jail, too."

Her husband then spoke up and said, "You can arrest me any time you want to, if you'll arrest her." [*Laughter*] He went on to say, "Every time I got into trouble, they'd come to get me but never did take her. You're the only one that took her!"

He told me several times, "You can come and arrest me any time you want to, now." [*Laughter*]

John "Tuffy" Snedegar, Bath County, December 11, 2009

RELUCTANCE TO PAY SCHOOL TAXES

This fellow came in to the office one day, and he was irate about the school taxes that he was having to pay on his tax bill. He said, "I want to pay my taxes."

I said, "That will be fine, but you'll have to talk with some of the ladies here in the office."

He wanted to pay the rest of the taxes but wasn't going to pay for school taxes on the bill. They finally called me, and I went up there where things were taking place. He said again, "I'm going to pay my taxes, but I'm not paying any school taxes."

I said, "We can't take partial payments, so you've got to pay it all or none."

Then he said, "Well, I'm going to sue you. I'm going to sue the county. I'm going to sue the state. I'm going to sue whoever I need to sue, but I'm not paying any school taxes. I don't have any people in school, don't have any children in school. I never did have any children, so I shouldn't have to pay no school tax."

I said, "Well, I understand that, but the state law says that's the way it is, and that's the way it's got to be paid, so you can't pay just a part of your tax bill. You've got to pay them all or none. You have a good day."

Well, he came back three or four days later and never said a word. He paid his tax bill, all of it. Didn't sue anybody!

Barney Jones, Barren County, December 21, 2009

Don't Rely on the Velcro

This is a funny thing that happened, and if I'd had a camera most likely I'd have been on *Funniest Videos*. I had this Velcro, which is an inner belt that is sticky and sticks to the outer belt to hold onto your gun. I probably had five or ten pounds on my Velcro. Well, we got called to a domestic dispute one night, and this time I had some helper with me. We'd always try to separate them. He'd get the guy, or vice versa, and I'd get the girl, and we'd separate them and talk to them.

Well, I had a mike hanging on my shirt, and you could cut their dispute with a mike. They were just flat going after each other; hollering and carrying on. This was in the summertime, and it was just getting dusk dark, so you could still see everybody and each other. I had this mike hanging up here, and it was tied onto my radio that was tied on my belt. I was sitting there ready to talk to this girl, and about that time my belt fell all the way down to my knees. There it hung with my radio, just sitting there bouncing up and down through my legs. My face got so red, and when I looked over at the other guy, he had tears running down from his eyes. He was setting there crying with his head on his car.

The two domestic-dispute people broke out in a laugh, and they got down on the ground! That's what solved their domestic problem!

We were then setting there talking, and while talking I reached down like a woman pulling up her girdle or something, and pulled my belt back up, wrapped it right back on, then went on talking. I mean, that was hilarious. We laughed about that for at least a week after that took place.

When I went back out there to talk to them later on, they were still dying by laughing about it.

LeeRoy Hardin, Boyle County, January 11, 2010

READ THE T-SHIRT

I get calls all the time from people asking me questions. Of course, I'll try to help them. Just two days ago they had a domestic problem out there on White Oak Road, a little ways from Junction City. When our home phone rang my wife answered, and the woman calling said, "Ma'am, is LeeRoy there?"

She said, "No. Can I help you?"

This lady said, "Yes, my husband is out here fighting and carrying on, and I'm sick of it, so I want you to get LeeRoy out here."

My wife said, "Honey, I'm sorry, but LeeRoy is retired."

That woman yells, "Damn!" then hung up the telephone. [*Laughter*]

I guess that will explain the message printed on the front of my T-shirt that I have on right now. It says, "RETIRED SHERIFF. Please don't ask me any law questions. I have no answers."

LeeRoy Hardin, Boyle County, January 11, 2010

IF THE PRICE IS RIGHT

This is about a fellow [name withheld] who was outstanding, but when he was young he drank a lot of whiskey. He came up the road two different times. Let me say that my mother was a Nazarene, and she was a teetotaler. One time when he came up the road he told my stepfather that he had broken this half gallon of whiskey that he bought down the road. He asked if my mother would sell him a half-gallon jar. My stepfather said, "No, she won't do that for you to be used as a whiskey jar."

This fellow said, "Well, I'm going to ask her anyway."

So he asked her and she said, "I'm not going to sell you a half-gallon jar to go get whiskey."

He said, "Well, I've already got the jar, and I've cracked it. But I'd give 50¢ for one."

Well, my mother was working all day for 75¢ a day, so she said, "Well, I'll see if I can find you one of them." [*Laughter*]

Another time, this same fellow went down that road to this man [name withheld] that made whiskey. His family don't care to tell about it now. That whiskey maker made it for many, many years, and they say it was some of the best whiskey ever made. He is dead now.

This man said he went down there to get a half gallon of whiskey, and when he got there he asked where the whiskey maker was. The man's wife said, "He's gone to town, and he's going to go to torment for making that whiskey, and you are going to go to torment for drinking it."

The fellow who was there to purchase the whiskey said, "Well, I wish he was here. I've got $3 I'd pay for half a gallon."

She said, "Have you got $3?"

He said, "Yes," then she said, "Then, I'll get you a half gallon." [*Laughter*]

Glynn Mann, Clinton County, February 8, 2010

Desirable Guns

Back when I was sheriff, I had this .357 Magnum, and I carried a .30-30 Winchester repeater rifle also. So I'd take a prisoner up to LaGrange, and they had a building there in which they checked you. You had to leave all your weapons and all your ammunition there with them. Well, they'd make fun of my .357 and my old .30-30 Winchester there at that place in LaGrange. They'd say, "You know you don't carry anything like that down in Clinton County, do you?"

I said, "Yes, I do. We try to carry a weapon that we can hit with. Some of these like you carry up here wouldn't hit the side of a barn!"

So when I took these fellows in there, before we got there this fellow whose name was Fitzgerald had a little package that had a pair of old shoes in it, and he took his new shoes off before we got there and put them old shoes on. He said, "When I get inside the prison, they'll give me a pair with these old ones in this shape. Take my new shoes back to Clinton County." See, he was slicker than they thought he was!

When you go in there, they drop the gate over you with the prisoner. Well, when I came back out of that little building to get my weapon and ammunition, the prison guards tried to buy my guns. They'd made fun of them when I was going in, then they wanted to buy them, which were a Winchester and .357 Smith.

Glynn Mann, Clinton County, February 8, 2010

HALLOWEEN PRANK ON SHERIFF'S NOSE

There's a hill out here that we all call Foster Mountain. A clan lived out there, kinda like the Garlands on the *Andy Griffith Show*. But these on Foster Mountain were all kinda kinfolks. Every Halloween they'd take trucks and fill the road up with logs and rocks. So in my office we all split up on Halloween. I said, "I'll take Foster Mountain."

I went up on the mountain and there were rocks and trees in the road. Well, I drove around there, got through them, and parked up there on the snow. Well, here comes an old station wagon full of their women. Everybody knew me, so they stopped. There were five or six of them, maybe seven, and all were drunk as haints. They were inside a home by now, so I thought if we turn them loose we'll have to come back. So I just loaded all of them up, brought them to Monticello, and put them in jail.

I went back out there, and their youngest brother, Junior, had a motorcycle that had no muffler, no nothing. He'd run from down in the flat, and get up close to me. I was just sitting there in the car, and on down through the woods he'd go, out of hearing. In a few minutes you'd hear his motorcycle going "zr-r-r-r, zr-r-r-r" coming back up the hill. Right toward me he'd come, then turn off again. I had me a paper, like I was reading. I said, "Next time you do that, ole boy, I'll nail you."

So he popped up in the road about one quarter of a mile below me, then started back up the road. I started my car up. He's come a little closer every time, and just as he was getting ready to turn, I took off toward him and he turned over. Well, he stood right there until I started to get out of the car, then he took off running like a scalded cat.

It was getting dusky dark, and down at his daddy's house around the house we went running, with me chasing him. I kind of thought he'd bobbed [jumped] up when he was only twenty feet or so ahead of me. Well, I didn't bob, but there was an old fence across the road down there and I hooked my foot in it. I kept running and went out through them skulled rocks and lost everything I had, including my flashlight. I scooted to a stop on the ground. There was an old building setting up above me, and they had goats. These goats started jumping on me! I got up and my nose was running, so I swipe it.

I finally got my flashlight but my hands were hurting. My knees were torn out of my pants. My nose was peeled down and just hanging, skinned by the rocks and peeled down. I pulled it off and covered up everything, and an old man comes out of the house and he is drunk. He hooked his arms around the porch post and says, "Are you hurt, son?"

I said, "No, I ain't hurt. I'm tough."

I got up and searched every house up there and couldn't find the man I was chasing. They'd go by and just open the door and go on in. Of course, I was skinned all over, and blood was running down my nose. I went ahead and hauled the motorcycle in.

About a year later one of the women I had put in jail that night asked me, "What did you ever do with Junior's motorcycle?"

I said, "Didn't he go get it?"

She said, "No, he was afraid you had a warrant for him."

I said, "No, he just outrun me. His motorcycle is still down there at so-and-so's. Let me call down there and save you a big storage bill."

I called and talked to so-and-so. I said, "Go and get it, and just pay the wrecker bill. There won't be a storage cost!"

Joseph Conn, Wayne County, February 13, 2010

Easy Arrest

Here is a funny story that will make you think about Andy Mayberry. When my office was in the courthouse, I was sitting there in my office and the state police called me and said, "We've got an accident on the highway down at Van. We have one vehicle, so can you take care of it?"

I said, "Yeah, I'll be glad to."

They said, "The troopers are tied up right now. They are down at Blackey with a SWAT team trying to get someone there."

I said, "I'll take care of it," so I go down there and worked a little 1045 accident with a woman that had run into a ditch line. I get all the information and everything, then go back to my office. Something like two hours later Dr. McDougal down here at the Mountain Comp Clinic called me and told me that he had a fellow there, and asked me if I knew him. When he told me his name, I said, "Yeah, I know him."

He said, "Well, he's down here at my office right now, and you need to come down here because he needs to talk to you."

Well, I never thought nothing about him connecting with the SWAT team at all. So I took my gun and went down, but left my gun in the car. My wife works there at the clinic as a registered nurse. So I just go around to the back and walked into the back of the clinic. The nurses are standing there, and Dr. McDougal comes out and said, "Just a minute." Then he goes back there and brings this guy out. The guy runs over to me and shakes my hand and says, "Danny, I'm so glad to see you. Those ole state police was down there at my house, and they had guns and everything."

Well, he had run off and left them there! He had come to turn himself in to me, and there I was with no gun on me. So the nurses start laughing at me and started calling me Andy.

What that was all about is that he had run off barefooted and run through the woods. So I said, "Well, come on," then put him in the Tahoe and brought him back to the office. I then called a good friend of mine on the state police and asked him, "Are you all looking for this guy?"

They said, "Yes, we're getting ready to go back down there. We had the SWAT team down there this morning, but he got away from us."

I said, "Well, I've got him up here at the office."

They said, "What?!" then they came up and arrested him for domestic violence threats. He'd make threats against his wife and also against police officers. But I just didn't put that together. He was coming to the doctor's office, so I just figured it was somebody down there that was a drug dealer, lived next to one, or something like that.

When I walked into the doctor's office, it was the guy the SWAT team was looking for.

Danny R. Webb, Letcher County, February 27, 2010

SHERIFFS KNOW EVERYBODY

When I was a trooper in Knott County, the sheriff was Taulby Pratt, and he was one of the first highway patrolmen for the Kentucky State Police. At that time I was working as a trooper in Knott County by myself, and I got a call telling me that this guy was over there shooting his shotgun and was drunk. He was raising sand in Rock Fork over in one part of the county. So I went over there and could see the guy's house over there in a bottom, so I parked my state police car over there on the road and started walking across that bottom.

When I got about halfway there, this man comes out on the porch drunk, then takes a shotgun and shouts out, "Hey, trooper, you'd better go back and get you some help because you're going to have to take me out of here feet first."

I said, "Yes, sir." And there he was standing on the porch with a shotgun! Well, I just sort of walked backward to my cruiser and called the Hazard post and said, "I need some assistance. This guy has got a gun, and he says he's not going unless we kill him."

So they sent me another trooper over there, but by the time he got there it was dark. We parked down the road a little bit and walked up there into the field and loaded up, like in the army. We then walked on over there to the house, and when we got there we saw this rock wall down below the porch, and the house was up higher. We crawled up there behind that rock wall, but hadn't been there but a few seconds until here he comes back out with that shotgun and shoots it a couple of times. We were thinking that he saw us and was going to shoot us. We were just two young troopers and were scared to death. We went ahead and got our weapons drawn and were behind that wall and just a few seconds from having a shootout as far as we were concerned. Then we saw this car coming and it went on past where we had parked our cars, goes on up, turns around, and comes right down there where we were at. What I didn't realize was that there was a road that came around and went on down to his house.

Anyway, we were there up against that wall hiding from the car lights. This guy pulls up and gets out. It was the sheriff, Taulby Pratt.

The sheriff yelled, "Frank, what are you doing?"

"Oh, they've been giving me a bad time all day."

"Put that shotgun away," and he goes up there and takes the shotgun away from him. Then he puts him in the police can and drives away. He never knew that we were there! After he pulled out we got back in our car and drove back to Hindman.

The sheriff knows everybody. So I've had the lieutenant over here at the state police, who is my good friend, say to me, "From now on, before I call the SWAT team, I'm going to call you to see if you know the guy." [*Laughter*].

Danny R. Webb, Letcher County, February 27, 2010

Woman Trails the Trooper

When you are a state police officer people like to know things about you. I was young when I first started as a trooper. My badge was just a little bit bigger than anybody else's, and my gun was slung just a little bit lower. That badge will stop just about anything, such as bullets. I call it the Wyatt Earp Syndrome. You go through it and when you come out you are going to solve all the crime in the world, and then you are going to start on sin after you get through with solving all the crimes!

It doesn't take you long to realize that you're not going to make much difference with anybody, because there're always going to be criminals and everything. The first thing that started happening to me was being told that people would say, "That trooper is going out with that woman." Of course, I was married and had one child then. People kept saying, "That trooper is going out with that girl," and "That trooper is going out with that woman." It wasn't true, but you can get on there and say anything, and it was viewed as good gossip in the town if you had a girlfriend.

So I had just started working after my training officer had turned me loose, and I am working by myself as a trooper. I was on the road, and this car was following me. I stopped and cars would go by. I'd get back on the road and this car was still following me. I thought to myself, "What's going on here?" So I pulled over and this car goes by, then I followed that car and pulled the driver over. I said, "Are you following me? Why?"

She said, "Yes."

Then I said, "Don't follow me," then I drive on.

A few days later the same thing happened, so I stopped. Well, back then we didn't have cell phones, so I stopped at a phone booth and called my training officer on the phone and said, "Listen, I've got this woman," then told him her name. I went on to say, "She's following me."

He said, "Well, go back there. Where's she at?"

I said, "She's sitting on the road right now. I just stopped here at the pay phone."

He said, "Go down there and say to her, 'If you follow me one more time, I'm going to take you to jail.'"

I said, "I don't want to do that."

He said, "You have to if you want her to quit following you."

So I go back there and tell her, "Don't follow me no more, or I'm going to take you to jail." After saying that to her I drove off, and she never did follow me anymore!

Danny R. Webb, Letcher County, February 27, 2010

COMPROMISING SITUATION

I remember one time when I was a trooper there was a rumor started that I was dating this woman, and her husband was real mean. As a matter of fact, if he caught somebody with her he'd threaten to kill them. I didn't even know who she was, as I had never seen her. I kept being asked, "Have you got a girlfriend?"

I'd say, "No."

This girl's husband was real mean, and he said, "Rumor is out that you are dating her."

One day I was over in one end of the county and got behind this car that didn't have taillights. So I pulled it over. The only thing I had was that girl's name, because I had been told what her name was. I had never seen her before. Well, I walked up there and she was in a Dodge car. I said to her, "Can I see your driver's license?"

She got her license out and hands it to me, and I looked at the photograph and said to myself, "It's her!" [*Laughter*]

There I was out in a rural area and had her pulled off on the side of the road. I threw her license back to her and said, "Get your taillights fixed."

I knew that if somebody drove by, that would be the end of it and that the rumor was true. So just in a few seconds, I was gone!

Danny R. Webb, Letcher County, February 27, 2010

HUMOROUS TIMES IN MONROE COUNTY

I had gone to talk to this man who had threatened suicide, and on the way there I saw a man standing in the field and I waved at him. For some reason my deputy giggled about what I had done. Well, after dealing with this man about suicide, we passed by this man still standing out in the field, so I waved at him again. That time my deputy just busted out laughing. I said, "What's wrong with you?"

He said, "Not only did you wave at that scarecrow once, you have waved at him twice."

I said, "That ain't no scarecrow, that's a man."

He said, "No, it's a scarecrow."

I drove on to the top of the hill, then turned around and drove back down there. I looked over there, and it was a darn scarecrow! It had a straw hat on, had on a pair of bib overalls, a sweatshirt hanging all the way down, and had on a pair of black gloves.

Of course, it was away from the road a little bit, so I just glanced my eyes over there and thought it was a man standing there. When I waved my hand, my deputy wondered why in the world I waved at that scarecrow. He thought I actually thought it was a man, and I did!

We went out there and took a picture and hung it on the wall here in my waiting room.

Here is another thing I thought was funny. This woman lived down here in the Boles community and she called to tell me about a skunk that she couldn't get rid of. So I called the game warden, and he was on his way to Glasgow. He told me to go shoot the skunk.

I said, "I don't want to shoot that thing. It will stink me up."

He said, "No, I want you to shoot so it won't spray out."

The deputy and I went down there, and the deputy is the one that shot the skunk. When that awful stuff started coming out of the skunk, we took a beeline in our cars!

In another situation, this lady called to say she had ticks in her yard, and in still another situation a woman called from Akersville about this guy that had a pony. However, he had never built a shed for this pony to get in when it rained, etc. She wanted me to go down there and make him build a shed!

We get these types of calls all the time.

One time this woman come in and told me she had $30,000 in the trunk of her car, and that her daughter stole it. I brought her daughter in here, and she admitted doing it. Actually, the mother had been drawing Social Security thanks to her daughter since her daughter, who was now fifteen, was a kid. The mother was drawing this money, but never gave any to her daughter. The mother said, "I bought her clothes and things like that," which normally you do.

We worked things out. I had two troopers here in the office, and the mother was sitting here with us. I said, "Now I'm going to talk, and when I get through, you talk."

So I talked about an agreement, and how she was to pay the money back, and things like that.

Well, she also wanted to talk, and then started out telling her side of the problem. Well, she didn't get to the point. What happened was, she come up with "I was attending Western Kentucky University when I was such-and-such an age. I was working at Houchens cutting meat . . ."

She talked for ten minutes telling stuff like that, so finally I said, "Look, go home and write me a letter about these things, and all that stuff."

Well, these troopers just cracked up. They laughed so hard that Ray just got up and got out of the office. I finally broke loose laughing and turned my head down. She said, "You're laughing at me."

I said, "No, I'm not laughing at you, it's just the way things come out when you were told to write me a letter."

That was a funny thing to all of us.

Jerry "Slick" Gee, Monroe County, March 18, 2010

Chapter 5

MOONSHINE, MARIJUANA, AND METH

The stories in this chapter detail the changing scene of illegal substances, ranging from the old days of moonshine whiskey to marijuana to the more recent—and more alarming—rise in the production and use of methamphetamine.

Although the days of moonshine are for the most part gone, stories of its heyday persist. These sometimes feature hardened criminals who would stop at nothing to protect their illegal interests; alternatively, however, making moonshine was often a family effort necessary for survival in hard economic times. One amusing story reveals two sheriffs whose own fathers were bootleggers.

Marijuana succeeded moonshine as the illegal drug of choice, and many stories reveal that sheriffs were kept busy searching and destroying patches of plants, which were usually hidden in secluded areas or grown in cornfields or other croplands. Often law enforcement officials had to burn the contraband before witnesses—or take photos—to avoid suspicion that they kept the plants themselves.

The sheriffs report that drug-related offenses increasingly involve meth—much to their distress, as experience has taught them that the danger meth poses to its users is far greater than that of moonshine or marijuana. The drug was originally manufactured primarily in rural pockets, but more recently meth labs are springing up anywhere and everywhere, all across the state. In response to what Daviess County sheriff John Cain refers to the "methamphetamine epidemic," Drug Task Forces have been established throughout Kentucky. These have had some successes, as the stories below indicate, but meth continues to be a serious problem.

No Need for Moonshine

Around 1981, which was the last year of my first term, I was told there was a moonshine still out here on Slim Island Road toward Jackson Orchard. So, I called ATF [the Bureau of Alcohol, Tobacco, Firearms, and Explosives] and told them there's supposed to be a moonshine still out on Slim Island Road. The agent said, "A moonshine still? Hell, I ain't never worked one of them cases, it's been so long ago."

We pondered around, and he wound up saying, "Just go out there and tell them we know what they are doing, so don't do it no more."

I went out there and told a fellow, "Hey buddy, you need to quit making whiskey."

He said, "Oh, I ain't doing that."

Actually, he did, but we haven't heard anything more about it. And here in Bowling Green, we were talking the other day about bootlegging, but I ain't heard anything like that going on. I guess that's because the liquor stores stay open till 2:00 in the morning, then open back up at 6:00. So there's not even a bootlegger in Bowling Green anymore, but there might be one up around Smiths Grove.

Jerry "Peanuts" Gaines, Warren County, July 20, 2009

Out with the Old and in with the New

On Saturday night during the first time I was sheriff, my wife and I and the chief Constant, who was police chief and who later succeeded me as sheriff for one term, went to the Grand Ole Opry. My boys said, "We're going to raid all the bootleggers in Smiths Grove." And that night they raided the bootleggers, about five of them.

When I got home that night my phone was ringing off the hook. These phone calls were from the people that had been buying moonshine whiskey from the bootleggers. They'd say, "You SOB, we got you elected, and now you've caught our bootleggers. We have to drive all the way to Bowling Green to get a drink."

Well, I thought, "Damn." We more or less got it through, and I said, "We're going to have to cut it down some. I'll bother you no more, and you won't bother me."

So I don't know what it's like in Smiths Grove now. That was the last bunch of bootleggers we had. I think we scared them out; they moved out. There was one that got too old to make moonshine whiskey, and he died out.

I don't know of any in Warren County now. We've got a Drug Task Force here in Warren County now, and they catch four or five meth makers every day. Persons make it in cars.

I've got a big bus in which I haul senior shoppers to Wal-Mart the second Thursday of each month. I had the bus down at the jail, and the trustees had washed it. The nose of the bus was facing Main Street, and the traffic backed up at that point. There was a four-door pickup truck that came through the intersection, and the traffic had stopped. A fellow said to me, "Hey sheriff, they're making meth in that truck."

I said, "What?" Well, the girls in the back of the truck had a hot plate hooked to the cigarette lighter, and they were making meth in that truck. They had the tanks right in the back, and so we just pulled them right into jail. One of the trustees said to the ones in the truck, "You all are going to be in here with us tonight." We arrested them right on the spot.

We've tried to cut meth makers, but they pop up every night. It's such a cheap thing to do, so persons in every nationality are doing it.

We now have a Drug Task Force here in Warren County, and three of my deputies are on it.

Jerry "Peanuts" Gaines, Warren County, July 20, 2009

MARIJUANA DISTRIBUTORS

Back when we had only a few officers, we got a complaint from a lady out in the county, out where there was a house that was awfully suspicious. People would come to this house, then leave pretty soon. And every now and then big trucks would come in. So the chief deputy and I decided we were going to conduct surveillance on that house.

One night the deputy and others went out there, but I was still here in the office. As soon as they got there they realized that there was a truck at the back door of this house, a big U-haul type of truck. My deputies watched as these people were carrying in big boxes. Then as the truck and car and stuff left, they walked up to the house. They saw this lady standing in there, and they asked her, "Can we search your house? Do you live here?"

She said, "Yeah, but you probably can't search. You might need to get a warrant, because you are going to be very surprised at what you find in here."

From all the information we had gathered, we got a warrant, but while we were getting a warrant, we were trying to track these guys that had left.

When we finally got our search warrant, we walked in and found more than two thousand pounds of processed marijuana that they had been shipping in from Arizona and Mexico—the route up through there. We were able to track down the guys that had left here. We called Elizabethtown where there were some Mexicans and stuff they caught up there.

The main guy got away. He lived in another county, and he fled. It ended up that he and his wife were wanted in Tennessee for the same thing.

Anyway, the DEA got involved, and months later we got the main guy captured in Florida. The DEA were able to track from a little town in Kentucky a network all the way back into Mexico. The shipments they sent here to Taylor County were distributed in New York, and they found out where it was distributed from there.

These illegal eighteen-wheelers had brought it up to Indiana, right there in the Louisville area. Then they distributed it to us, then these trucks would go somewhere else.

Well, we captured over two thousand pounds. I guess it was the biggest marijuana drug bust in Kentucky, and it still is the biggest. I'm sure that type of illegal activity is still going on.

The funny part is, it just happened that this woman called and we were just lucky enough to go the same night that they were making the delivery. The reason she called was due to the traffic in that area. It is usually quiet, but since these people had moved into this house, there was much noise.

The owner of the house lived in Marion County but was renting it out to the fellow that lived here. The one who owned the house was involved with people associated with Cartel. But in a small town in Kentucky, you'd be surprised what goes on.

John E. Shipp, Taylor County, July 30, 2009

WOULD-BE MOONSHINE MAKER

I found one moonshine still that was in this guy's closet, but he hadn't got it into production yet. This guy had pulled a gun on me at another time, and after that happened he told his cousin that he knew I drove there from Campbellsville. This fellow lived right there on the road, and he said, "I'll be waiting for him. He will shoot me."

So I heard about it, and grabbed his cousin up and took him to the county attorney and said, "I want you to issue a terroristic threatening warning on his statement," and he did.

I jumped in the car and headed out there, and didn't wait for any help or anything. I slid up in front of his house, dove out of the car, and hit his front door and busted it wide open. He was setting there, but had his shotgun apart, cleaning it. He looked at me and said, "Oh, crap," and the fight was on.

You had to do that to bullies back then. If you didn't, they'd run all over you. If you backed down one time, you'd had it. So I got him, whipped him, and put him in the car. Actually, we had a heck of a fistfight. But as I was in there, I saw something sticking out of the door. I opened it up, and he had a full moonshine still setting there. He just hadn't got it in operation yet!

John E. Shipp, Taylor County, July 30, 2009

Success against Meth

We work seven days a week on the methamphetamine problem, which has been ongoing, but I think we've got a handle on it. When we took over this county was on its knees as far as the meth problem was concerned. We've had many meth arrests, but it has slowed down tremendously during the last couple of years. I don't think they are making it and selling it like they did at first, but that is my opinion.

A lot of the makers have left the county. One fellow had moved out of the county because we were putting so much pressure on him. What happened is that he caught an apartment complex on fire. He was making meth and the apartment burned down. I think that took place in an adjoining county. We've had a lot of people come and tell us the meth makers left the county because we've been so aggressive in drug enforcement.

Before I took over you could go somewhere and tell them where you were from, and they'd say, "That's where Bonnieville is." They said that because it was famous for its meth makers. We've been so very effective because we get good information from people that trust us. They'll call us on our drug tip line. They call us anonymously and we act on that information. If somebody just calls in about one thing, we won't go. But usually we get information from two or three different places. We've been real successful in dealing with meth makers.

Boston B. Hensley Jr. and Deputy James Veluzat,
Hart County, July 30, 2009

WHISKEY MAKERS KILLED OFFICIALS

This is about a revenue agent and a city policeman. I recently put up a monument in Johnson County to all law enforcement officers killed in the line of duty. Back in 1921 there was a revenue agent in the U.S. Treasury Department that responded to Slate Branch, located in Johnson County off of Highway 172, to a moonshine still report.

A Paintsville policeman was close to the location, and they went to check on a moonshine still in this hollow. When they got close to the operations shots rang out and it developed into a gun battle. The federal agent and a police officer were killed, and another police officer was wounded but survived.

William D. Witten, Johnson County, August 7, 2009

"MR. AND MRS. CRYSTAL METH"

A young lady I want to tell about was addicted to drugs in Johnson County, and the sheriff's office had dealt with this problem on many different occasions by arresting and taking her to jail. I personally had several discussions with her, talking about what the impact of drugs would do to her life in her future.

She had gone through some classes on narcotics, and had gotten cleaned up at one point. However, many of these folks relapse. Very seldom does one person go clean for a long period of time. They relapse three or four times before they ever really come out of it, and some never do.

I got a call one morning about the young lady, and apparently she had overdosed and died. What I learned after her death was that she was in jail once, and her father brought me a very long handwritten poem that she had written, or copied, while she was in the Floyd County jail. The title of the poem is "Mr. and Mrs. Crystal Meth." The first few lines of the poem reads like this:

I destroy homes; I tear families apart.
I take your children and that's just the start.
I'm more valued than diamonds, more precious than gold,
The sorrow I bring is a sight to behold.
If you need me, remember I'm easily found,
I live all around you, in school and in town.

The final two lines say,

I can show you more misery than words can tell,
Come take my hand, let me lead you to HELL.

As the *Paintsville Herald* did a newspaper article about her, they found there were different versions of the poem on the Internet. While she was in the Floyd County jail, she may have copied something, but in fact she did have it in her possession in her own handwriting at her death.

We do drug classes several times a year in Johnson County churches and schools in different communities. When teaching these classes, I always use this poem because it's got so much meaning in it, and describes in detail what happens to parents, family, and what happens to you when you pay this price.

William D. Witten, Johnson County, August 7, 2009

Guns and Moonshine

We had received a call here late one evening, and the person calling told us that a father and three of his sons had disturbed the church in their area, which was very remote at that time. It was located on the Tug Fork River, which separates West Virginia and Kentucky.

Two deputies were dispatched to check on the disturbance at the church. When they got there it was a little after dark. They found that these three fellows had gone in and disturbed the church, and the church people left. These fellows had shotguns, and they were firing up in the air near the church.

When the church group left one of the deputies said, "Now, you just sit here in the car. I know these people, so I'll just go in and get them and bring them back, then we'll take them to jail."

When he walked in the door, they disarmed him immediately. They took his weapon and shot him between his legs. He was sort of bowlegged, and he'd get upset with us if we called him "Bowlegs" after that. Those fellows also took that other deputy's weapon and fired at him. He ran off and left to get to the phone and called me. After telling me what had happened, and I told him to pick up the deputy and meet us at another place.

Two other deputies and I proceeded to go over to that area, and as we reached the house every light in the house was on. I said, "Now, turn your red light on."

He turned on the light, and about the time we pulled up to the gate to get out, we heard a *kaboom, kaboom* noise. They had shot our light out. "Dome light!" I hollered.

We went in the house, and at that time the old man, who was the noisemakers' father, had passed out drunk and was laying on the couch. So we put handcuffs on him, but the three boys run out the front door with their shotguns. I told the deputy to stay in the house and keep the old drunk man from leaving.

At that time there was gunfire going off with the three boys shooting their guns. We went behind the house and saw that they were firing up into the air, and those buckshots were falling down on us.

The deputy that was in the house walked to the back door to see what was going on. When he did that the father of the three boys ran out of the house with his handcuffs, just hollering and cussing and telling his boys to get us off his property. He was using profane language while he was shouting. So these boys hid higher up and fired again.

I was afraid they might shoot their father, but one of my deputies was standing behind a tree. Of course, the other three of us were laying in the weeds. He thought he was well hidden behind that tree as they were shooting, and wanted to fire back.

The deputy said, "Sheriff, can I shoot them? I can see one of them."

"No, no, let's let them run out of ammunition," I replied.

Finally they did run out of ammunition, then took off and ran across a railroad bridge that crossed into West Virginia.

I understand it, they had obtained those guns from a catalog mail order, so they were trying them out that night. They threw their guns in the river that night.

We went on to arrest the father, and as we were walking by we noticed a fellow that had passed out flat in the seat of another old junk car there. We brought him and the boys' father to the jail.

The road we were on was very narrow, and as we went through

it we met a pickup truck. It seemed almost simultaneously the driver's side and passenger side doors came open and two suspects ran, leaving their lights on and the truck running.

We thought we'd run a license check, but the truck didn't have a license plate, and because of that we didn't know who it belonged to. But in the truck bed there were probably twenty half gallons of moonshine and a horse saddle. We loaded the moonshine and brought it with us, leaving the saddle behind. Later on a few people took a sample taste of it, but we didn't.

Believe it or not, four or five years later, the same two deputies and I were sitting in a restaurant here in Pikeville, and began talking about getting that moonshine liquor. Someone came up behind me and patted me on the back and said, "Let me tell you something, Fuzzy Keesee, that was my liquor you got," laughing as he told us.

That is a true story. There was a lot of moonshine liquor made in this county when my father was sheriff, and also during my first term. We looked for it when we'd get a report, and we found a few active situations.

Back in my early years there were several coal mines that were no longer working here, so a lot of former coal miners and others did make moonshine liquor because they needed the income. What little corn they did grow was converted into moonshine liquor. I knew several families that were raised by making moonshine liquor.

Charles E. "Fuzzy" Keesee, Pike County, August 7, 2009

MARIJUANA AND METH

We used to cut marijuana a long time ago, and we cut quite a bit of it here in the county. State troopers, National Guard guys, and my other officers, we all had a good time doing that. It was hard work, but we had a good time doing it, so we joked and laughed about it amongst ourselves. There were a few times when George Pat Profitt, who was in a state unit, and I had hard times.

One time we got into a valley cutting some marijuana and could hardly breathe down there. Of course, the helicopter came over to give us some air and stuff, and we finally got out of there and cut it.

A lot of marijuana was grown and sold in the Kettle Creek area, and also in the Pea Ridge area where I was born and raised. After I became sheriff, we cut a lot of marijuana plants in those areas, and also up on Jones Ridge. There were just several places all over Cumberland County where we went to cut the marijuana, but most of our activity took place in the Pea Ridge area.

Meth making takes place in different parts of the county, as meth products are now much more popular than marijuana. There are different versions of meth labs, the way they fix it, etc. The makers put different types of ingredients in their meth containers, little cans, pots, etc. They put their pot on top of these heater things, put different ingredients in it, then let it set there and cook off. They put things like rat poison and other things in it such as red iodine. They just use anything that is poisonous in order to fix it up the way they want it. When they get it done it has turned into a liquid thing.

The stuff they mix together to make the liquid makes people sick, causes their teeth to start falling out, their hair to come off, and they get really skinny. For example, if a person that weighs like 250 to 300 pounds uses that stuff, in about two, three weeks or a month, he is down to 140 to 150 pounds, if he lives that long.

People tell me the reason why they use it is because they get a big "high" out of it. It calms them down, and they don't worry about nothing. To me, I'd rather be fat and alive than to be nothing. It is dumb that people are doing their bodies that way.

James Pruitt, Cumberland County, August 10, 2009

NAKED PRISONER

One time back in 1988 or 1989 I had a call about this lady who was coming from the Clay County, Tennessee, area, and was around Ashlock, a community here in Cumberland County. She was on drugs, and was driving toward Burkesville on drug charge 148. I started south on Highway 61, and got past Willis Bar-B-Que, then met the car I was looking for.

I turned around and came back, stopped her, and she pulled in at Willis Bar-B-Que. Well, as soon as she got out of the car I could see that she didn't need to be driving. So I got her out of her car and tried to do some tests, but she couldn't do any, so I placed her under arrest for driving DUI on drugs. I put her in the back seat of the car and headed toward Burkesville. I radioed my miles to the dispatcher—how many miles I was out and how many minutes I hoped it would take to get to the city hall.

When I pulled up at city hall, got down behind the building, and this lady had pulled all of her clothes off. She was sitting in the back seat of my car with no clothes on. Miss Joan Smith was the dispatcher at that time, and she is still dispatching today for us. We got this lady inside and tried to get her clothes, but she wouldn't put her clothes on. So we had a hassle with her there. Transportation officer Hobo Branham came by, and he and his wife took her to the Adair County jail. And she still had no clothes on!

That was one of those deals where I asked her if she had anything in her pocket, and she just took all her clothes off. There she was in the back seat of my car with no clothes on!

James Pruitt, Cumberland County, August 10, 2009

Meth Lab Barn

We've also had quite a few meth cases since it has gotten bigger than marijuana and has overpowered marijuana production. Meth production became more popular around 2000 AD, but maybe a little later than that. However, we've had a lot of problems with it, and thankfully have captured a lot of meth labs.

I remember one time I was out in the Ashlock area here in Cumberland County chasing a guy on foot, and he ran through this little barn opening and I was running behind him but wasn't able to catch him because he was outrunning me big time. There were three guys setting in the barn making meth at the time.

This guy ran through, and I got halfway through and then turned around, then these guys went out each door that they could find. I walked back, and there was a meth lab setting there in this little old barn in the Ashlock area.

James Pruitt, Cumberland County, August 10, 2009

Scared Straight

One particular story about a meth maker comes to mind. I'll not mention his name, but he was a good friend of mine. He got involved with meth and was selling it. So we had an undercover agent to buy meth from him two or three different times, then we placed him under arrest for selling it. I had him down at the city hall, booking him by writing out a citation, took his fingerprints.

We've got posters on the city hall wall showing people where meth had blown up and put big blisters on them, people with their teeth coming out, and other posters like that. The fellow I'm talking about was a good basketball player in high school. He was looking at those pictures, and he said, "Why would anybody do that?"

I said, "Well, why would you do that?"

He said, "What do you mean, *me?* I'm not on meth."

I said, "Go in that bathroom and look in the mirror."

He went in there and looked; then I said, "Now smile."

Some of his teeth were done gone, had fallen out, and he was in his twenties. His hair was also coming out. I said, "Come back out here and look at those posters again."

He didn't say anything else to me.

So he went to court and got put in jail for several years. He's out of the jail now. He came into the courtroom here in the Justice Center about two weeks ago, came up to me, shook my hand, hugged me, and said "Thank you."

That made me feel good and I almost cried because he said I had saved his life. And he was just a young man. He's alright now, and he weighs about 240 or 250 pounds.

James Pruitt, Cumberland County, August 10, 2009

MOONSHINER DADS, SHERIFF SONS

I didn't think I'd ever be sheriff of Cumberland County, because my dad at one time was probably the biggest bootlegger in Cumberland County. I carried a lot of mash, malt, water, and everything to him for him to use it in making liquor. My uncle, Jett Spears, also made liquor with him. They made a lot of moonshine back then, and that was truly a way of survival.

Another state trooper right now is like a brother to me. He is David Long, and he worked for me awhile when I got to be sheriff. His dad, like my dad, was a bootlegger. David and I sit around sometimes and talk about what our fathers did. We get to laughing a little bit, then say, "Here we are on this side of law, and we thought we never would be."

Time truly changes things. But back then making moonshine whiskey was really a necessity for families to be able to financially survive.

What few acres of land they had on which corn could be grown was used to grow corn that was used in making whiskey to be sold.

James Pruitt, Cumberland County, August 10, 2009

THREE PATCHES OF MARIJUANA

Back when I first started as a sheriff, when going to marijuana patches there was no trouble getting shot at about every time you were going into one of those, especially if it was a good patch, or what we called a plot. They'd shoot over your head or something.

I had this one gentleman to tell me one time that he grew three patches of marijuana every year.

I said, "Three patches?"

He said, "Yeah, I grow one for you, one for marijuana thieves, and one for myself."

He grew three of them, thus he finally got one for himself! In other words, the sheriff's office got to cut down one patch, the thieves got to steal one patch, then he had one patch for himself that could be sold.

He told us, said, "Now you know why I grow it."

I said, "Yeah, I'm going to try to catch you while growing it."

He said, "Well, you got close one time!" That way, he joked about it.

What I want to say now is not related to him. Anyway, we still have people growing marijuana today. As a matter of fact, about three weeks ago I was out in this little area and I come across eighty-six plants. Of course, there was nobody around, and it was on another guy's property. There was a path that went through there, so I followed the path and found a plant here and there, kind of scattered around. It took a little while to get it, but I found eighty-six plants and cut all of them.

James Pruitt, Cumberland County, August 10, 2009

GOOD HIDING PLACE

These people were hauling moonshine whiskey through Shelbyville in trucks. They had big tanks on them. Back when I was a deputy, I asked the sheriff, "They said they was moving moonshine, so what do you want me to do?"

He said, "Well, work the case."

Well, that's what I did. I knew where the truck was coming from here in Shelby County, so me and two other deputies walked and walked while a heavy rain was coming down. But we couldn't find no moonshine still. But what we were doing was probably illegal, because we didn't have a search warrant. We were just out there in the dark walking around in the fields, and really couldn't have done anything.

Anyway, some cars come in and went out. We went on back and got in our vehicles, and I said, "Let's find out who lives in that house. There's got to be a warrant on this guy somewhere." So I started calling all around the surrounding counties and found out there was a warrant on this guy in Oldham County. So we go back in there and drive right up to the front door of this house. Me and one of the other deputies go in, and the others stay outside.

The people in that house had been doing a little remodeling and had worked on a cistern and other stuff. So we arrested this guy and take him in, and then some people came to try to get him out of jail. They knew him and thought he was a good guy, and he probably was. We had nothing against him. It was just a warrant, so we had an investigation going on. Anyway, we took him to jail but he didn't serve any time on the warrant as far as I know. He might have stayed in jail one night.

Later on, in a month or two, I run into this guy and called him his name, then said, "You know, we was looking for that whiskey. Where was that whiskey?"

He said, "It was in that cistern that you and the deputies were standing on top of." [*Laughter*]

Well, that truck never did go in down there any more! [*Laughter*]

Back then people needed to make some moonshine whiskey, because they needed to make a little money to live on. They had laws against it, but when they sold the moonshine, the government wanted the revenue off of the sales. But that's the way those people made a living back during the Depression, especially in the western section of the county. But they weren't making it out there; they'd bring it in from somewhere else, then put it in that cistern and then pump it back out into that truck.

I don't know where they took it to sell it. As law officers, we never did get that far! [*Laughter*]

Harold E. Tingle, Shelby County, August 14, 2009

METH MAKERS

When I was sheriff I never ran into any meth makers, but I'm sure they made it here in Shelby County. It could be around one subdivision up there. A fellow told me that you could smell what these meth makers were doing. They told me what area it was in, but nothing was done to catch the makers. Of course, they could make it anywhere, even in an automobile. Making it is getting to be big stuff now, all around the state.

Harold E. Tingle, Shelby County, August 14, 2009

Delayed Arrest

This story is about an individual who was growing marijuana. He lived in the Jabez area of Russell County. The only way to get to the Jabez area is to go through Pulaski County, and then come back west into Russell County. The reason for it being hard to get to is due to the coming of Lake Cumberland, after Wolf Creek Dam was built. The old roads were blocked, and you had to go a long way around in order to get to Jabez.

There was an elderly gentleman over there who was likeable, but he had a reputation of growing marijuana. He lived next to the lake, and his property joined the government property. So I took a boat and went around the lake in order to come in on the back side. When I got there I looked around and found what I thought was his marijuana patch. It was not too far from where he lived, and a path went toward his home. The patch was rather small at the time, so I thought I'd come back later and stay there for a few days and see if I could catch somebody coming in to cultivate it.

In the meantime, when this individual would come to Jamestown, he would always come by the sheriff's office. When he got there he would say to me, "Larry, when are you going to come to Jabez to see me?"

I said, "Well, I'll be over there one of these days."

Time would pass, and he'd be in Jamestown again. He always came by and said, "Larry, why don't you come by to see me?"

I said, "I'll be over there one of these days to see you."

I'd already found his marijuana patch, so I took a pontoon boat and crossed the lake to go over there again. I stayed on his marijuana patch for three days. During the third morning I was probably ten feet from the marijuana patch, hidden behind a log with a camera. It was just coming daylight when he comes down the path and walks into the marijuana, checking it out. He's looking at the leaves and buds on it, and I'm taking his photograph as he is looking at and examining it.

My .35 mm camera would make a noise when it would fast-forward.

Every time that camera made that noise, he would look up in the sky like he was trying to see where that noise was coming from.

He also smoked cigars, and when he walked, he'd just got out of bed and his hair was sticking straight up. He was in his seventies. When he got there I raised up and said, "How are you doing this morning?"

He paused, then said, "I wasn't expecting to see you here today."

I said, "Well, if you'll remember, I kept telling you I was going to come to see you!"

So we had a big laugh, and he helped me cut the marijuana and then carry it over to the lake and put it on the boat. When we were finished he said, "Can I go back to the house and get me some cigars and tell my wife where I'm going?"

I said, "Yeah, we'll walk up there and tell her."

So we went back to his house and he told his wife, who was much younger than him, that he was going to have to go to jail. He got some cigars, and he never got mad at me. Down through the years we were always friends.

He pleaded guilty and got some time in jail for growing marijuana. He was sentenced to five years in jail, but he stayed only a few months in jail. Later his probation officer was at his house after he got out on probation and found a rifle there. Due to that he had to go back to jail and spend some time.

This is kind of funny, as his son came that night to see him in jail. Well, he was very intoxicated, and walked into the sheriff's office and said, "Can I go over here to the jail and visit with my dad?"

I happened to glance down, and he had a pint of Old Crow whiskey sticking out of his pocket. He was already pretty drunk, but I said, "Yeah, we'll take you in and let you see him."

So I took him to jail and locked him up for alcoholic intoxication, and he got to spend time with his dad!

Larry L. Bennett, Russell County, September 18, 2009

WIFE RUINS ALIBI

I've got another marijuana story here. I found this patch of marijuana that was really large. The grower had done an outstanding job growing it. This was in the Eli community of Russell County. I was going to try to set on it to see if I could see somebody coming in to cultivate it.

This was about the time that Hurricane Andrew came through. It was really rainy, windy, so I thought this marijuana is so big I'll bet whosever it is will go to it to see if the wind had blown any of it over. So I go and set down there on the patch. By the middle of the morning two or three of these big plants had blown over, and I seen an individual walking down through the woods. He had a pistol and holster strapped on his right side.

He walked into the marijuana patch, and when he saw the plants that had blown over, he cursed two or three times to himself. Of course, I drew my pistol and stepped out of my hiding place and said to him, "Sheriff's department. Don't reach for that gun, and don't do anything stupid."

Well, he didn't, but said, "Can I set down on the ground?"

I said, "Why?"

He said, "I don't think my legs are going to hold me up." [*Laughter*]

So I disarmed him. Well, his excuse was that he was just squirrel hunting and didn't know that marijuana was there. So he stuck with his story. He repeatedly said, "I was just out squirrel hunting. I didn't know that marijuana was there."

So I started back up the road and we went by his house because he wanted to tell his wife. We got out of the car and walked across the yard, then his wife came out of the house, looked at him and said, "I told you you was going to get caught growing that marijuana." [*Laughter*]

He went to jail, but I don't recall how much time he spent. After he got out, a few years later I was in the same area looking for marijuana again, and I found a moonshine still this same guy had. Well, he had two fifty-five-gallon barrels of peach mash at work.

I charged him for manufacturing whiskey. That used to be a federal act, but now it's just a Class B misdemeanor.

Larry L. Bennett, Russell County, September 18, 2009

CATCHING MOONSHINE MAKERS

I've caught two moonshine stills since I became sheriff in 1989. There was a guy who was sheriff back in the 1960s, Bob McClanahan. After I caught this first moonshine maker, Bob told me he had tried to catch this same guy for moonshining back in the 1960s, but they were unable to catch him.

The only way I caught him was that I knew he was making it, but never could find out where his still or anything was. There was an elderly man that knew him, so he took me one night to show me where this fellow had his moonshine still. He had it covered up with brush bushes piled all over it, so we couldn't see it.

I got a search warrant for his house, and the still being on his property. I charged him for making moonshine whiskey.

Larry L. Bennett, Russell County, September 18, 2009

USEFUL INFORMATION

I had a deputy whose name was Charles Mann. He worked for me for sixteen or seventeen years, and was a really good deputy. One day he was out searching for marijuana because he had been told where there was some growing. So he went and checked it out. Sure enough, he found a small marijuana patch and destroyed it. After he did that he wrote a note on the back of one of our cards that said, "We know who you are. Come to the sheriff's office and turn yourself in." And he left it where the marijuana was.

So the next day this guy walks in and said, "I'm here to turn myself in."

We had no idea who it would be! [*Laughter*]

For your information, if caught for growing under five plants, it is a misdemeanor, thus up to a year in jail or a $500 fine. If it's over five plants, it is a felony, and the sentence is from one year to five years' prison time.

The size of marijuana plants vary. It's like some other crops. Some people grow bigger tomatoes than other people. It depends on what type gardener you are. I've seen some plants twelve, thirteen, fourteen foot tall, and I've seen some that are short.

They don't want the male plants. A good grower doesn't want the male plants. A good grower can tell the sex of the plants, and if there's any male plants in the crop, they cut those down. They don't want the buds to pollinate and turn to seed.

Larry L. Bennett, Russell County, September 18, 2009

DRIVE-IN BOOTLEGGER OPERATIONS

When I was elected sheriff there were a lot of bootleggers in Russell County. In fact, there were three drive-in windows. You didn't have to get out of your car, just drive up and get it. So we worked hard to shut all those down. Two were in Russell Springs and one in Jamestown.

We really put a lot of pressure on them, and sometimes we'd raid them twice a day. Those dealers had done that for so long that they thought they had a right to sell beer and whiskey. One in particular had this little small building located right beside a barn. Well, you could drive up there to this little sliding window, tell them how much you want, and they'd just hand it out the window to you. That was like going to McDonald's.

We raided them several times, and they finally got to where they were being really careful. They'd turn the lights off, point a flashlight in your face when you drove by. They'd just be real careful because they were raided so many times.

So, me and one of my deputies who had been off work for a couple of days, and let his beard grow out, he put on an old pair of overalls that had paint all over them. He'd been painting many times. He had a sling he'd put on his arm to pretend he had a broken arm, and he had a partial tooth plate in front that he took out so he wouldn't have any teeth up front.

I also disguised myself by putting on an old set of glasses, put on a cap that I turned sideways, and kinda put on some old clothes, and we borrowed an old pickup truck and pulled around by this window. That was at night, so the guy inside slides the window open and shines a flashlight in my eyes, and shines the flashlight in my deputy's eyes. He says, "I hate to do that, but the law is watching me awfully close—so what do you want?"

We said, "Give us a bottle of vodka," and when he handed us the vodka, we arrested him! [*Laughter*]

When he said, "The law is watching me awful close; I've got to be careful," we almost laughed.

Larry L. Bennett, Russell County, September 18, 2009

MOONSHINE BURNS

This is about a moonshine still. I got a call on Christmas Day, 1985. I was told that this guy had a stolen tractor and trailer at Ready, Kentucky. So I went down to investigate that, and while investigating the theft of the truck I found this moonshine still, and he had two or three gallons of moonshine whiskey in the still.

It wound up being a pretty good case, and in the hands of federal agents, because he had stolen the truck across the state line. That's what brought the federal people into it. The boy that stole that truck and moonshine wound up in Indiana.

I had two or three gallons of moonshine, and brought it back to my office and put it in my locker. The rest of the story is that people would come in from out of town and had never seen any moonshine. So I would pour some in an ashtray and light it with a lighter, then it would burn a blue flame. Yes, moonshine whiskey will burn.

After I lit it I noticed my flame kept getting weaker and weaker. It wasn't burning like it should. Well, a few years later I found out that a constable I had working for me was drinking the moonshine and pouring water back in the jug!!

I will jokingly say that I never did anything to that constable.

I did find some other jugs setting along side the road, but I never did find out the place where they were being made because I never found a moonshine still that was used in making it.

I ate lunch with Big Six Henderson, a revenue man, on one occasion. Across the years he had caught a lot of people that made moonshine, so I asked him, "Mainly, how did you catch them?"

He said he would go to stores to see who was buying the biggest supply of sugar. That was the way he would get after them, because it took a lot of sugar to make moonshine whiskey. Now, if I'm not mistaken, he had a finger missing. I believe he told me that he got after a moonshiner one time and started to jump over a fence, and I think he said that the guy turned around and shot at him and shot his finger off.

Qulin K. Escue, Grayson County, September 22, 2009

MARIJUANA BUST

The National Guard in eastern Kentucky got so hot on these marijuana growers that it pushed them out of eastern Kentucky, and they moved down our way. When they got here in Grayson County, they'd rent farms and grow big marijuana crops.

Myself, Roy Clodfelter, and Buford Stafford, who were state police, had been looking for marijuana patches that day. It was getting kind of late in the afternoon, and somebody was calling in complaints, telling us they'd seen marijuana. Well, about whatever place we went to, what they were seeing were mole beans growing in people's gardens, and they thought it was marijuana.

I told Buford, "I've got one more complaint that we need to check."

He said, "Hell, I've had all of this I wanted. We'll just drive up there and ask them if they are raising any marijuana."

Well, that's what we did. We drove to this house trailer, and I hadn't got out yet because my back door was locked. They had to be opened from the outside, and I was setting in the back. When we opened those doors we heard the worst racket that ever was. They jumped out and ran around, and this old man in this trailer was standing knee deep in marijuana they had already stripped. What happened was, he had kicked the screen door off the trailer when he seen us pull up. And this fellow we were after was barefooted, but he got in after him. Then there was another one that took off running, so I had to have them come back and let me out of the car.

I had on a western-type holster, and I had on blue jeans, so I unbuckled my gun. I got after this one guy, and when I reached down to get my gun to fire a warning shot, my gun was gone. So I had to stop chasing him and go back and find my gun. It had jumped out of my holster.

We piddled around there for I don't remember how long. We also called in some extra help in, including the game warden, to help us. Well, we got to piddling around there, but finally caught the old man. I told Buford, "If that old man hadn't been barefooted, you would have never caught him."

We got in the back of the game warden's truck, but Buford and some of the others stayed up on the hill. I said, "Let's just drive down and see if we can find the patch." So we drove down to the patch, and there were four boys down there cutting and stripping marijuana. We just drove right out in the middle of them, as they had no idea that anybody else was around.

We got after them, with some running this way and some running that way. I run after mine until I got plumb out of breath, so then I fired a warning shot. During that chase we didn't catch any of them.

When we come back, that old game warden said, "Hell, I could wring your neck!"

I said, "Why?"

He said, "Well, I had reached my hand out to grab mine, and when you fired that warning shot that guy throwed dust all over me."

But we finally caught them. Some of them was walking down the road, and they were from eastern Kentucky, but they didn't have no idea why that the guy that brought them in there to strip that marijuana had blindfolded them and brought them in there at night. They had no idea where they was at, or how to get home.

I remember one boy saying that he had made so much money just stripping marijuana for people that he had bought his mother a new house. He was one of the four that we caught.

That all happened between Short Creek and Leitchfield, and we found numerous marijuana patches in that area.

Qulin K. Escue, Grayson County, September 22, 2009

METH PROBLEM

Marijuana was our biggest problem when I was in office, then when I came out meth started. We didn't have any meth problems when I was sheriff. So right now meth is their biggest drug problem. It is widespread across the county, and there's not an outbuilding left in the county. They've blown them all up trying to make meth!

They get arrested frequently, and the law is pretty strict on them here. One guy that I know of was given a life sentence for making meth. The local people buy it from them, I guess, or the makers are on it themselves. They do it for themselves, plus they probably sell it out. It's a big, big problem, not only in Grayson County but also in other counties.

Qulin K. Escue, Grayson County, September 22, 2009

KENTUCKY LEADS THE WAY

I busted a few moonshine whiskey stills on the east end of Daviess County back in the 1970s, but moonshine liquor has never been an issue in western Kentucky, as it is over in the Appalachian sector of eastern Kentucky. People were more inclined to grow marijuana than making moonshine whiskey.

During the last decade since I've been sheriff, the major problem has been the clandestine manufacturing of methamphetamine, and that has been a tremendous problem in western Kentucky in general, and especially in Daviess County. In fact, we had the dubious distinction in Daviess County of being the leading producer in clandestine methamphetamine within the entire commonwealth during the early millennium of 2001 to 2005. One reason for this is that we took an aggressive approach to enforcing the laws and combating meth, thus we seized a lot more laboratories and arrested a lot more people who were involved in that crime. Thus, the stats indicated there was a bigger problem here; we were somewhat a victim of our successes.

But we were very aggressive in our approach to engaging the community in assisting us with that problem. I was also very active with the state legislature in statutory laws to combat meth.

When we first encountered methamphetamine in Daviess County, it was largely a rural phenomenon. They cooked it out in isolated areas in the county, but not much was cooked in the incorporated areas in Owensboro due to the likelihood of being detected due to the odors, etc.

Let me say that all of that has changed. Now then, the production of meth fuels the reversed availability and we see a lot of it now in the city also. They cook a lot of it in hotel and motel rooms and elsewhere. One of the present-day big problems relative to the methamphetamine epidemic started along about 2000, and it continues to be a problem as there is more of it being produced locally. Actually, the first methamphetamine laboratory was seized here in Daviess County in 1999, and I was there. Virtually all of the methamphetamine [before] then found its way across the heartland of the Midwest and into western Kentucky, came from California. So people here depended upon an external source back then, but now people here make it in their own backyards, and there is more of it. So when there is more of a drug available, the use and abuse of that drug rises dramatically also. That is what has fueled the "methamphetamine epidemic."

So we set out to try to incorporate laws that would help us limit the production. We did a number of different things, but one of the primary things we did was to take the precursor drug, which is the drug [pseudoephedrine] that is converted into methamphetamine, and pass laws to limit how much of that you could buy. Instead of being out of the counter now, you go to a pharmacy and fill out a log that includes your name, date of birth, address, then they enter that information onto a log. You can only have nine grams of that in a thirty-day period of time.

Within nine months of that law taking effect in Kentucky in 2005, we reduced meth production in Daviess County 67 percent. But, here's what happened. When we passed a law, people found a way to get around it. So when we limited the availability of pseudoephedrine in Kentucky, people then moved over to other states where they didn't have these laws. Then began to buy mass quantities of pseudoephedrine in other states and bring it back into Kentucky, then cook their methamphetamine.

So what we did to counter that was to work with our federal legislature, and in 2006 they passed the Combat Methamphetamine Epidemic Act that did the same thing we did in Kentucky in 2005. Kentucky led the fight against production of methamphetamine, and I've been very proud to have been a part of that initiative.

What has happened now is that because these paper logs are so laborious to write and to check, we're working on legislation that will mandate electronic reporting on the Web Internet nationally so that we can track these people that go out to buy it and bring it back in. Kentucky, again, has led the way. We have that law, and all our logs now are electronic. But because we can limit it here, the offenders can go back out across the states. So we are trying now to get individual states to mandate electronic reporting so that we can tie all this information and provide it via the Web. So that's an ongoing battle.

Keith Cain, Daviess County, October 1, 2009

Western versus Eastern Kentucky

Marijuana is the mainstay of illicit drugs, as it is readily available and the most commonly abused. Here in Daviess County we have a like or synonymous problem as you'll see across the country with people using marijuana. We have somewhat of a marginal problem with people cultivating marijuana. But we don't have near the problem here in western Kentucky as they do in eastern Kentucky, because over there they grow marijuana in remote areas up in the Appalachians, the Daniel Boone National Forest, and other places.

I'm not speaking negatively against my neighbors in eastern Kentucky, because I've got a lot of good friends over there. But Kentucky has been the number two state in the United States for several years for the illicit production of marijuana. California is number one. That's because of the much larger landmass in California. Kentucky has been number two for at least a decade, if not longer. Much of that marijuana is then shipped to jurisdictions across the country.

Eastern Kentucky has never had the problem with methamphetamine we've had in western Kentucky. The reason for that is the catalyst used in production of methamphetamine is anhydrous ammonia, which is a source of nitrogen that farmers use in the cultivation of corn. We grow a lot of corn in this part of Kentucky, and there's a lot of anhydrous that can be stolen and used to make a lot of methamphetamine. Because eastern Kentucky does not have the availability of the anhydrous, their meth problem will never reach ours. Of course, they have a problem, but it's just not on the same scale that we have.

Keith Cain, Daviess County, October 1, 2009

MARIJUANA AMONG THE CORN

I had a deputy who is now the jailer here in Butler County, Terry Fugate. He and I started a horseback patrol back in 1990. When we were on horseback patrol we'd get out in the summertime, along with two or three part-time deputies, and ride through the county areas looking for marijuana. We sure did find a lot of marijuana, because for awhile there they were planting it in large plots. But we got rough enough on them that they started growing it in smaller patches.

That was our main drug in Butler County at that time, that and prescription drugs. We didn't do too much about meth around here until the latter part of the 1990s. Meth started getting real popular here around 2000.

We even arrested people from other counties who were coming in here to grow marijuana. What they did was get an isolated area on somebody's farm, on the back side of a farm. Or, another popular thing was to take a farmer that had a large cornfield and draw themselves a little map, then count off twenty or thirty corn rows deep and then go down and cut off forty to fifty plants of corn, then replace them with fifteen or twenty plants of marijuana. Then, they would go on down a little farther and do the same, then go over and do a couple of more rows. And they had this map to show where they could go in this field to get the marijuana out of there within a matter of hours. So we'd have to search the whole field.

The farmers did not know what was taking place. A lot of times the farmers would call us to let us know they got into the field and were harvesting the corn before the marijuana growers had got it out of the field. But most of the time the marijuana growers were watching close enough so they could get the marijuana out before the farmer harvested the corn.

A lot of the farmers didn't know what was going on until we started educating them a little bit.

We arrested one group of guys who were from up around London, Kentucky, Laurel County. This bunch of guys was renting a motel room over in Ohio County, and later when we took their vehicles we found maps in what we call "in the patch." We waited for them, and had a guy watching for them in a car. They had maps of Butler, Ohio, Logan, and several other surrounding counties where they were growing marijuana in these cornfields. These maps showed them where they could go to any cornfield and find their marijuana.

They had a motor home. As a matter of fact, the day we captured them we found a lot of stuff they just left when they headed back toward the London area. I believe it was three of them that had a $50,000 cash bond, and it was on a late Friday afternoon when banks had done closed, around 8:00 a lady rolled in with an attaché case of cash money and bailed all three of them out.

We got one nearly new truck out of this deal and another one that was older. We confiscated those and sold them, then used the money to buy equipment for the sheriff's department. Most of my cars during my first twelve years in office were purchased by confiscated drug money. Used to, before they changed the law, we'd have a public auction every year of guns, scanners, and anything else we caught in our drug raids. Every now and then we'd buy a cruiser or two. Had it not been for those auctions, we walked. We didn't have funds to do anything better.

These outlaw people don't pay any taxes, so it's only fair that they help support law enforcement! That's the way I look at it. A few people didn't like the idea, but I think it's a darn good idea. Technically, the statute says you are supposed to confiscate their equipment.

Kenneth Lee Morris, Butler County, October 11, 2009

KENTUCKY'S BIGGEST MARIJUANA BUST

Back when I was a deputy, the big marijuana bust in Butler County was on Dunn Store Road back in 1977, I think. A coon hunter had found some marijuana, so I, another deputy sheriff, the sheriff, and a state trooper went out there. We thought it was a little Mom and Pop organization. We got there, and were really lucky because they had rented this farm, and it had a really nice two-story house.

When we got there I saw one guy running, so I took off after him. He had a pretty good head start, so I couldn't catch him. Anyway, later on we found out that inside of the house was an arsenal. In there were five or six assault rifles, shotguns, pistols, and they also had a process-ing center in that house. They hadn't started processing the marijuana yet, but they had four or five acres of marijuana and the stalks were as big around as my arm. That was the older type marijuana before they went to Afghan.

People were harvesting it in other places, but they hadn't started harvesting it here. But where we were, they had set up different plots. They had a big barn set up, so we had to destroy the harvester. They were drying the marijuana, then after they got it dried they put it in garbage compactors and put them in bales. All bales weighed five pounds or so.

We had it processed, and loaded up an old Dodge truck they had there, so we confiscated it. We had it stacked over the top of the cab when we went to burn it.

I forgot how many officers were there, but at that time that was the largest marijuana bust in the state of Kentucky. We got all their names and started arresting them, and some of them were college students from different states that were going to Western Kentucky University. Several were arrested, but I don't know very much as to whom they were.

Kenneth Lee Morris, Butler County, October 11, 2009

"WIGGED OUT" ON METH

We've had people that are hooked on meth. One of the deputies went on call about two years before I left the sheriff's office. Some gunshots were fired up off Sugar Grove Road. When the deputy got up there this guy in a house had a .30-30 rifle, and he'd done fired two or three boxes of shells. He was high on meth, and he told the deputy who was arresting him that they were out there in a field trying to get him. He was shooting at him, but nobody else was around. He actually ran out of shells and busted the stock of his gun on the window frame, thinking somebody was coming in the window. He was just "wigging out." It was called "wigging out" because he was out of his mind.

That fellow had not had any sleep in about five or six days, and that was due to the meth he was hooked on. Meth was and still is our biggest problem. I testified before the state legislature committee back when they were pushing matters about having to go behind counters to get Sudafed, or pseudomethamphetamine. That helped some, but nowdays they have got different ways. They'll take a bunch of kids and go to different places to get pseudomethamphetamine. As a matter of fact, for a long time you could go to Canada to get it, like two hundred to three hundred pills in a bottle. I think just about all the states are tied down now.

But the users use other things, such as tranquilizers. One of the main ingredients while it was here was anhydrous ammonia. That was something that the farmers used to put down in the ground. It's ammonia nitrate, or similar to that. So it's in a gas form, whereas the old ammonia nitrate used to be in liquid form.

I found a large tank of it on Guy Road early in the morning during the summer. I thought it was empty, so I put it in the back of my cruiser, went up to Country Corners, got out, and went in the store to get some coffee or something. When I came back out and got in the car—and just as I got in the car, it hit me. It had warmed up enough that it had started coming out again. I had to roll all the windows down and stay outside for awhile before I could get back in the car.

Kenneth Lee Morris, Butler County, October 11, 2009

Popular Moonshine

The last moonshine whiskey still I know of here in Butler County was found approximately two miles from my house. Some people moved out of an old house, and I reckon that right after they left the owners of the house, or somebody else, moved a moonshine still in. Nobody knew they were gone. Everybody thought they were still living there. Of course, they didn't pay any attention to the smoke coming out of the chimney. That was probably back in the 1960s.

There was a big still set up there in the house, and we don't know how long that had been going on before the still was found. It could have been going on for six months or so. When the officers got the still they started trying to catch them, but I don't think it was still going on. It was a pretty nice still, but it was left there by the people who had operated it.

That still was displayed for a long time in the old courthouse, and was still there in the early 1970s. My understanding is that now, if you make a gallon or two just for your own personal use, nothing is said. But if you start selling it, that's when they will get you. It's just like wine, as a lot of people make their own wine, but moonshine whiskey is still pretty popular in eastern Kentucky.

Kenneth Lee Morris, Butler County, October 11, 2009

Woman Moonshiner

This happened on the Butler-Warren County line, but actually in Warren County. Back several years ago there was this woman who was actually making moonshine whiskey. On Saturdays they'd take it to Bowling Green with them. They'd go up there to grind some feed, and underneath was hay and corn materials under which she would stick her quarts and gallons of moonshine in an old truck.

The law stopped them on the road just before you get to Bowling Green, because I guess they were suspicious. When they found the whiskey the woman started crying and called her husband's name, says, "Everett, I told you and told you they was going to catch you for doing this."

Well, he went to prison, and she just made whiskey while he was in prison. Actually, she was the one who was making it all along! Her name was Blanchet before she married. She had two brothers that got into a shootout with city marshal, Uncle John Smith, back in the 1930s or early 1940s. That took place where the old city hall and old theater used to be.

I reckon they had dared Uncle John out, or was trying to get him. They said that he'd take a puff on his tobacco pipe every time just before he'd fire a shot. I seem to recall that he killed one of them, and wounded the other. From what I hear, he was a character, and never got too excited. He killed one of the brothers of the lady that made moonshine whiskey. Nokie Beck was her name, but she was a Blanchet before marriage. Nokie and Everett lived in the Hadley community, Warren County.

Kenneth Lee Morris, Butler County, October 11, 2009

Elected by a Bootlegger

This is a story about a bootlegging event in which I was involved early on. I lived in the Cropper community in Shelby County, and it was a well-known fact that a guy that lived in the Cropper community seemed to be a bootlegger. I'm sure that he had "shine" from time to time, but he always had beer or something like that. My family and I never actually saw what he did, but we pretty much suspected that he was bootlegging beer and other things like that. It seemed he obtained it from someone else, then sold it himself.

Shelby County was dry, and he was running his own little wet store out there. I was elected back in 1989 and took office in 1990. During the first year or so, what he was doing was one of the things I felt ought to be addressed. Interestingly enough, along the way this fellow was always your friend and buddy. I felt as though he assumed that people looked the other way, etc. However, we did bring in some individuals that worked out of Frankfort, worked with the Kentucky ABC [Alcoholic Beverage Control]. We got those fellows involved, so over a period of time one of these fellows, dressed up in old clothes, would stop in that man's store on a late Saturday afternoon and convince him to sell him some drinks. He'd say he'd tried to get home, but so-and-so had told him he could buy a drink at this store.

So you could pull in and get that drink, then move right on. It wasn't too hard to buy it there, as it was in a grocery store.

The only bad thing about all that was when this nice young lady kinda got caught in the middle of this while working for this man that liked to bootleg on the side. She got caught selling it, but I think it worked out okay for her in the long run.

Once that man was caught, and once he was put out of business, the thing that he wanted to tell everybody in the community was that he had worked so hard to get me elected, but after I was elected I turned against him. That's the thing he wanted to stress to everybody. But let's just face it, I was just doing my job. The thing that aggravated me in that whole situation was that he was bootlegging on one side of the street, and law enforcement was teaching DARE, which is a drug-resistance program, on the other side of the street, which was right across from the school.

So he was doing things like that, but he was a gentleman that didn't mind to do that. He had always bootlegged, gambled, and played cards. However, the thing to me was that I actually took pride, and he thought he had helped me get elected. As I understand it, he was a convicted felon and couldn't vote anyway. But he felt he helped me get elected, and that I then turned on him and got him caught.

His business was penalized, and he ended up being put out of business and had to move on. Eventually, he was a good friend of mine! As a sheriff, sometimes you have to deal with friends. After that event happened, I think people began to realize that as sheriff, I was going to uphold the law. Numerous people throughout the county thanked me for how I handled that situation, and most likely I received more thanks for that than for any thing I've received thanks for since that time.

Mike Armstrong, Shelby County, November 6, 2009

WHAT NOT TO REPORT TO THE SHERIFF

One day an individual called here and talked to me. There is an individual in the county I had dealt with a time or two, and arrested him a few times. His call was to report to me a theft of money, something like $50 or $100. He told me the name of this individual and told all about him stealing his money. In the process of talking to this young man, he told that he had paid so-and-so a certain amount of money to go to a certain place and buy some marijuana for him. He went on to say that the fellow had not come back, and that he had kept his money.

He was considering theft, but after we talked to him it was so ironic that he thought he could report that that fellow was doing something illegal, and was trying to purchase something illegal. See, he was wanting to report this other guy because he had taken his money and didn't bring his dope back. After he told us all that, we advised him that if he wanted to go any farther with it and admit these other things, he might be the one in trouble. We never did hear anything else from that guy.

Not related to him, but back in the 1990s we could go out here in the county and find truckloads of marijuana. Years ago there were farmers in Shelby County that used to grow hemp, then cut it and put it in shocks, put it on a train and send it to Texas, I think, to have rope made out of it.

So over the years there were a lot of places here where marijuana and wild hemp grew. A lot of times we would cut those hemp plants and have mounds of it that we would burn. However, it didn't have much of a street value like marijuana plants did. There was a little THC [tetrahydrocannabinol, the main psychoactive substance of the cannabis plant] in it, but not as much as marijuana plants. Producing all that stuff doesn't take place very much in this county anymore. Overall, we still have more marijuana and cocaine around here than anything else. Some meth is still here, but not like it is thirty miles south and southwest of us in other counties.

Mike Armstrong, Shelby County, November 6, 2009

OVERZEALOUS PILOT

Sam Catron, who was Pulaski County sheriff at that time, and I, probably cut more marijuana than any sheriffs I know about. Of course,
we had a plane and we really, really worked in Casey and all the other
adjoining counties. We found thirty-seven patches of marijuana one day
in Russell, Casey, and Pulaski counties.

Sam would fly the plane, and I was the looker. Of course, we'd
switch back and forth. We'd be very tired while doing this. I remember
the time we were over on Highway 49 when Sam was supposed to be
flying, and I'm the looker. I had a pen in my hand, and we were finding
patches of marijuana on this hillside at what we call Steels Knob.

I don't know what made me do it, but I just happened to look up
and all I could see were treetops. Well, Sam had forgot about his job as
flyer, so he was looking, too. I hit the throttle and opened it wide open,
and Sam said, "We're going to make it, Carl. We're going to make it."

Believe it or not, we did take some limbs out of the tops of these
trees with us back to the airport. When we finally landed at the Russell
County Airport, these treetops really jarred the plane. What happened
was, there was a limb that had like a fork in it, and that limb was stuck
in each wheel. When we landed those limbs started turning, and smoke
started coming up, and made me think the plane was on fire. Those tires
were just about worn out due to those limbs. If we had gone another two
hundred feet, the limbs would have ruptured the sides of those two tires.

That was the closest thing that we ever did that almost killed us in
an airplane. But Sam and I have been on many, many marijuana episodes.

Sam was killed by a sniper in the 1990s. I'll not go into any detail
relative to his death, but one of his staff members was involved. Sam's
daddy was also killed when he was a policeman, or maybe chief of police,
there in Somerset. He had gone out onto the porch to get some wood,
and someone shot him there on the front porch.

Carl E. Meece, Casey County, November 12, 2009

SCARY STILL

Moonshine whiskey was no longer in practice when I began serving as
sheriff, but there were several persons here in Bath County that made
moonshine whiskey. When I was a little boy, me and my cousin was riding
horses one time through the woods on another guy's farm. We ran up on

a moonshine still, but didn't know exactly what it was at first. Of course, we saw smoke and things coming from it, so we took off and ran home.

When I got home I told my dad what we had seen. He said, "Don't you ever go back down through there again. If you do you'll probably get shot, because they're making moonshine back in there."

Well, that scared me and my cousin to death. I mean, we didn't know what was going on! Just seeing that smoke is what scared us.

Most moonshine whiskey making took place in communities like White Oak and Peasticks.

John "Tuffy" Snedegar, Bath County, December 11, 2009

Marijuana versus Meth

Growth and use of marijuana is still taking place here in Bath County. We pulled a lot of it up this summer on people's farms. They'd call me and say, "We've got something down here that we don't know what it is."

I went down and looked, and there was one farm down toward East Fork community, and I pulled up and saw seventy-six plants down there. They were all about one foot and a half tall.

People are still growing marijuana if they don't get caught, but that is not nearly as bad as this meth pill stuff that is used these days. Using marijuana was about the same thing as just sitting down and smoking a cigarette. Marijuana won't kill anybody, but these pills will. Some people here in Bath County have died from taking overdoses of these pills. They sure have.

John "Tuffy" Snedegar, Bath County, December 11, 2009

Active Meth Makers

Awhile back we caught a meth maker right out here on Har Pike. When we got word about that Buffalo Trace organization, we went in and found it. We arrested two men for making meth pills, but I don't know what their prison sentence was because Buffalo Trace went to it all over.

As far as I know, the trailer is still empty and nothing has been done to it yet. I mentioned Buffalo Trace, and that is a drug association that takes care of and distributes drugs and things. It is still an active organization. The state police caught a fellow in that organization not long ago out here at Preston, but the organization was not active there, but they did have stuff in a building there. They were getting ready to set it all up to be sold in a meth lab.

People tell me that if you take a meth pill once, it is hard to not use more of it.

John "Tuffy" Snedegar, Bath County, December 11, 2009

Moonshine in the Old Days

I never made moonshine whiskey, but I always jokingly thought I would probably see an active moonshine still, but I've never seen one, have never got any information of one in Barren County. I've been told by a friend of mine that if you want to see a moonshine whiskey still, you need to go to Monroe County, Kentucky, or to Clay County, Tennessee, and could still see them. I was invited to go over there one time, and I decided it would be my luck that they would be raided by the time I got there, so I never did go to see one in operation!

I understand there's possibly some stills still in operation in that area today. In earlier times people that made moonshine whiskey had to do something in order to make a little money to help them survive hard times. That was especially true back in the 1920s to 1930s.

I've been told that back in those days in the area in which we live here in extreme western Barren County, there are several water springs that are used for water supply, etc. I've been told that on some particular mornings, you could get on this hill here and see seven smokes coming up from seven different moonshine stills that were in operation. I've been told stories about all of this by some of the older people.

Barney Jones, Barren County, December 21, 2009

Coon Hunter Finds Marijuana

When I first became active in law enforcement, marijuana was on the scene, and we did a lot of field searches based on information that we had received. We were somewhat successful in our searches. If the information received was not very helpful, we might walk for days and not find anything. However, in the latter years when I was sheriff, what I would do was get this good friend of mine who was a pilot. I'd have some good information, so I'd go out to the airport with some information indicating where, possibly, marijuana was being grown, particularly in cornfields, wooded areas, and those types of places.

My pilot friend and I would fly across the county and check out these spots in the county. That took four to six hours, and I'd have people on the ground. So while flying, if we did spot something, I'd just tell them the location and they would go in there and stay in the area until we pinpointed them as to exactly where the marijuana was located.

Marijuana was very distinctive in cornfields. There is always a pattern, so we found a lot of marijuana like that. That took place all across the county. Of course, Barren County is a very agricultural county, as it has a lot of grain farmers and dairy farmers. So a lot of corn is grown across the county. We have farmers raising up to one thousand to fifteen hundred acres of corn and/or soy beans in rotation. But a lot of fields may have only a hundred acres in them, and that's not a large field in some states, but it's pretty large in Kentucky. Some of these cornfields would have marijuana in them, but some wouldn't.

I had a coon hunter to call me one morning to let me know he had been going through this cornfield the night before while coon hunting. He said, "You need to check this cornfield out. I found something last night you might be interested in."

He gave us a good location, so me and one of my deputies drove and drove to within five hundred feet of the area about which he had described. It was a long cornfield along the side of the road, and the marijuana was only from waist to shoulder high at that time. I remember it very well, and there were 753 plants in one row continuously, and they were about three or four feet apart. (When it gets larger they need to be six to eight feet apart.) They had pulled all the corn up, and it was easy to see the long row of marijuana. It took us awhile to pull it up, cut it, take it, and harvest it.

Barney Jones, Barren County, December 21, 2009

BURNING MARIJUANA

The biggest marijuana I ever saw consisted of only twenty-three plants. This fellow had it in his backyard, and another fellow knew he had it there and was attempting to steal some of it. The guy that owned the property on which the marijuana was located was guarding it. The other fellow that was going to steal the marijuana was going across the field, and the owner shot at him with a high-powered rifle. The bullet didn't hit him, but in just a little while he called me and said, "You need to check so-and-so's property out."

We went out there, and the marijuana was covered up with a canvas that was kind of like a tobacco canvas. The plant was sort of pulled over, and he had this canvas pinned down with wires. The stalk at the base of the plant was as big around as your wrist, so we had to use tobacco knives in order to cut it down and trim it up. It was just like a big tree. When we straightened those plants up and measured them, one of them was twenty-three feet tall. Well, we hauled that marijuana in two pickup trucks. Those plants loaded both pickups, and that was all we could get on them. We hauled the plants down to the County Road Department barn, and it was after regular work hours.

We were trying to burn all that stuff. I had a five-gallon container, and we started pouring five gallons of kerosene and diesel on that marijuana. Well, it's hard to burn green marijuana, because it won't burn very well! I seem to remember that we burned twenty-five gallons of kerosene and diesel on that marijuana before we got all of it destroyed. In addition to that kerosene and diesel, we also threw on some old tires and wood that were stored there at the county barn onto the plants in order to help get the burning finished.

The fellow that had the marijuana had processed it in the basement of his house, where he lived with his mother and his two children after his divorce. He also had some smaller plants in an outbuilding just behind the house. So we made a felony arrest on him.

Barney Jones, Barren County, December 21, 2009

Helpful Marijuana Grower

I had some information that this fellow had some marijuana growing in his backyard. Or close to his backyard, and I had a warrant on him. I went to his house, but went to the back door instead of the front door. That way I could walk through the backyard to see whatever. It was summertime.

So I went to the back door of this old farmhouse in which he lived. I don't think he had air-conditioning, but it was a nice farmhouse, even without air-conditioning. Anyway, the windows were up, and I knocked on the door. Well, he and this girl were there in the house, and he said a few choice words indicating there was law enforcement there at the back door. I mean, his curse words were really something!

He came to the door, and I walked in and stayed pretty close to him. We walked on into the living room, and he had a shotgun over there in the corner. I got between him and the shotgun and began talking to him, telling him I had a warrant on him. I told him what the warrant was for, and that he was under arrest.

I didn't have anything on the girl that was there. Anyway, he put his shoes on and he was fixing to leave, going out through the front door. I said to him, "I'm superstitious, and because of that I don't ever go out a different door than the one I came in through. So we need to go out through the back door." Actually, I didn't really think that was the case, but I wanted to go out through the back door.

So we went out through the back door and walked by five big plants of marijuana in five-gallon buckets. I guess the plants were six feet tall. I already had him handcuffed, so we just walked right on by the marijuana and went on toward the vehicle. He said, "What about that marijuana there?"

I said, "You are under arrest for cultivating over five plants of marijuana also."

He just couldn't stand it any longer. We were walking right through this marijuana, so I put him in the vehicle. Then I pulled the plants up, raised the trunk of my vehicle, and put the plants in there. Well, they were so big they were hanging clear out on the ground from the vehicle. I looked all over the other part of the yard and didn't see any more plants. But he said, "Well, you might as well get the rest of it. I don't want to be arrested again."

I said, "Well, I don't see any other plants."

Well, he had some tomato plants stuck up next to an outbuilding there, so he had this other marijuana behind the tomato plants so you couldn't see them. Anyway, there were five or six more plants back there, for a total of ten or eleven.

I thought that was interesting that he couldn't stand it anymore, so he had to tell me more about this marijuana. To me, that was rather interesting.

Barney Jones, Barren County, December 21, 2009

MARIJUANA GROWERS AND METH MAKERS

Growing marijuana takes place just about everywhere. It's hard to catch people growing it. You get some out there, and you may catch them coming back to where they are growing it out in a field, and you try to set on it. You can wait two or three days and maybe not catch them. The biggest crop we ever found was down in the Forkland community, just right outside of Junction City. We caught two or three guys there, but I don't think they were growing it but were there to steal it.

So we caught them and charged them with it, but about all you get anymore is the little man. You never get the big man.

When we arrested these guys, they were convicted for growing marijuana and were sentenced to prison for a brief period.

I don't know a lot about meth making, but it just started around here in this county three or four years ago. I'm not really up to date on that meth stuff, but all I can tell you about meth is that it is an instant killer. Within ten years you'll be dead.

LeeRoy Hardin, Boyle County, January 11, 2010

STILL EDUCATION

The first year I took over as Adair County Sheriff in 1994, I got my first moonshine still on Sand Lick Road over on Melson Ridge. I arrested this guy who had moved in here from Indiana about a year earlier. The way I understood him, making moonshine whiskey ran in his family. His grandfather made it, as did his father.

He had one of these little portable moonshine stills that used a pressure cooker to cook it off in, and he made yellow corn moonshine. I got word that he was selling some of this moonshine for $10 per quart.

One of my deputies and I went over on Sand Lick Road, and we got out of the car and went up to this fellow. I approached him, then told him what information I had. He said, "Oh, no, I ain't doing that."

Then I said, "Would you mind if I look around?"

I did not have a search warrant, but he gave me permission by signing a consent to search. I walked out to a little building behind a trailer and looked through an old glass window, and saw the worm in the barrel of the moonshine still. I went on to look a little farther there, and said to him, "Well, I found part of it here." Then I went into the building and also found a pressure cooker.

Well, I had this moonshine still, but still lacked one piece, so it was incomplete. There was a little air compressor setting there, so I thought maybe he used that to blow the lines out with. I told him, "I'm going to take this air compressor. I believe the air is connected to this."

So I did get the moonshine still, but didn't arrest him at the time because we thought the feds took care of this. So I called the feds, and they said they were busy and that if I wanted to, just go ahead and handle this through district court, and I did.

The man paid a big fine and got his days probated. But I still lacked one piece of that still, so I went in between the lines up there, but didn't know enough about a moonshine still to know what it was about. So I told him, "You tell me what that one piece is that is needed to complete the still, and I'll give you this air compressor back."

He went home and brought me a gallon tin can that had two holes in it, and that is what they called a puker that went to the still. The fluid went up through that tin can, so if it had any debris in it, it would fall to the bottom of that can and the heat would keep the liquid going up through the top of the can out the other line into the worm of the still.

So I got that taken care of. Anyway, we found out this man had a mental problem, and about a year after that he moved to Florida. About a year later I heard that he had died down there.

James Ralph Curry, Adair County, January 11, 2010

PROFITABLE DRUG BUST

During my first year as sheriff in 1994, I made a big drug bust during the fall of that year. I got a trooper, Jimmy Dale Cox, who is my neighbor, to go with me. We went to this guy's house on Highway 55 South, and turned onto Christine Road. When we got there he was drunk and had left his house. He had a wreck over in Russell County, and there was bag after bag of marijuana in his car.

We got this call from Russell County and they told us about this fellow who had come from Adair County. We looked into the tax books and found that he owned two pieces of property, one on Christine Road (Highway 531) and one on 55 South, about two miles from Columbia.

When this trooper and I went out there the back window of the house was up, and the scent of marijuana was coming out of there like crazy. He had grown five hundred plants of marijuana in that house, and we busted that by taking it down. Then we went up on Christine Road, and he had a big garage built behind the house, and I guess he had another five hundred plants there.

We made a bust out of that, too, and the total sales on that property brought $57,000, and I got around $40,000 out of that for the sheriff's department. With that I bought a new vehicle, new SUVs, and that really helped this department because it had never had anything like that before.

The man lived in Somerset, and he pled guilty and received seven years' prison time. He also had operations in four or five other counties east of Somerset. So, all total, we busted up a big marijuana ring. He was actually growing marijuana in all these houses, using indoor lighting.

My deputies and I also made a lot of arrests on smaller drugs while I was in office. I actually went to Texas and bought a drug dog that the county purchased for us, and it cost $3,200. The dog's name was Doc, and I used him for four years and did right well with him by discovering and capturing drugs. After we had Doc for four years he got melanoma and died.

James Ralph Curry, Adair County, January 11, 2010

Motorcycle Leads to Still

During the year 2009 I made another moonshine still bust here in the county about six or seven miles from Columbia. I got word a year before that this man had a moonshine still. So I called this guy, who had never been in any trouble, and asked him, "Do you have a moonshine still out there?"

"Oh, no, I ain't got one."

I said, "Okay."

So about a year later, which was last year during the spring season, my deputy came in one morning, and I said, "Well, we've got an incident that happened over the weekend." A bunch of guys who live out there not too far from where this guy makes moonshine whiskey got some of that moonshine and got drunk. One of the guys got down, couldn't even get up, and is in bad shape. He was riding his motorcycle down there to this place where all the others were located. He told one of them, "You take me home, and I'll give you my motorcycle."

So this boy and another guy took him home, then they came back and loaded up the motorcycle. It was an antique motorcycle with antique paint on it. About two days later this drunk guy gets sobered up and comes in and reports to me what happened. He said, "My motorcycle is missing, and somebody told me that I gave it to this guy down at Breeding to take me home. You know, he could not take my motorcycle when I was drunk."

I said, "No, you can't do that. That ain't right."

So I got hold of this guy in Breeding, and he said, "Yeah, yeah, he gave it to me."

I said, "You can't do that. That man was drunk. He couldn't give it to you."

Well, he [the owner] went down there to get it, but that fellow had already gone to Wal-Mart and bought a bunch of red paint and painted the whole motorcycle red.

When he saw what had happened, he just about died. He said, "Well, it is ruined." Anyway, he got the bike, took it home, and he knew somebody who told him that Wal-Mart paint could be removed, so he went and had all the red paint taken off. After that the bike come out alright.

So that was what instigated me to go find this still.

James Ralph Curry, Adair County, January 11, 2010

CAPTURED STILLS

I've got a piece of an old moonshine whiskey still, and here is a story about it. Our county attorney, Ray Hutchinson, had been in office here for about thirty years, and he is assistant county attorney now. His daughter, Jennifer Corbin, is county attorney. Her father still comes in as her assistant and still helps her.

By the time I got this old still, it had been twenty-seven years since one had been captured in Adair County. Frank Nell, who was sheriff way back before my time, captured this still, then fifteen years later I captured this one.

After Frank stopped serving as sheriff, he was elected as Circuit Court Clerk.

James Ralph Curry, Adair County, January 11, 2010

MOONSHINE DEALERS ACROSS THE YEARS

Here in Adair County, we had one family that was into bootlegging way back in the days of earlier sheriffs. And some of them are still delivering moonshine whiskey. Nowadays they don't sell it through a drive-in window like they used to do. Actually, they don't make it themselves, they simply buy whiskey that is hauled in here by a bootlegger, or they'll go over to someplace like Lebanon and purchase a carload of it. That way it's already in a bottle and ready to be sold.

They still have deliveries around here, and you could probably still buy it down here at the same old place. You could drive out there in your car, and they will bring it out to you.

That's what has taken care of a lot of the whiskey business here. But if somebody makes a complaint, I go out and bust these dealers.

There was one guy here that, I guess, took control of sales better than any of the others. He's dead now, but he'd come every year and say, "Well, Ralph, I hear you are running for sheriff again. Do you need anything?"

I'd say, "Well, coming from you, no." I wouldn't take a dime from him; no way.

James Ralph Curry, Adair County, January 11, 2010

Marijuana Production in Clinton County

Marijuana is still out here in Clinton County. However, former judge Larry Hatfield told me that I got more of that stuff than any other sheriff in Kentucky, and that he was proud to be a part of what was done by me and my deputies.

I hadn't been sheriff for three or four months when this boy got killed at an intersection of Highways 90 and 127. That bothered me, and I was told a lot of those young people were using marijuana. I didn't care if old people smoked marijuana, but the young people were ruining their lives, so we started getting marijuana.

I had been a coon hunter, rabbit hunter, and squirrel hunter, and that made it possible for me to track marijuana growers down. These young fellows wouldn't go to the same way to marijuana patches. Actually, they'd go in different paths. So I got to where I could track them, and on some occasions I'd run into a patch of marijuana accidentally. Back then, before helicopters started flying over so much, marijuana growers would put out large patches and I got more marijuana than has ever been gotten before or since in Clinton County.

The growers would put a lot of marijuana plants out on government property. They grew it there since you could not prosecute farmers or the government. They still grow it there. I would go to find a path where the dogs and coons and foxes had run, and you could tell there had been a lot of traffic on that path, but growers never put their marijuana close to the path. I had to get down below or up above, and that way I could find their marijuana patches. Several state policemen would go with me lots of the time.

I came up on some booby traps, which are made of dynamite with a charge, so if you hit a trip wire when walking the dynamite will go off. There were a lot of those booby traps around patches of marijuana. A lot of them put dynamite wire around those patches of marijuana, so I learned to walk around them and go in at the same spot where the growers went in. However, most of those booby traps were false, as they just put that wire around the patches in order to scare people and keep animals out. The state police and I did find one patch that was really booby-trapped up on Coal Mountain, as we called it.

We got truckloads after truckloads of marijuana. I've had the city police to bring a truck to help me bring a load in. Marijuana was grown in just about all parts of Clinton County at first. By the first I mean back in the 1980s. It was also heavily grown here in the 1990s, and is still grown but not as much. These days, instead of putting it in large patches where marijuana is grown, I also learned that the marijuana has got to have sunlight. So if you come out to an opening in a field, it looks suspicious. If there's a little cedar tree there, they put the marijuana plants where the sun can hit it in the morning and afternoon. They wouldn't put it where the shade was located. They'd put it in the sun. So they had to clear them a path for the marijuana. It was grown everywhere, and I guess in all states, but Kentucky has the perfect climate.

A state trooper, George Cravens, taught me that when you burn marijuana, always have a witness. If you find a patch of little small plants that are one foot high, people tell that it is ten feet high, and you've sold it. So his advice was to always have a witness when we burned marijuana. We'd burn marijuana in different places, a lot of times in public, and a lot of times at the radio station in Burkesville. We'd let people come out to see us burning marijuana. And we've actually smoked some people out of their homes due to all that smoke going toward the ground. See, marijuana smells. I didn't smoke cigarettes, so I could smell it.

One night I was up on this mountain right here near Albany with these troopers looking for marijuana down at the bottom. I said, "I smell marijuana."

They said, "How do you smell marijuana? We don't smell it."

I said, "There's marijuana somewhere up there."

We went on up on the mountain and found a large patch of marijuana up there where the wind was blowing it toward us.

We couldn't arrest most of the people that were assumed to be marijuana growers, because you couldn't prove it most of the time. You may have an idea whose it is, but you can't prove it. Thus, you have to have proper calls. So, what you do is to go in and cut it, then burn it.

Glynn Mann, Clinton County, February 8, 2010

No Hard Feelings

Back when I was sheriff, these kids were cutting things up during this big ice storm. So I ran out there with a flashlight and tried to flag them down. The first four-wheeler went on, but I jumped on behind the next one and the driver was yelling, "Don't, Glynn! Don't, Glynn!" He knew me, but I didn't know him because he had on a mask. I was holding on for dear life until we got down to an Amoco station. He was twirling around, and it slung me off. I guess I slid on the ice one hundred feet. I was going to shoot over his head and scare him, so I pulled my old .357 gun out, and it was full of ice. I couldn't fire it. Since then one of them came and told me who he was. He said that he was the first four-wheeler to go by, and Pickey Means was the next one.

I didn't hold that against them boys, nor the marijuana growers I caught later on. When I was young, and if I didn't have any money or something, you don't know what you would have done. I tried to be honest always, because my mother would have beat me to death. So, I didn't hold it against the ones I caught, and these days most of them are friendly with me.

This one guy we sent to the penitentiary for several years was out at Jones's Restaurant here in Albany not long ago. He was a pretty good friend of mine, although we prosecuted him. Anyway, there at the restaurant he went up to pay for his food, and I heard him say as he pointed at me, "That old man over there cost me $40,000 one year. I ought to go over there and beat the 'H' out of him!"

Of course, I was sitting there in a booth, and he said to me, "I'll tell you what I'm going to do. If he lives to be ninety years old, I'm going to beat the 'H' out of him."

I said, "Ole boy, when I'm ninety years old, all I can do is just barely pull the trigger."

He said, "You'd better do it now," and just laughed and laughed. [*Laughter*]

Of course, when they know they are breaking the law, as he did back then, they don't hold it against you. Be sure you have probable cause to stop them. You can follow nearly anyone a couple of miles and they will make a bobble.

The same ole boy told me later on that when he and his buddy were growing marijuana, they sat over there on a hill and watched me cut it. Later on, the dispatcher told them boys, "You didn't get all that marijuana down there."

They said, "Yes, we did. We stayed over there and watched them get it."

He told them, said, "I can still smell it."

Well, these boys told me that they went back and found one patch of marijuana that we missed! [*Laughter*]

Marijuana is still grown here in Clinton County.

Glynn Mann, Clinton County, February 8, 2010

SHERIFF DETRIMENTAL TO THE ECONOMY

The funniest thing about marijuana production that happened when I was sheriff was that a lot of good church people complained about me getting all this marijuana. They said I was hurting the economy. The church had a bunch of business people, and two or three of them right here in Albany complained about me getting people's marijuana because it was really hurting the economy. Judge Larry Hatfield told me that he actually got calls in his office from people saying, "Can't you do something with the sheriff? He's hurting the economy because he is busting the illegal pot growers."

Hatfield, who was a former state police officer, told me that he said, "No, I'm for him 110 percent. A lucky thing to be would be to catch somebody in the patch."

Glynn Mann, Clinton County, February 8, 2010

JAIL ON WHEELS

This happened at Static, Tennessee, when I was sheriff. Static is located right on the Clinton County–Pickett County, Tennessee, border. Static was running wide open with a lot of beer bars and illegal whiskey, but most of them have burned since then. It has really slowed down and has never really gotten back on its feet. There were three or four roads that came from Static into Clinton and Wayne counties. People were having wrecks, and these ladies were drinking and injuring their children. So the state police and I started roadblocking when I became sheriff. The state police brought this jail on wheels down there from Columbia, Kentucky.

This lady had wrecked over there, and had hurt her children and everything just a few days before that. I had to go to Static to work that wreck. Well, there were wrecks on the other roads. Soldiers were coming in, and they had a lot of girls that would sell flowers and wear those shorty, shorty clothes over there while they peddled the flowers. Those girls were coming from everywhere, like Casey County, Pulaski County. They were coming from everywhere, even Tennessee, to do those shows at Static. Static was in a wet county, but Clinton County was dry.

We started road checking, and they brought that jail-on-wheels bus to near Static. It had jail cells in it, and a breathalyzer. Actually, it carried the name of Cells on Wheels. The first night we got so many males and females, young and older, that they had to sit on the floor and everywhere there in the jailhouse. There just wasn't enough space to put them. Well, they had to sit in the jailhouse that night. I never will forget it as the floor was full of them. Some of them were cursing me, and some were friendly to me.

We waited a week or two, then got only about one-half that many, and then it started dropping down to only one-third that many later on. And when the state police brought the jail on wheels down here for the last time, we just arrested only two or three.

Glynn Mann, Clinton County, February 8, 2010

Marijuana Growers versus Bootleggers

Most of the marijuana growers would squeal on the other man in order to keep their personal production all to themselves. I've had people up in Duvall Valley, who were growing it themselves, tell me where other patches were in order to get them away from theirs. Up there in the valley they were pretty slick, and if they had a large patch of marijuana they would kill a deer and let it rot, hanging close to the patch. See, you could smell the deer, but couldn't smell the marijuana.

I found these patches like that, and I've had them yell out at me and say, "Hey, if you go down a certain road in a certain place, you'll find a patch of marijuana." Well, sure enough, I'd go down there and find it.

One time I had two state policemen with me; actually they'd come get me to go with them because I didn't smoke and could smell it better. When we got down there we smelled this deer and I said, "There's probably a patch around here."

Well, we found it. They said that there was so much marijuana in that patch that we should burn it right here. So we cut and piled it and set the patch on fire, using brush and everything.

This state trooper had a portable radio that he gave to me, and I laid it on a stump that was pretty far from the pile of dope, and there was such a hot fire it melted that radio. Oh, he complained to me, saying I just ruined his radio!

See, that's the way we found patches of marijuana. One guy that had some would squeal on another bunch and tell you where to go to find it.

See, the difference in marijuana growers and bootleggers is that bootleggers would not squeal on another man. And most of them would drink it themselves, and everyone knew that it wasn't poisonous if the bootleggers drank it. Some of those bootleggers where I come from were the most honest people you've ever seen.

Glynn Mann, Clinton County, February 8, 2010

Family Moonshine Business

I grew up knowing what moonshine was, because a lot of my people made it and a lot of them went to jail over it. At one time there were so many of my kinfolks in prison at LaGrange that's where we had the family reunion. [*Laughter*]

Here is something that was told to me by my daddy, who died several years ago. When he was young, all of his family members lived down on Harmon's Creek here in Wayne County. He and his brothers, his daddy, two of his cousins, and a work hand were making moonshine whiskey, big time. They sold it by the keg.

Well, one of Daddy's work hands got to stealing his chickens, and Daddy caught him making moonshine one night, so he filled his butt full of birdshot. Then he come into town and turned the work hand in, and received $100 dollars for turning in that man's still. (It was a federal offense at that time, but in July 1982 it became a state offense because drugs were taking place back then.)

Well, the law came down and began searching. Something happened that burned the house, maybe it was a still that blew up. Anyway, they were making this stuff in the woods, and they had a barrel setting in the horseweeds by the barn and they were batching in the barn. When that was taking place, my granddaddy was cooking breakfast and he kept moonshine all the time. He had a half gallon setting there, but when he saw the law coming he stuck this half gallon of moonshine in a sack of flour and covered it up with flour.

Deputy Windy Jim Casteel walked around to check the premises around the barn. He started in this big horseweed patch that was as high as the ceiling in this room, and said a chicken snake run out from under his feet. That's why he missed that. They got him for a half gallon, brought them all to town.

My granddaddy had three farms on Harmon's Creek, and he was well off financially. In order to keep everybody from going to a federal penitentiary in Atlanta, Georgia, he spent everything he had to get them out of jail.

Joseph Conn, Wayne County, February 13, 2010

Red Moonshine

My daddy and my uncle on my mother's side got to making moonshine on a hill under a waterfall. One day they began drinking and got into a fistfight and throwed rocks at each other. That split them up!

All of my people on both sides of the family, at one time or another, were well acquainted with moonshine and moonshiners. My granddaddy on my daddy's side and a neighbor would load up a load of corn in little wooden kegs that held thirty to thirty-five gallons and bring them to Monticello. If they got old whiskey barrels and put moonshine in them and let them set there for a month, it turned red. Well, everybody went crazy over that red moonshine. My granddaddy made it for years.

Joseph Conn, Wayne County, February 13, 2010

Good Moonshine

Sunnybrook here in Wayne County was probably the last moonshine whiskey holdout, where it was made last. There could be a small still or two still out there. Commercial moonshine is about a thing of the past. The Yankees up north still go wild over it. A good moonshiner will make it from 100 to 120 proof. He cuts that half and half with water. The last account I had was that it was selling back then for $40 a gallon. I don't know what it is now. A fifty-five-gallon barrel of mash only makes you seven gallons of good moonshine.

Joseph Conn, Wayne County, February 13, 2010

Dog for the Deputy

Here is a good marijuana story. When Sheriff Boston was a deputy he was involved in this. I got a call from out in Sunnybrook about these people that were originally from Michigan or North Dakota. They had moved in out there and were growing pot big time. I've got pictures of it out my house. When I got this call, they said this fellow had gone out there to steal some, and they put the lead at him. He didn't stop until he got in here, so it was a holiday. Anyway, we went out there, and we had to cut our way into where it was being grown way back in the country. When we got there we found this camp. Believe it or not, they'd cut my picture out of a newspaper and had it stapled to a tree!

They had two tents, guns, tillers, and a big Doberman pinscher dog that was meaner than the devil itself. So we cut some topnotch marijuana, then got to reading some of their mail that said that was going to be their last crop because of law enforcement.

We gathered all that patch up, then that night, unknown to us, they were at an old house place where there was a cellar and they had a bunch of bagged marijuana sacks in it. These fellows hit the woods when we got there, but these neighborhood thieves were going in to steal the bags and they all got into a gun battle. When we went back there the next day, we'd taken everything the evening before except the dog. We couldn't catch him.

Deputy Charlie Boston goes out there and he fools around, then pretty soon he hollers, "I've got him!" Well, I walked back down to where we had parked, and the dog is setting in the back seat of the car just like he had on a white shirt and tie, and Charlie takes him home with him and keeps him for years.

Well, about a month later I got a letter from Milwaukee or somewhere, and they said, "We hear you've got our dog and we want it."

So I fired a letter back to them, saying, "Yeah, we've got your dog, so just come on down and get it." Well, they didn't come down to get it, so Charlie kept it for years.

However, Charlie and his wife, Phyllis, told me that the original owners came to their house and knocked on the door. Standing there was a little bitty fellow and a woman with him. Phyllis said that the dog was down there just barking at them when this fellow told her that they had his dog, and he wanted it back. Phyllis told him, "You just hold on, mister, and I'll call my husband, who is a deputy, and he'll be right out here to give it."

Boy, they jumped in their car and took off!!

But that dog would bite a hole in a car tire. He was mean, but not to Phyllis and Charlie.

Joseph Conn, Wayne County, February 13, 2010

Marijuana Replaced Moonshine

From the time I started as a deputy in the 1970s, moonshine was going out. Marijuana was replacing moonshine. There were a lot of bootleggers in Wayne County that sold beer and whiskey, even up into the 1980s when Joe [Conn] was sheriff. However, the moonshine was about gone. All I know is that we found one still when I was deputy working for Joe. The one I found wasn't in operation, it was just hidden away under a brush pile. [Joe added that he found two stills in operation while he was sheriff.]

Charles L. Boston, Wayne County, February 13, 2010

Medicinal Marijuana

Meth making began here in Wayne County perhaps in the late 1990s. Back in the 1980s marijuana and bootlegging were the biggies. We stayed busy raiding people who were bootleggers and growing marijuana. I've got photos of some of it. I was standing in this patch where we got the dog [see "Dog for the Deputy," above], and I had a shotgun in my hands that wouldn't reach the top of those plants when I pointed it upward.

We had to have hatchets to use when chopping it down. They grew it all over Wayne County, and just about everywhere else. To give you an example, I was riding along through the Cabell community one day and looked over in a tobacco patch, but the tobacco had done been topped, so there were only marijuana plants there. We stopped and cut the plants, and I left word to the ole boy to come on in during the morning because I've got a warrant for you. Well, he came in.

I know a lot of family members and friends who used marijuana, but I never personally used it. I've got a sister in Indianapolis who has had leukemia for years and years. She is just a walking skeleton. About ten or twelve years ago, she had a stepdaughter who told her, "Marijuana might help you." So she went and got her two marijuana cigarettes and smoked one of them. She said she thought she was going to die, and she's still got the other cigarette.

I've got a cousin who lives here on Castle Street, and he's retired from the navy. He worked in a hospital in Louisville and took lung cancer. He then went with his wife to Mexico ten or twelve years ago so that he could use marijuana legally, and he stayed there six months. He was told in Louisville that marijuana would help his lung cancer, but he finally wound up losing that lung. He told me that he thought it helped him when he first started using it, but before he quit using it the doctors had done told him he should go and come through El Paso, Texas, where he could be checked by an American doctor to see if his cancer was going backward or forward. It never did help him, but he thought it did for a couple of months. He came back to Louisville and had his lung removed, and he now lives here in Monticello.

Charles L. Boston, Wayne County, February 13, 2010

Meth Methods

Just this week we arrested two people for operating a meth lab. When I was a captain as a state police officer, meth was a big problem in western Kentucky. You could see it on the map, but if you put a red pin where meth labs were being found, most of them were in the western part of the state. Within more recent times, it started moving east, so you could see a red dot here and a red dot there, but then it got into alignment and in 2001, when I retired from the state police, it started coming into Perry County. I think I was involved in two cases while I was captain during my last year.

When I got to be sheriff here in Letcher County in 2003, we had never had a meth lab. During this past year or two, we began getting reports that somebody was making meth up in the mountains, like where they used to make moonshine whiskey. They'd go up in the woods and make this meth, so we started getting complaints like that. Well, we found a few places out in a rural area, like in a graveyard back in the woods, where they were making it. Within this past January we arrested two people for actually making meth, and just recently we got another one. We think it's moved into our area, and I think it's just people learning how to make it.

The first guy that we brought in for making it, the deputy had him back here in the office when I came in. I knew him, for I had sent him to the penitentiary for selling cocaine since I have been sheriff. I said to him, "What are you trying to do? Kill yourself making this meth?"

He said, "I was just trying to make me something that would get me high."

I said, "Where did you learn how to make meth? I know where you live, so I know you don't know nothing about the Internet and things."

He said, "Oh, I learned when you sent me to the penitentiary."

I said, "Are you telling me you learned how to make it while you were in the penitentiary, and now you've come back up here and started making it?"

He said, "Yeah, that's where I learned how to make it."

I guess he learned it from the other prisoners there who had been arrested for making it.

I think making meth here in Letcher County is just starting, but we are beginning to get more complaints about it. We've got neighborhood watches here at which we make presentations in order to let people in the neighborhood watch know what to look for. Just about everything you make it with can be purchased at Wal-Mart, such as Sudafed, that is used for the pill. Also used are Coleman fuel, lighter fluid, Drano, coffee filters, etc., all of which are at places like Wal-Mart. The community watch programs have made people more aware of meth making, so people are looking for it and I get calls telling that people are in a house and have their windows covered up, and they think they are making meth. See, that gives us someplace to start looking.

I think we are going to find more and more of it here in this county, as it is just like anywhere else in adjoining counties where the sheriffs are dealing a lot with it.

When we go out looking for meth making, we look for a propane tank. I always thought they used them for heating purposes, but that's what they use for making meth. They've got a hose on the tank, and they turn the tank upside down in order to drain the liquid propane out of it, then put the meth stuff in there in order to cool it down.

In addition to the propane tank they also have a generator. A lot of times they'll use a bottle, like a Gatorade bottle, and put all the chemicals in it to let it react. Then they steam it off, and that leaves a powder residue which is the meth. Sometimes we don't find that, but if we do we have to call the state police so they can come with a cleanup team that has to handle the meth materials. When my deputy arrests the meth maker, the state police will write a report and attach it to the deputy's affidavit.

Danny R. Webb, Letcher County, February 27, 2010

SON SELLS OUT MOONSHINING DAD

My hometown is Millstone, Kentucky, a little mining camp. There was a fellow there who was always a moonshine maker. He'd have his still back in the woods, and he sold the moonshine in pints and half pints, quarts, and gallons. That was in the late 1960s when I was still in high school. He had a son that was a little bit younger than I was, and the ATF revenuers and the state police came up there to their house. They searched all around, trying to find where the moonshine was.

When they got there this little boy was running around there, and they asked him to come over to them. They said to him, "We'll give you 50¢ to tell us where your daddy has got his liquor hid."

He said, "If you'll give me a dollar I'll tell you where the still is located."

When they gave it to him, he took them right to the still. They arrested his daddy and sent him to the penitentiary.

Moonshine whiskey is still made in eastern Kentucky, but I don't know whether or not they still make it in Letcher County. Actually, we've raided drug dealers, and they had quarts of moonshine that they were selling, but it is my understanding that it comes from either Knott County or Floyd County. I am told that there are people that still are making it in the mountains right now.

Danny R. Webb, Letcher County, February 27, 2010

PRESCRIPTION DRUG ABUSE

Marijuana is still a very popular thing in Letcher, Knott, Breathitt, Perry, and Leslie counties here in eastern Kentucky. The [Drug] Task Force, National Guard, and state police come every year to fly over in a helicopter and cut marijuana. This is one of their biggest areas. I'll get a report from someone, and they'll say, "I know where a marijuana field is. You go up this hollow, turn off here, then go back there." Well, you take five deputies up there and stay all day, but you still can't find it. So we have started reporting it to the task force. They'll bring a helicopter and we give them the areas that we're getting reports from, and they fly over it.

If they go up there in these mountains where these people travel around four-wheeler trails, they see these things and start trying to draw us a map as to where it is located. But when you get back in there you can't find anything. You end up just burning up. Everybody is miserable, but if we can follow a map right to the location we try to go and check it out. However, most of the time marijuana was grown back in the mountains, and they clear it out before we get there.

Marijuana growth has been a big-time business in this area. Some people say using it isn't harmful, but I feel that using it leads to other uses. Everybody that I deal with now that are addicted to drugs, or are selling drugs, I try to help them if they are addicts. After they get started on marijuana, they have marijuana parties and somebody pulls a pill out and the others try that. The next thing you know they are on cocaine, but our biggest problem here is prescription drugs. It's so easy to get pills. Many of them go to West Virginia to a doctor and get a hundred pills that they bring back here to sell. Well, our doctors here are really good. They've got Kasper, which is a computerized system that connects all the pharmacies and the doctors. So if the doctor is suspicious of this guy that comes in, he'll turn him down. These doctors here check them out before they prescribe any pills. But when turned down these guys go to West Virginia because that state doesn't have that system. So they just go over there and the doctor will prescribe anything they want. I hear that they are now going to Florida. I got a complaint last night that these four people had just got back from Florida with a thousand pills a piece. They were down there selling them and taking them. Most of them are pain-pill prescriptions, and people are addicted to the pills that they purchase and use. These people that get these prescription pain pills sell them here for $30 to $40 each. I saw on television the other night where these people went down there, and every few miles, or every block or two, there was a pain clinic, and out in the parking lot were all these Kentucky cars! So they're going to the doctor and you know what they are doing.

The Drug Task Force in this area is working on that problem these days. Me and my deputies help the task force, because when we catch people with Florida pill bottles and stuff, we add them to the illegal list. I'd say 90 percent of our biggest drug problem is prescription drug abuse. Many things are stolen these days by people who sell what they steal, then use the money they get from the sales to purchase pills.

Danny R. Webb, Letcher County, February 27, 2010

BUSTING THE JUG

When I was out campaigning for sheriff, Letcher County was a dry county. Now in Whitesburg City they can sell beer and drinks in restaurants only. They passed that since I've been sheriff, but when I came into office it was a dry county. While campaigning I was driving all over the county and would go and knock on doors. I'd go way over here in the rural part of the county and drive up this hollow. It was just at the edge of night, and I heard loud music playing. I'd drive by and look, and there's this nightclub in there.

They had built this building and it served as a roadhouse. Through the windows you could see people sitting in there drinking at a bar. I'd say, "You can't have this in this county. It's a dry county, so you can't sell beer and liquor across the bar."

When I'd drive by, I started asking people about what it was.

They said, "Oh, that's the jug."

I said, "Jug?"

They'd say, "Yeah, that's the name of it."

One time I was talking to this guy that said he was down in Perry County and was at one of the bars. This guy came up and handed him a card that had on it, "Jug, Cherokee Lane in Letcher County, Kentucky." They were advertising by handing out cards.

So when I got elected sheriff, my first mission was to shut the Jug down. The best way to do that is to have somebody go in and actually purchase a drink and everything. So I had hired this deputy from Knott County, and nobody here in Letcher County knew him. Well, he goes over to the Jug and takes a girl with him. He was to call us when he actually purchased a drink. I had the search warrant already written up, and was waiting for him at the judge's house. My deputies were waiting out there with a state trooper, waiting for me to call them since I had the search warrant.

So Kenny called and said he had actually purchased beer, so I got the search warrant signed. I called the deputies and said I'm headed that way.

After I called the deputies and troopers ran in and said, "Search warrant, search warrant, search warrant."

Well, my deputy that was in there asked them, "Where's your search warrant"? He knew that I hadn't got there. They're looking around at each other because they don't have the search warrant yet. It took me fifteen minutes to get there.

By the time I got there the deputies were all tore up. Anyway, we didn't arrest everybody, but we did arrest the guy that was running the Jug.

I said, "Well, let's get everybody's name as witnesses and everything." The deputies began taking the names and addresses of these people who were there drinking, dancing, and all that stuff.

My deputy, who was doing his job undercover, began smarting off. Those people were all saying to him, "Shut up or you'll get every one of us put in jail."

He said, "I never seen no search warrant," then he kept smarting off to two of my other deputies that worked with him. He went on to say, "I thought you had to be taller to be a police officer," referring to the state police height requirement years earlier.

One of those deputies came over to me and whispered, "Do you want us to rough him up a little bit to make it look good?"

They got so mad at him they wanted to get him, because he was in there as a troublemaker!

It was written about in the local paper that we busted this Jug. The Associated Press also picked up on it. I had a buddy in Florida who heard about it, then called me and said, "I heard that you, the new sheriff in town, busted this bar up."

Danny R. Webb, Letcher County, February 27, 2010

MOONSHINE A THING OF THE PAST

I've heard that Felin Ford, a sheriff several years back, was always a big moonshine getter around here. However, when I got into law enforcement several years ago, moonshine was a thing of the past. But we did have what were called bootleggers. Back when I first started it was bootleggers and marijuana growers that were the primary things. The bootleggers sold government whiskey, and the marijuana growers sold what they grew. Bootleggers would go to Bowling Green and buy whiskey down there and come back here and sell it for double price.

I've never seen a moonshine still, nor have I ever had a report about a still here in the county during my years of service. However, I've heard about two persons that were found dead after drinking poisoned moonshine years ago.

Jerry "Slick" Gee, Monroe County, March 18, 2010

MARIJUANA IN MONROE

Marijuana is still grown in Monroe County, but not like it once was. Back before I became sheriff, marijuana was one of the biggest problems in Monroe County. It wasn't a dangerous drug like meth is today. Marijuana was grown all over Monroe County, so you really couldn't pinpoint one particular place.

During my first two terms I guess we confiscated somewhere between $15 or $20 million of street value marijuana. I remember this one patch we got into was booby-trapped, so we took care of that. Actually, when we were going down the field to look for marijuana, it was easy to spot because it had grown so high. It grew above the rest of the grass, brush, or trees, just whatever was down there. The big stalks of plants ranged from thirteen to fifteen feet high, and had big buds on them that were about twelve to fifteen inches.

When we cut the marijuana plants we brought them into town and burned them down here behind the jail. We always got someone from the newspaper to come and take photographs to show that we had destroyed marijuana, so people couldn't say that we kept it ourselves.

One year we were busting marijuana plants every day. People would call on the hotline here to give me tips as to where some marijuana was located. We'd drive out there and drive right up on it, all over the county in communities such as Center Point, Rock Bridge, Bugtussle, Akersville, Gamaliel, Fountain Run, Sulphur Lick, Boles, and Harlan's Cross Roads.

I finally figured that this guy who was always calling us to report growth activities and where a marijuana patch was located—he never mentioned his name—but I finally believed he was a marijuana grower who turned everybody else in. That way we didn't get him but we got everybody he turned in. He continued to grow his crop and got away with it. Since I never figured out who he was, he could sell his crop after reporting all the other growers and telling us exactly where the other crops were located.

That was during 2003, the year we stayed hot on marijuana. In the last couple of years we've not found much marijuana being grown, probably just three, four, or five hundred plants.

Jerry "Slick" Gee, Monroe County, March 18, 2010

PRISON TIME FOR METH MAKERS

Meth making here in Monroe County these days is not as bad as it was back in 2002 to 2005. Back in 2002 we busted 222 meth labs and made about eighty arrests. We found labs in barns, horse trailers, outhouses, basements, abandoned houses, in the woods, and just anywhere. The arrested persons typically got about ten years in jail. I remember one guy was sentenced by the jury for fifty-five years in prison for manufacturing meth. Some of the others were sent to prison for ten to fifty-five years. Thus most of them are still in prison.

They serve prison time all over the state of Kentucky. These prisons are located in LaGrange, Eddyville, Green River Prison, Holly's Forester Camp, and other camps all over the state of Kentucky. A lot of Class D felons, the smallest sentence you can get, serve time in local jails.

Jerry "Slick" Gee, Monroe County, March 18, 2010

DANGERS OF METH

I've talked to and interviewed several persons as to why they purchase and use meth pills. They tell me they reach this certain peak that is unbelievable, and they keep taking more to get back to that high peak, then after they get that high, they are addicted to it and can't turn away. It is highly addictive. I'd say we've had ten or twelve people to die over a period of two or three years because of being hooked on it.

When taking meth pills, the first stage is loss of weight; second stage is scalp's appearance, then teeth rottening out and eyes going back in. The meth users typically expect only seven, eight, or nine years of living, but meth makers expect only four or five years. What happens is that they all breathe the pollution that results while making and taking it.

My workers and I never go into a meth lab unless we have our gas masks with us. The certified persons who take down meth labs, they get meth suits from Pennirile Task Force. Their masks are different from the ones I have. I always wear a mask, even after the meth-making equipment is taken away. These masks help keep you from breathing the fumes.

Jerry "Slick" Gee, Monroe County, March 18, 2010

PAPAW'S SECRET STILL

My papaw used to have a moonshine still, but he wouldn't tell his kids where the still was located. I have asked them several times, "Where was that still?" Actually, the old farmhouse and the land is just up from where we live now. I've asked my mother and my uncles, "Where did he have that still?"

Well, he never would tell them where the still was located, so they couldn't tell me. But they did tell me that he had a still and made moonshine whiskey, but he just would never tell them where it was. Anyway, he decided to quit making moonshine.

That took place over on Hatton Creek Road about three miles from Stanton. Papaw had a farm that had approximately 175 acres, but not much of it could be farmed due to mountain terrain. I was going to go out there and look to see if I could find anything that was left, but didn't do it. None of us ever found out where his still was located, because he never would tell. He was a quiet fellow.

Danny Rogers, Powell County, March 27, 2010

ILLEGAL PRESCRIPTION DRUGS

The most recent arrest I made dealt with a drug dealer. It was a female drug dealer that we've had so many problems with. Her activities dealt with prescription medications. She would pay people to go to Florida to bring back prescription medications. When they brought these pills back to her, she would give them so much money and a few pills, and she would keep the rest of the pills. She made a lot of money doing this.

We investigated her for several months, and finally got enough information to get us a search warrant. We activated that search warrant, and on the affidavit we filled out we stated where the drugs were and that she was hiding the drugs. Actually, she was hiding them down in her bra. So we executed the search warrant as soon as we pulled up, and she was coming out the door. She was headed toward the creek that ran alongside her house. I knew that she was going to get the pills out of her bra.

When we saw what she was doing, we handcuffed her and conducted the search on her. Well, she had about $1,800 worth of cash in
her pockets, but she don't work. We said, "All right, we know you've
got some pills on you."

"No I don't," she said. "There's no pills on me."

"Yeah, we know you've got some down in your bra."

There was another female there, so she finally said, "Yeah, I got
some down there." That other lady assisted her in getting the pills
because she, too, was handcuffed.

The lady we had gone to arrest had over 260 pills down in her bra,
right where we knew they were going to be. She just reached up and
got the pills out of her bra.

Her bond was $100,000 cash. She's in prison for a little while—at
least I hope so. She was a thorn in my side, because people called my
office four or five times every day to complain about her. She was tough
to catch, but we finally got enough information to arrest her.

The pills she was selling were Oxycodone and Xanax and they were
prescription meds she got from Florida. That's how most people are doing
it these days. They're going to Florida and getting all these pills, then
come back home. And it's legal to go down there to do that if you keep
them in their prescribed containers. A lot of people who go down there
and get their medications split them up between three people. There will
be three persons, and one person will have control of the pill bottle with
likely one quarter of the pills in it, and the other two will have the others.
So, that's how they get caught a lot of times down there.

Danny Rogers, Powell County, March 27, 2010

METH BUST I

For awhile marijuana was a big problem here in Powell County, and that
was before I was elected as sheriff, but right now it is not a big problem.
It is just about a thing of the past, as we don't find much of it anymore.
However, we do find some every now and then, as we did especially
while I was a police officer. Sometimes people were caught with a small
bag of marijuana plants, and they sold it for approximately $40 per bag.

I sure didn't use marijuana back when it was more popular than it
is nowadays. I did drink a little alcohol in my early days, but that was
before I became a police officer.

Meth is not a problem around here. However, I'll say that we did have one really big case dealing with this fellow who was a big meth dealer in Wolfe County as well as here in Powell County. He moved into Stanton, where I was a city police officer at that time, working third shift.

We had a bunch of complaints about him for selling meth in Stanton city limits. What I decided to do was do a trash pull, which means that when people set their trash out for the sanitation guys to pick up on the edge of the road it becomes public property, more or less. So when we did a trash pull, we'd just go and get the trash and take it back to a place where we'd look in it. You can tell a lot about a person when you are going through his trash. That's a fact!

It was 3:00 in the morning, so I was driving a cruiser and just run by this driveway and reached out the window and grabbed one of them bags. I took it back to the police department, then went back to do that for three nights each week. So I picked up three big bags of trash. I was driving down the street and was holding a bag of garbage outside the cruiser so he couldn't see me. Anyway, we went through his trash and found where he had been making meth. We got all the evidence laid out, photographed it, and all that stuff, then got a search warrant based on all that evidence. We went back to his residence three or four hours later and found some stuff where he was making meth in the house.

He actually wasn't there, but his brother was. We started searching the residence, but we also had some officers outside that were looking around. Well, this car pulls into the driveway, and it was the meth maker himself. So the officers got him right there, and he had some more stuff in his vehicle with which to make meth in his vehicle. We arrested him and charged him, and I turned it over to the federal Drug Enforcement Association, which was good for me because he'd get more prison time and would have to do more time than what he was given. You have to serve more time on federal charges than you do on state charges.

We took him to court, where he got a little more than six years, and he had to serve every bit of it. However, he is out of prison now, as that took place back in 1995. He was originally from New York, then moved down here and began making that meth stuff.

Danny Rogers, Powell County, March 27, 2010

METH BUST II

Another event about meth that aggravates me very much happened when this guy from Laurel County–in that county they do arrests for meth makers all the time—anyway, this guy had moved up here to Powell County from Laurel County and lived just up the road from here. There is a little store that sets right in the Y of two state roads, and right behind this store is a church. The church has got a little building that has a little bunch of materials and other things where the ladies go to sew and make quilts, etc.

We got word that he was making his meth in a residence located right beside the store. Well, we got enough evidence in order to get a search warrant. When we went inside the house, he wasn't there. We didn't find anything in the residence, but outside the residence he had been burning that stuff and we found some stuff there. That was early in the morning when we did that, but later on that evening I got a call from the pastor of the church telling me they had gone into that little room where all the ladies' materials were located. Well, that man had been making meth in a little room located by the side of the church. The building actually belonged to the church. That's why there was nothing in his house.

When the officers went in there they said, "Lord, we went into this building, and it smells awful. It will knock you down." All that stuff really smelled awful due to the chemicals.

I said to them, "Don't go back in there, just stay out. Don't breathe that stuff. I'll be up there in a minute, so hold on."

So I went up there and that's what was going on. He was making meth in there, and when he got done with the stuff, he was burning that out behind the store. So the officers had to throw all that stuff away. I guess all that material was worth about $1,000.

Well, finally the man ran away from us, so we obtained some warrants for him and finally picked him up back in Laurel County. He is now in the penitentiary, but I don't know which one.

He was using part of the church property to make that stuff! That happened in 2009, and it was the last time we took care of meth making.

Danny Rogers, Powell County, March 27, 2010

Chapter 6

MAJOR PROBLEMS AND SIGNIFICANT ACCOMPLISHMENTS

With the job of sheriff comes a host of problems. The issue of inadequate finances is a recurrent theme in the stories below. Sheriffs often struggle to fulfill their duties properly when personnel and equipment are not what they ought to be. In addition, the sheriff's position has become increasingly administrative over the years, as paperwork and "politics" occupy more and more time.

Population growth in the sheriffs' communities has also changed the dynamics of county law enforcement. From a time when sheriffs generally knew the perpetrators they dealt with personally (as so many stories throughout this collection attest), sheriffs find their jobs increasingly impersonal as social demographics change. Changing social and cultural factors further complicate the issue, as the face of crime itself has in some ways altered, with drug-related crimes (particularly the astronomical increase of meth labs) on the rise.

This chapter also highlights some signal accomplishments of sheriffs in response to the new difficulties, including the establishment of successful Drug Task Forces and one sheriff's staging of a successful rally to help his county during an economic downturn.

Personnel Difficulties

If you ask any sheriff in the United States as to what is their major problem each year they'll say, "Keeping up them damn deputies!" We have a turnover, not so much in road deputies but bailiffs. It is a problem to find good qualified men. I can go out on the street now and pick up anything I want, then run a background check on him, and do this or do that, and something will check out down the road.

So your personnel is one of your biggest problems, keeping them going. Warren County began changing in 1993. I used to work every weekend just like the rest of the boys. Then it began growing so big. When I started out, I had eight deputies on the road; now I've got thirty-three. And I had two bailiffs on the road when I started out, and now I've got thirty-three.

I could see a big change, so I quit working the road. Now I'm an administrator. We have something like forty cars, three buses, a truck, two dog trucks and two dog wardens. I've got to keep the money going, keep the training up.

I worked a case when some man broke into David Garvin's house. We caught him. He stole Garvin's Rolex watch. I was in trial down there for four days, during which time people couldn't call me—couldn't do this and couldn't do that.

So my biggest job is serving as administrator, holding things together. See, during tax season, there's eight persons that work here in the tax office. We also inspect cars, and have two workers that does that only, such as checking serial numbers on out-of-state cars. I'm more of an administrator now than anything else.

Jerry "Peanuts" Gaines, Warren County, July 20, 2009

ADMINISTRATIVE DUTIES

As a state trooper I worked at various problems in all the counties in and around here, but as sheriff I only work one county. You are elected by the people, and you get to know the people in your county. Like in some other states, Kentucky is lacking in sheriff's responsibilities. As in some other states, Kentucky sheriffs just handle courts, roads, and taxes. But in Florida and elsewhere, sheriffs run the jails. Kentucky is the only state in the United States that had a constitutional jailer. All other states are under the sheriffs. Maryland was the last, along with Kentucky, but three or four years ago they also turned the jails over to the sheriffs.

I guess the greatest priority of sheriffs is to serve the court systems. We have to have bailiffs in every court proceeding that goes on here in Taylor County. Then all the papers, such as warrants, summons, small claims, and emergency protective orders, we sheriffs are responsible for serving them. Actually, any police officer can serve a warrant, but they all are sent to us and we distribute them out.

Nowdays, the sheriff's job is getting to be more office connected rather than going out on service calls. The sheriff's job is to make it easier for the deputies by being able to get money, grants, go to fiscal courts, give reason why we need more money, more officers, etc. I hate politics, but I take care of politics here so that it doesn't affect the officers and deputies that are out on the road. I want to let them get their jobs done without having people on their backs. I handle that part, and also the administrative parts.

In connection with administration, we're handling $7 or $8 million in taxes. Every year our fee budgets are audited four different times by the state.

John E. Shipp, Taylor County, July 30, 2009

KENTON COUNTY FAIRLY SAFE

I'm pretty close to the sheriff in Hamilton County, Ohio, and the chief of police in Cincinnati. We get together for lunch on occasion. There's a very pro–law enforcement community over there, that are mostly made up of big businessmen. They invite us to have lunch with them at the Queen City Club on a rather regular basis.

Cincinnati and Hamilton County have a hard time right now. They are not being financed or supported by the local governments as well as they should. Here in Kenton County and Covington, we don't have as much trouble as they do. I was sitting next to one of these fellows, who was a civilian, and he asked me, "Why is it that I feel very safe when I go over to Covington with my wife, but I don't feel safe when I go into downtown Cincinnati?"

I said, "Well, that is probably because when we arrest someone they actually go to jail, and they typically don't come back."

We had one sting operation on a guy that was going to sell some dope to our undercover agent, and he wanted to do it in Cincinnati. He didn't want him to come across the bridge into Covington, and that was like teasing an animal that was trying to take a little bait. He finally did come on over, and we arrested him. When that happened he told us, "I knew as soon as I crossed that darn bridge that I was going to get arrested, but I just couldn't help myself."

Kenton County, Kentucky, is much more under control now than Hamilton County, Ohio, is. The sheriff in Hamilton County told me a few months ago that he had to turn loose eight hundred prisoners because he had to close the jail since it was overcrowded, and he had to lay off three hundred deputies. A couple of weeks later the chief of police over there told me that he had to lay off two hundred officers. That's five hundred they had to lay off because they couldn't afford to pay them. So, that's a catch-22; you have less presence on the street with law enforcement, so you have more crime. It feeds on itself, something terrible.

In Kenton County we are finally getting a new jail, because our old jail is overcrowded, too. The new jail will be ready probably in one year, or maybe one and one-half years. In Covington, Erlanger, and other places here in Kenton County, we now have a total of fourteen police departments and three dispatch centers.

Charles Lee "Chuck" Korzenborn, Kenton County, September 17, 2009

FINANCIAL WOES

Robert Miller Jr. was on his second term as sheriff when I got old enough to know him. I learned that he was a very bold sheriff, because he would tell it like it is, and in his own terms. Sometimes what he did just sort of stepped on people's toes.

Looking back through all the sheriffs, the main thing I found out was one of the things I wanted to change if I could seek the office and obtain it. In other words, I was looking back at all the heartaches and woes all the sheriffs have had in Todd County. Robert Miller Jr. had the money, but he probably had to borrow it from himself. Some of the other sheriffs would have to go to a bank and borrow money to run the office on through the year. Across the state, there are sheriff's offices that still are fee offices, and some are fee pooling. In other words, the fiscal court paid all their bills, but the sheriff still stayed in the same budget. The fiscal court sort of plugs you when you are low, but you pay it back to them when the taxes come in at the end of the year.

The way we still have to operate is to still operate fee offices. That's one of the main things I wanted to change, because we've struggled and struggled and struggled over the years in our individual capacities as sheriffs because we had to borrow money. The state has relieved some of the interest burdens by coming up with what is called state advancement. However, I refused to take it after my first year in office, realizing that my name was on the bond as the principal, and it didn't say nothing about a sheriff, fiscal court, or government. It just said Billy Stokes, as principal, his heirs, executors, and basically my estate, would be responsible for paying the bonding company back, or should I die before it gets paid back, or if anything happened. I pay my own sheriff's salary as a fee office, if I have the money. And if I don't have the money to pay myself, by statute the fiscal court is required to pay my salary.

So, since refusing to take the state advancement loan for the last two years, I sort of put a little of Robert Miller Jr. into me, and all the sheriffs in between whom I have known. Seeing their struggles, their heartaches and struggles, and now looking forward to the future of the sheriffs, we don't need to have to worry about that. They don't need to worry about how they're going to finance their office until the tax money starts coming in. All they need to have to worry about are their statute and duties, such as law enforcement. Unfortunately, a lot of people in rural counties think sheriffs are still only responsible for law enforcement and patrol of the county. But the sheriffs have the duty of collecting the taxes, seeing that elections are run properly automatically on the county election board, seeing that the courts are run correctly, that everything that goes on in the courtroom is performed correctly, and that the convicted that are sentenced to do prison terms are transported to prison by the sheriff. There are prisoners throughout the state that have to be transported to and from the county for court sessions, and the sheriff is responsible for that. Tax collection, of course, is the number one job for the sheriff, as he has to be responsible for collecting taxes. I see that now more than I did before I became sheriff, because when you sign that you are going to handle someone else's money in large amounts, you want to be exactly to the penny.

My number one goal was to go in there and try to figure out a way to work with our court, but it hasn't worked. I guess you might say I've done put too much vinegar in it and not enough sugar with our county government. Thus, I've tried to change things to where the county would have the desire to go to fee pooling, but since they are the county body, it is up to them. If they would want to do that, it would allow us to have more law enforcement protection.

W. D. "Billy" Stokes, Todd County, September 17, 2009

Meritorious Achievement Award

One Meritorious Achievement Award was issued by the Kentucky State Police, February 14, 1992, which reads as follows:

Sheriff Kenneth Morris, several deputies, and state troopers, located an armed and dangerous suspect and attempted to talk with the man. The suspect told Morris unless he had a warrant, to get off his property, or he would shoot one of his state troopers standing nearby. The suspect then began counting to five, and Morris continued to negotiate with the man, but on the count of three he took out his hand held radio as if to call for a warrant. The suspect walked toward Morris, and when he got close enough, Morris grabbed the man's gun and wrestled the suspect to the ground and Sheriff Morris displayed calm professionalism and courage that was instrumental in successfully resolving the highly volatile situation. Be it therefore ordered that the honorary title of Colonel aide-de-camp to the Commissioner of the Kentucky State Police be conferred upon Sheriff Kenneth Morris, along with the everlasting admiration of the Kentucky State Police for his dedication to duty and exemplary courage in keeping with the highest tradition of the Commonwealth of Kentucky.

Signed: Billy Hoffman, Commissioner of the Kentucky State Police, May 13, 1992

Kenneth Lee Morris, Butler County, October 11, 2009

THEN AND NOW

Going back to when my father was a deputy sheriff, and looking at the different things I have realized, I can see in each generation its own right in the way they handled things. Probably back in the 1960s and 1970s, there were a lot of "Good Ole Boy" programs. I don't mean anything bad with that term, as I consider myself a good ole boy, but I look at those sheriffs and those deputies as officers that pretty much knew everybody in the county. If something was going on in a community, you pretty much knew who was doing it, and how to deal with it. All you had to do was give them a call and they would show up here at the office.

Now that we've moved into this era, there are so many things you have to deal with. One of these things is that you don't know everybody in the county because it has grown so much, there is no way you can know everybody. There's also a lot of other things you deal with, such as drug use and the things they do while on drugs, and the way they act. All of these have to be dealt with.

The sheriff's office has moved itself from that early situation to the way it is now. I'm still a country fellow at heart. I'm still a Shelby Countian that grew up here; I know how the good ole boy system used to be, but the way it is now we have to deal with matters professionally.

I would say that the big changes took place in 1990. To illustrate how it has grown here, back in 1989 we had a dispatch center through which all the formal calls came. Back then we received something like four hundred calls through the dispatch center. Today, my office is getting fourteen hundred contacts per month.

Mike Armstrong, Shelby County, November 6, 2009

TROUBLEMAKING COMMUNITY

There is a community here in Casey County that was just bad, bad. Burglaries, drinkings, fightings, cuttings, arsons, and things like that. Persons that did those things burned a guy's house one time. We sent thirty-two prisoners to the penitentiary, and I think twenty-seven of them came out of that community or the immediate area.

When I was county judge, a job I didn't like at all, we didn't have an ambulance service, no road department, no water lines out in the county—we had nothing. The worst winter I remember us having was in 1978, when we had floods like we did in 1977. Well, I promised the people if they would elect me as sheriff again, I'd clear up that bad community (whose name I won't mention), if I had to buy me a tent and stretch it out on the courthouse square. Well, due to all the people I put in jail and in the penitentiary from that community, you might think I wouldn't get any votes there. Believe it or not, that community and surrounding area was one of my better precincts!

I was over there a few days ago, and all the boys there were telling stories about me arresting them and putting them in jail and in the pen. Why, you'd have thought they were the best friends I had anywhere! We really had a big time.

I was elected sheriff in 1982, and a gentleman in that community had been selling cocaine, marijuana, beer, and liquor in a poolroom up there. I was staying up there in that community all night, and about 4:00 a.m. I was setting back in there, and this fellow, who was one of the worst ones back then, was originally from Lincoln County. Somebody pecked on my window while I was still dozing there in my cruiser. I rolled my window down, and he said, "Carl, can I talk to you?"

I said, "Why, sure," then got out of my cruiser and said, "What can I do for you?"

He said, "Well, I can save you some money, so I thought I'd just tell you."

I said, "Well, how are you going to save me some money?"

He said, "Well, I've ordered me a new gate truck, and I'm supposed to get it Thursday. If I can get the poles put on it in time for them to load me with gates on Friday, I'm leaving out of here. You may not believe me, but I have not sold a can of beer since you were sworn in as sheriff again, and you won't have to buy that tent, because I'm leaving here."

He turned out to be a friend, and was a good informant in helping me catch people, even guys from out of state.

Carl E. Meece, Casey County, November 12, 2009

Strange Call

Probably around 2001–2002, we received a call at the sheriff's office telling us that there were some people behind this guy's house in the woods, and they would sneak around hiding from, but watching, him. He said that they looked like state police troopers, and said that they also looked like they were from the task force. He went on to say, "I don't know what's going on with them, and you're not going to believe this, but I saw a snake eat a deer."

I said, "You saw a what?"

He said, "Yeah, I saw a snake eat a whole deer. The deer was standing up, and a snake ate it."

Well, we didn't know what in the world was going on. So we hung up the phone and went out to check on him. After getting out there I talked with the old boy, and he seemed fine. I didn't understand what the call was all about, as he seemed fine. He never mentioned anything about a snake, or men. He just talked like anybody else would.

Anyway, that's been one of the strangest calls we've had in a good while. And I certainly don't want to run into any snakes like that.

Wayne Agent, Crittenden County, November 3, 2009

Establishment of Drug Task Force

Meth was just beginning to come onto the scene about five years before

I retired. We got to hearing about it, and that it would be coming from the west to the east. It was just migrating from California and Arizona, and it was like a plague. You could get to talking about it a year before we saw it in this area; we received reports that it was beginning to show up in western Kentucky, and it just came on across the state. And it was a tremendous problem.

During my last term as sheriff, one of the things I did was to work very hard to get a Drug Task Force established in Barren County, recognizing that it needed people working on it full-time. I was successful in getting that done. I had people who were in agreement with the fact we needed the task force. We got the money approved, then applied for some grants and did get a Drug Task Force established during my last term as sheriff in Barren County.

We incorporated the task force at the beginning with the police department in Glasgow and Cave City, and the local sheriff's office and the Kentucky State Police. We invited Metcalfe County to become a member because the commonwealth attorney is for both Barren and Metcalfe County, thus it made sense to have those two counties together. However, Metcalfe County officials didn't feel like they had enough money to be involved at that particular time. Then we worked with Edmonson County, and Edmonson County came into the Drug Task Force with us. As a result, the organization is presently known as the Barren-Edmonson Drug Task Force. Metcalfe is not yet included, but they have expressed some interest in joining. I'm still on the board of directors of the Drug Task Force. In fact, we have sent the director to talk with Metcalfe County people, and they have expressed some interest in trying to come on board now. That may materialize within the next six to twelve months.

Staying in the Drug Task Force means we get grant monies. The way it is presently set up, I had a full-time deputy who was assigned to the Drug Task Force out of the sheriff's office. The Glasgow City Police Department has pulled out, primarily because of monetary problems, I understand. However, they have expressed an interest to come back in as a member. Edmonson County has one person assigned to the task force, and Barren County now has two members out of the sheriff's office right now.

Barney Jones, Barren County, December 21, 2009

STAFFING PROBLEMS

A lot of the problems I had here in Boyle County had to be covered 24/7, but I'm understaffed. I have only seven or eight road deputies, who help me cover twenty-four hours daily, seven days a week. We didn't have state police helping us, but if we needed help, they would come. That was one of the things I campaigned on, because back before we would leave work and go home, they'd call us out on the basis if they needed us, they call us at whatever time they needed us. I did that, so that was one of my campaign things, and I stuck to it throughout my years in office, and we had people out there all night long.

The main problem I ran into was that I also had to provide help in the court systems. I had to provide the bailiffs, transport drivers who had to go and get them and bring them back for court. When court was over, we had to take them right back to places like Hopkinsville, which is a good four- or five-hour drive or more in one day. We had to bring them up here to let them plead guilty or not guilty, then turn right around and take them right back to where they were picked up. Then we had to go back the next week to get them and bring them back for a pretrial conference. When that was finished, we had to turn around and take them right back. It didn't matter, because the fiscal court had to pay the costs for all that transportation. In other words, it was paid for by local taxpayers here.

LeeRoy Hardin, Boyle County, January 11, 2010

TURKEY RUN

Prior to me taking office on January 3, 1999, there had been occurring an unauthorized event in Lewis County known as Turkey Run. For over seventeen years Turkey Run took place the day after Thanksgiving. This event had grown to where over two thousand people gathered with their ATVs and other vehicles for approximately four days. Lewis County is a large, rugged county with a sparse population base, and ATV enthusiasts have flocked to the Briery area for years. Briery is an area approximately ten miles, extremely rugged and rural. The site had been posted on the Internet, and people came from other Kentucky counties and also from Ohio, Tennessee, West Virginia, and Indiana. Landowners in the area and gas pipeline authorities had complained to law enforcement authorities for years to keep the ATVs off their property.

In my first year as sheriff my deputies and I confronted the viola-
tors, which numbered over a thousand. I informed them that we would
return in three hours and if they couldn't produce authorization, I would
make arrests and have their vehicles impounded. The vast majority of
them understood, and informed me they had been coming there for at
least seventeen years, and that no law enforcement officer had informed
them not to.

We returned three hours later, and only three or four remained
and produced a letter from the landowners to remain.

William D. Lewis, Lewis County, January 13, 2010

Successful Economic Rally

In February 2000 Lewis County was struggling economically because of
the loss of manufacturing jobs and other economic issues. The unem-
ployment rate in Lewis County was 18.3 percent (highest in the state)
when the state and nation were enjoying an economic boom. The U.S.
Shoe Corporation had recently moved two factories to Mexico. Their
factories were about 90 percent of the manufacturing jobs in Lewis
County, causing a loss of 850 jobs. Cuts in tobacco quotas and cuts in
the six-year road plan also had devastating effects on the economy. I
felt as a public figure, I had an obligation to do something to help the
citizens of Lewis County. I informed other county officials, along with
the state senator and representatives, as to what I was going to do, and
that scared the hell out of them.

The Kentucky legislature was in session at the time. My plan as
sheriff was to cause a symbolic gesture that would draw attention to the
economic plight of Lewis County. On February 12, 2000, after contact-
ing the media regarding the press conference, I did the following: A rally
was held at the Lewis County courthouse, where I spoke approximately
twenty minutes about the problem. I informed them that I was going
to turn the American flag upside down as a symbol of distress. I turned
it upside down and ran it up the flagpole at the courthouse. Hell, it was
like the shot that was heard around the world. In addition, I encouraged
people to turn their Lewis County registration plates upside down, which
is not illegal, in order to draw attention to our problem.

My office immediately began receiving phone calls from individuals
and companies from all over offering to help. The state senator and representatives, who were too afraid to attend the rally, started feeling the

heat. The governor's office was also getting questions from the media. Being in session, the legislature also received pressure from the media. The cuts that had been made to the six-year road plan were put back into the plan. The state economic development cabinet sent a team to Lewis County who assisted in preparing a plan to assist Lewis County with our economic problems. Two manufacturing factories have located in Lewis County because of the economic condition of Lewis County being brought to their attention.

This story has many voluminous issues that are too numerous to mention. Just let me say, the position of Lewis County sheriff is powerful when the sheriff sincerely gets involved with an issue.

William D. Lewis, Lewis County, January 13, 2009

RECOVERING STOLEN PROPERTY

Back when I was a deputy I worked on a lot of burglaries, thefts, and bootlegging. I saved insurance companies thousands of dollars, as I recovered a lot of stolen property and things such as livestock, vehicles, items stolen from homes. I had a good name here in Adair County for doing that. People knew I was good at recovering stolen property, and a lot of them praised me for what I was doing.

I still did the same thing when I took over as sheriff in 1994.

James Ralph Curry, Adair County, January 11, 2010

METH TROUBLES

A big problem here in Wayne County is getting enough deputies to help us, but our major problem is dealing with meth makers. In the lab of the last meth makers we caught, I believe there were 151 bottles that had been filled with meth. They were still in that house when we got there, and that's where it was made. I don't know a lot about making meth, and don't want to know much about it, but we drove into that meth lab, that was in a house that has been there about ten years and is still unfinished. This guy works on it just as he gets a chance.

So we were out there looking for another meth lab in a place where we thought there would be one. We stayed there until around 11:00 that night, but nobody showed up. So we stole all their stuff and left, including their ingredients with which they made it. As we were coming back toward town, we came by this house, and the lights were on.

Ronnie said, "I've never seen lights on in this house before. Let's turn around and go see if somebody has broken in the house or something." So we just turned around in the next driveway and went back. We pulled in the driveway and went up to the house and knocked on the door.

This guy came and opened the door and he had on rubber gloves. When he opened the door that smell would knock you down. We also had the Drug Task Force officer with us, too. So we went in and saw there was nobody else in there, then decided it was a meth lab. There was no one there, but the lab was running wide open when we got in there.

Well, we left after we were there for about fifteen hours to get it cleaned up. They called two crews from Louisville to come down here and clean that up.

Charles L. Boston, Wayne County, February 13, 2010

Money Hard to Come By

When I came into the sheriff's office my first day, I had nothing. I walked in the door. There were no computers there, no equipment, no guns, and no uniforms. The cars I had were old state police cars that had 180,000 to 200,000 miles on them. Any of the old four-wheel drives they had bought had 180,000 miles on it. One of the jeeps they left for me didn't have a four-wheel drive on it. It was snowing outside, but the jeep had no heater in it. So I started out with nothing, not even any money. The sheriffs that were going out of office would leave and all accounts are closed. Excess money goes to the fiscal court. So when a new sheriff started out, we had zero amount of money in the bank.

I had to go and borrow $20,000 at the bank to start the sheriff's department. Now then, I've applied for grants and done all these things. I now have three four-wheel drive vehicles, two Dodge cruisers, and have accumulated uniforms, guns, computers in the cars (each deputy has his own computer) that are connected with the state police. We type all our cases to the state police, scan the driver's license, and help out the state police all we can.

I now have six certified deputies, and have two deputies that take care of the bailiff. I also have a deputy as a certified school resource officer.

The sheriff's office is financed by the tax base, and I get only 4 percent of the tax money I collect, which amounts to $280,000, but my budget is more than $700,000. So there's no way that I can have what I want to have in terms of deputies. But with the help of the local fiscal court, the judge, and magistrates, I get a certain amount of money to help.

I have worked drug cases and we take drug forfeitures, like from drug dealers if they get caught. We were involved in a case in Knott County. My deputy is on the [Drug] Task Force, and they took a motel out of which drugs were being sold. The deputy got part of the forfeiture and they sold it for $210,000 on February 24, 2010. My sheriff's department got 20 percent of that. Since my deputy is on that task force, I may not get 20 percent of every case in which he is involved, but I get at least 5 percent.

All the money that comes in from these cases is put in the bank in the forfeiture services account. I get a fee account from taxpayers, but I have this special account that I get from the federal forces. With that money I can pay for my cars, my gas, my computers, supplies, uniforms, and anything that I need in the supply line to run this office, but I cannot pay salaries out of it because it is not guaranteed money.

If you talk with the 120 sheriffs in Kentucky, you will find out that the biggest problem is financing and keeping relations. So we are fighting a battle every day in trying to keep the doors open and trying to provide a service to the public.

Danny R. Webb, Letcher County, February 27, 2010

Chapter 7

MISTAKES

Stories in this brief chapter describe instances of human error: one sheriff mistakenly informed his bailiff that his beloved son was dead; others failed to arrest drunken drivers, wore inappropriate attire on the job, lost convictions through avoidable mistakes on search warrants, or drove recklessly in pursuit of suspects. In one particularly thoughtful story a sheriff muses on his disordered priorities as a younger officer.

No doubt many more stories of mistakes could have been told by sheriffs, but it is completely understandable why they chose not to relate them for publication.

BEFRIENDING DEPUTIES

Likely the biggest mistake I ever made as a sheriff was running to be sheriff! Now, once you get into politics, if you're going to stay, you'd better stay. Actually, the biggest mistake I ever made—and I don't mean this the way it sounds, but it has also happened to other sheriffs as well—what I'm talking about is that when you get to be a sheriff, you become buddies with the deputies, and when they get in trouble, you are automatically in trouble.

During my first term that happened to me in two or three instances, so now I just talk to them and everything, but stay away from them. That way they show me more respect. So that was some of the biggest mistakes I made while serving as sheriff.

Today, if I have trouble, I try to explain it and redo it so I won't have to do it again. But I always stick up for my men. When a deputy comes into my office the first time he's screwed up, I back him up whether he's right or wrong. I figure he's messed up because he didn't know any better. But the second time he messes up, I get on him, and when he messes up the third time, he's fired from his job. Or he also has the choice of submitting his resignation to give up his job.

The sheriff's office belongs to the people. I'm elected by the people. I work for 110,000 people here in Warren County, and they're my bosses. But the chief of police gets his job when only three city commissioners appoint him. State policemen are appointed by a couple of persons on the board. But the people look at the sheriff as their police officer. People call me, and I answer more stuff than lawyers do.

I tell people when I hire them, "Treat people like you'd want to be treated. Don't be smart with them." I get onto them all the time when they do something they shouldn't do; I just don't fool with them. I want to be nice to people, but firm with flexibility.

Jerry "Peanuts" Gaines, Warren County, July 20, 2009

BORDERLINE

I never did get into any trouble while serving as sheriff, but I'm sure there were some situations on the borderline. Sometimes just going out on these calls, you just don't know what to expect, so sometimes you'll make an arrest on a borderline something. However, truth of the matter is, you might stop a lot of other things from happening, but you may sometimes get condemned for doing what you do. In your mind, you know that you're probably doing right.

Harold E. Tingle, Shelby County, August 14, 2009

MISTAKEN IDENTITY

I will tell about a tragic mistake I made. I wasn't in office more than a few months when I got a phone call from the Ft. Wright Police Department and they told me that the son of one of my bailiffs, an older gentleman, had committed suicide by shooting himself in the head. I said, "Now, look; I want you to verify this."

The fellow said, "The policeman that found him knows the man. His identification is exactly the same as the man he knows. He was found down toward the river bottom in Boone County."

I asked the man three or four times, "Are you really sure this was the person?"

He said, "Absolutely, there's no question in my mind. This is the man."

I said, "Okay," then had another of my deputies to go get the bailiff out of court and to bring him over. I told him this terrible thing had happened, and you can imagine how upset he was. I dismissed him and told him he could go home, or whatever he wanted to do. He left the office, and couldn't have been in his car more than a minute when another deputy sticks his head in the window and said, "Wrong man."

I had to get in my car and beat him to his house. I got into his house just after he walked in. He just had time to tell his family what had happened, and I got to explain to these people that I told him by mistake that his son was dead.

You can imagine how I felt telling this man that his son was dead. Of course, he was completely upset with me. That caused so much pain in the family. That was a terrible mistake, and I don't know what I could do to not do it again, because I was thoroughly convinced that the policeman that identified the body was right. And the driver's license name was identical to the same name as the man's son.

I think that's the worst mistake I ever made.

Charles Lee "Chuck" Korzenborn, Kenton County, September 17, 2009

Priorities

When I was a young officer I made a lot of mistakes. I have counseled my young officers not to repeat these in their lives. One of the mistakes I made is that I loved this job too much, and this job became my priority. It became my life. Because of that, my family and other things that should have been more important to me took second place. Ultimately it cost me dearly.

I went through two failed marriages. Well, I'm not proud of that at all. In fact, I'm embarrassed about it. But I learned from those mistakes, and I'm married to a young lady now that I've been married to for six years, and she is absolutely the love of my life. Between her and my two granddaughters, my priorities now lie where they should be. And as much as I love this job, and all the things I do, it will always come second place to my family.

That's the way it should be, and that's the way it should have been.

These days, I tell my young officers, "Keep your priorities where they need to be. Keep your faith first and foremost; look to your family, and *then* do the best job that you can as deputy sheriff in Daviess County. You'll be better off because of it."

Keith Cain, Daviess County, October 1, 2009

BAYONET THREAT

This is a story about my wife. When I first went into the sheriff's office, I had arrested some of the city council members, and they were paying fifty-six hours each week on their dispatching in the sheriff's office so we could have twenty-four hours' dispatching. The county furnished fifty-six hours, and the city furnished fifty-six hours, then the sheriff did the rest of it.

After I took office in January 1974, the city came over there and did away with their part of the dispatch. Thus that dropped all the burden on me. That caused my wife, Carol, to work seven days each week, and doubled over two nights a week. Our oldest son that had a double lung transplant, who was a little fellow in high school, would get off the school bus and come in and dispatch for me until 12:00 p.m. so I could bring him home, and I did. It was really, really tough back then.

Well, one night I brought this woman into my office. I never did search a woman, so I didn't search her. But she was crazy drunk. Of course, my wife was dispatching on the second shift. Of course, she collected taxes during the day, and then she doubled over to fill in dispatching.

I was getting a breathalyzer set up to give this drunk woman a test, and she started giving Carol a cussing, then jerked this big long bayonet out of her pant leg and asked Carol, "What in the so-and-so are you doing here at this hour?"

That like to have scared Carol to death. I didn't know whether this woman was going to use the bayonet or not, but Carol thought she was going to use it.

I arrested her for drunk driving, and should have searched her before she pulled that bayonet out. That was my mistake since I should have at least slowed her down a little bit.

Carl E. Meece, Casey County, November 12, 2009

DRUNK DRIVER

Nobody ain't perfect, I don't care who they are. You make mistakes. You can look back, then say, "Well, I wish I had done this" or "Wish I had done that," but it's too late now.

I went out here one time and got a guy that was drinking and driving. I should have brought him in and put him in jail for DUI, but I didn't. Instead I took him home. I said to him, "I'll take you home this time, but if I catch you again, you will go to jail."

Well, he became one of my friends! I never caught him again. He was thankful for the way I treated him when he was driving drunk, and he apologized several times.

Actually, they all thank you when you treat them respectfully.

John "Tuffy" Snedegar, Bath County, December 11, 2009

ARREST AT CHURCH

The biggest mistake I ever made hurt me the worst. We had this guy that had allegedly killed a man. He was in prison for murder, and that happened before I became sheriff. He was in the Brushy Mountain Prison, located in Tennessee. While he was there he escaped. They said that the sheriff here in Clinton County before me knew where he was located but wouldn't arrest him, so they said.

So, when I got in office, I found out that he was going to church. I took my deputies to the church house and posted them at the windows and I went on through the door. This man I was looking for was sitting up next to the front row there in church with his wife. So I just sat beside him and flipped a handcuff on him, and I already had mine on. That cuffed him to me.

His wife started screaming and yelling, so I felt bad. We didn't want to shoot him since we assumed he would run. When I was bringing him out his wife was screaming and yelling and pulling on him. The Sunday school teacher, I'll not call her name, or superintendent there at church, went out with me and begged, "Please, Glynn, please, Glynn, don't take him from church."

I said, "Well, I have to."

Then she said, "Would you care to have prayer before you leave?"

Well, I pulled off my old cap, stood there, and we had prayer with him. When we finished I was taking him out and putting him in a car, but his wife was pulling on him. She held onto him and the car, screaming and crying, "Don't take him! Don't take him!"

Well, we took him. I can't think whether I took him or sent him back to Brushy Mountain. For some reason I don't understand, it wasn't long until they turned him loose from prison. He then sent word to me that locking him back up was the best thing that ever happened to him, because he was an escaped prisoner. Not long after he was taken to Brushy Mountain Prison, they turned him loose. He had allegedly killed this person, but they turned him loose. I think he has been in a little trouble since, but he told me that was the best thing that ever happened to him.

Well, taking a man out of a church house was the most embarrassing thing I've ever done.

Glynn Mann, Clinton County, February 8, 2010

Racing Sheriff

I'm a jack-of-all-trades and master of none. Back before I was sheriff I was driving a racecar, and I liked to chase these young fellows here. I shouldn't have done it, but traffic wasn't as heavy as it is now. What you should do is get their license number and not run them, but I would chase them. I would chase them until their car got hot or something.

One time I was chasing them up through Duvall Valley, and the city police was also after them. I passed the city police and caught the car on top of the mountain. They were good ole boys, and had a hot car! Well, when they hit that mountain, the smoke boiled from their car. They stopped at the top of the mountain.

I liked to chase them back then, but now officers won't chase them because that is dangerous and might kill somebody.

Anyway, in reference to my chasing these fellows in Duvall Valley, a citizen called Frankfort and told them I was driving too fast. I'd let off to about ninety miles per hour, and the fellow I was chasing went on up the mountain, but I caught up with him again up there. Well, they didn't call the law on this young boy, but they called the law to tell what I had done. The charge was that I was driving reckless through the populated areas. However, there was no problem, as the sheriff is the chief law enforcement officer from county line to county line.

Glynn Mann, Clinton County, February 8, 2010

No Uniforms

I guess I've made a lot of mistakes, but I guess the biggest mistake I ever made was not listening to my parents, if you want to know the truth! No, truthfully, I'm not bad to make mistakes because I try to clear things before I start. But the biggest mistake I've made in this profession was not wearing a uniform or having a pistol when I went to arrest people.

When I first started serving as deputy, we didn't wear a uniform and I don't remember whether I had a gun or not. There was a racetrack out here in Oil Valley at that time, an old dirt track where they run those stock cars. Well, my first day on the job nobody knew I was working except me. I went on out to Oil Valley, and all the drunks from Foster Mountain were down there, and they got out of hand, so the other deputy and I decided to arrest them and bring them to jail. But because we wore no uniform, they didn't know that we were members of the law enforcement when I went up and started talking to them. So we proceeded to have our fight with several of them. Part of them ran away and part of them got put in jail.

That was a big mistake, not letting people know us and who we were. Anyway, this was my job to go do that.

Charles L. Boston, Wayne County, February 13, 2010

Technicalities

Some of the biggest mistakes I have made as a sheriff is goofing up on some of my search warrants. I worked on one case for a long time, and I got a search warrant on this fellow who was dealing with narcotics—illegal coke, crack, meth, marijuana, and other things. He had about three hundred pills of everything. Pills are a big problem here right now.

I got the search warrant and we busted him with all those pills. On the search warrant it said that the Commonwealth of Kentucky and the Circuit Court of Kentucky, Tompkinsville, Monroe County. This man we arrested was impounded by the Monroe County Sheriff's Department, and his license number was on the warrant. Some lawyers from Louisville got the charges against him kicked out because it didn't say Monroe County, Kentucky Sheriff's Department, because there is a Monroe County, Indiana Sheriff's Department, and a Monroe County, Tennessee Sheriff's Department.

That was the most disappointing mistake I had ever made. The word *Kentucky* was all over the search warrant, along with where the buys were made in Tompkinsville, Kentucky, in Houchens parking lot.

I've had three or four cases kicked out on that little technicality. I had one I really goofed up on, but I told commonwealth attorney Clay Hundley that I wanted a plea bargain, and that we would lose the case if he didn't verify it. I had got the wrong entries on the search warrant. I had gone by at nighttime to get needed address information, but the infrared cameras I used to get the address sort of confused me, so everything I wrote down was incorrect.

All that cost this man $10,000 cash. He was a marijuana dealer down here at Bugtussle. I said, "Offer him ten years' probation, because we don't know who is holding the money and everything." He had a good lawyer from Glasgow, Bobby Richardson, and he didn't even think to catch that because he wasn't going to go to trial. So this marijuana dealer took the ten years' probation, and we got the $10,000. My office got $7,000 of that amount, Clay Hundley got a certain percent of that $10,000, and the state police got their money back on the deposit box.

That was just one of those times we bluffed. But I make mistakes all the time, but I can't recall making many serious mistakes.

Jerry "Slick" Gee, Monroe County, March 18, 2010

Chapter 8

OTHER SHERIFFS

Folklorists truly appreciate stories people tell about individuals of older generations, as such accounts contain much information about people and places that is typically not available in full detail in formal sources. The stories herein, told by present-day sheriffs and former sheriffs, reveal what circumstances were like for their elderly or deceased predecessors, who served in a more informal era.

In the stories below we meet old-time sheriffs: some were corrupt; some were remarkably brave; one had to carry out his duties on horseback when he lost his license for driving under the influence; one dressed as Santa Claus to make an arrest; one didn't like to carry his gun.

Humorous Sheriff

There was a sheriff in Louisville who got in trouble and served a little time in jail for something. But he was humorous, and I'd laugh just by looking at him. I don't know what he got into, but being a sheriff you're supposed to be the cream of crop. So when you get into trouble, they try to pour it on you. I think that's what happened to him.

But he was really humorous. Just by looking at him you could see what he was like.

Jerry "Peanuts" Gaines, Warren County, July 20, 2009

Improper Use of Funds

There was a sheriff in a western Kentucky county. He's down there now, and was sheriff for about two terms. Well, the FBI gave him some money, about $25,000, with which to buy drugs from a bunch of drug dealers. Well, he kept the money!

They waited about three years, and then there was a train wreck down there. Well, this sheriff guarded things when it happened. Not any sheriff can make more money than their salary. I could go out here and work for you while doing something else, but in the line of service as a sheriff I can't charge you. Well, the sheriff charged a rate per hour for the deputies that were working, and he personally charged $10 an hour. So, instead of the railroad company paying him, he let the sheriff's office pay him. Well, they had a trial on him for that, and he served nine years in the penitentiary.

But it goes back to the $25,000 that he stole. It isn't funny to him, but it's funny how he took that money and run away with it.

Jerry "Peanuts" Gaines, Warren County, July 20, 2009

ORIGIN OF AMERICAN SHERIFFS

This is a story about Big Six Henderson. I knew Big Six and just loved him. They had a car ring theft here in Bowling Green several years ago. I was already sheriff then. I first met Big Six when he was an ATF man, and he was a marshal at that time.

People had come down there at the courthouse, as they had been told to be there by 1:00 and it was already 4:00. The judge was still in his chamber, and I'd never seen this done before. Big Six went in there and beat on that door and told that judge, "Get the hell out here and arraign these people that have been here since 1:00. I've got to go home."

I thought, "Good God," but the judge did come out.

But a judge can't do anything with a U.S. marshal because he is appointed by the president. See, the only one that can fool with a U.S. marshal is the president of the United States. Thus, a U.S. marshal is a national sheriff. They do the same things as local sheriffs do. He does it on the federal level. At first the U.S. marshal was sheriff, given the fact that the sheriff position is the oldest office in the United States.

The first American sheriff came over from England. The word *sheriff* came from the word *shire*, then they put *riff* on there. So they came from England, and they kind of kept the law around/in wherever they were, and they had swords in those days. The first sheriff here in America was John Nixon, and he delivered the Declaration of Independence to the British. The ones that wrote the Declaration of Independence said, "Why, they [the English] will kill us. Give it to the sheriff." Well, Sheriff John Nixon was the one that delivered it. Thus, they organized the sheriff's office like the ones in England.

Jerry "Peanuts" Gaines, Warren County, July 20, 2009

THE MEANEST SHERIFF

There is a sheriff from Phoenix, Arizona, who claims he's the meanest sheriff, but he ain't. He wants to make people think that. I saw him two weeks at the Sheriff's Convention in Florida. He knows me real good. He might be mean and active, but he ain't all that mean. I don't know why, but he just wants to be known as the meanest sheriff in the United States. He locks prisoners up in tents, feeds them a bologna sandwich. That's being mean to the prisoners.

A lot of people think the worst you can treat a prisoner, they like that. But I run our jail for six months when our jailer got into a little trouble. I found out that if you keep prisoners happy, keep them fed, and keep them watching their television and, as Judge Griffin used to say, "Keep the door locked so they can't get out," then you'll get along good with them. And I treated the prisoners like I did everybody else, and that's good.

We've never had any mean sheriffs in Kentucky that I know of. But in most towns in the state, the sheriffs and other law enforcement employees just don't get along as good as we do here in Bowling Green and Warren County. I just tell all our employees that as long as they acknowledge that I'm the king, everything runs fine. [*Laughter*]

Jerry "Peanuts" Gaines, Warren County, July 20, 2009

SHERIFF ON HORSEBACK

One sheriff in Taylor County got a DUI about two terms ago, and he patrolled on horseback! I knew him, and I went up through there one day. Taylor County is kind of off my beaten path here. I don't go through there to go anywhere. I bought a couple of truck tops for my pickup from them, and I've been there on other occasions. It's a beautiful town, but you just don't go through there. But when this sheriff got a DUI, he rode on his horse for about a year, I think. As long as he didn't have his license, he rode that horse!

Jerry "Peanuts" Gaines, Warren County, July 20, 2009

BEER BREAK

The Larue County sheriff arrested a drunk one night. He had one of those '75 Plymouth cars that had no screen. It had a switch like a toggle switch down on the dashboard that locked the door. He would just barely hit it and it would lock the door, but other people always had trouble with it.

He went out to this little jail one time and hit the switch by mistake. He walked up to ring the bell, and when he did he walked back to the car to get his prisoner out. When he got there he found the door locked, so he hollered at the prisoner, telling him to unlock the door.

The prisoner said, "What do you mean?"

The sheriff said, "The door is locked; unlock it."

The prisoner said, "You can't get in?"

He said, "No, I can't get in."

The prisoner said, "Are you sure you can't get in?"

The sheriff said, "Yeah, dang it; open the door!"

That fellow said, "Just a minute," then reached up and got the beer the sheriff had taken away from him. He sat there in the back seat and drank the whole six-pack before he opened the door. Then he said, "If I'm going to jail, I'm going to drink it all." [*Laughter*]

John E. Shipp, Taylor County, July 30, 2009

SHERIFF SHOT AND KILLED

During my lifetime in Johnson County we've had two sheriffs that were killed. One of them was Walter Meeks, who was twenty-five years old, and at that time he was the youngest sheriff ever elected in Kentucky. He was killed November 26, 1966, the year I graduated from high school. He was a young barber in the area.

As sheriff, he was serving what was at that time called a lunacy warrant. He walked up to this guy that he knew really well. Our present county judge is Tucker Daniel, and he was a good friend of the sheriff. Tucker came to the sheriff's office that day to visit his friend. The sheriff told him he was going to serve this warrant, and told him who the guy was, that there was no problem, so he asked Tucker to walk out there with him.

So the sheriff, a deputy, and Tucker Daniel went out to this guy's house on Route 40, just outside of Paintsville. To get up to the house there was a kind of steep incline that you had to walk up in order to get to the house. Tucker told me that as they were walking up the hill, all three of them were just talking, and that you could look up and see the house.

As they got near the top of the bank, the door come open and a shotgun barrel come out. The sheriff was standing in front of Tucker, and a deputy was standing beside the sheriff. Tucker said he saw the gun, and just about the time he wanted to say anything, the gun went off. Being on a steep incline like they were on, Tucker said his head was down two or three feet below the sheriff. The sheriff received a full blast from the gun, right up in his face. The shots hit the deputy also.

The sheriff was back on [chasing] him, and they all went down the hill. Of course, they stopped their vehicles along the way, and law enforcement was called.

They were building a new version of U.S. 23 through Paintsville at the time. I was eighteen years old at the time, but had no idea what was happening over on the old highway route out of Paintsville. Cars were lined up on the side of the road across Paint Creek. There were probably some three or four thousand feet between these two highways.

I remember stopping, and people said there was gunfire over there. You could see police cars coming into the area, and one was officer was Jack Musice, who was a state trooper in the area. They shot tear gas into the house. There were shots exchanged, but they were shots of tear gas, and from them going into the house. As the sheriff approached the house, he was struck and fatally wounded by a shotgun blast.

The story says that the assailant then committed suicide, and was later found dead inside his house. But whether or not he committed suicide has always been a question.

William D. Witten, Johnson County, August 7, 2008

KILLED IN THE LINE OF DUTY

Another sheriff that was killed was Cecil Eugene Cyrus. He was in his third term as sheriff when he was killed March 19, 1992. He was the first sheriff in the twentieth century to serve more than one term. The first time I ran for sheriff I ran against Gene, and he defeated me.

He had a guy in court, and I think it was his case. It was child molestation they were dealing with. During the break for lunch the accused guy somehow got away and went back to his home.

Upon hearing that, Gene immediately got in his car and went to a section off Highway 580 here in Johnson County. Gene and a deputy got out of their car, and as Gene approached upon the porch this guy stuck a shotgun out the door and shot Gene in the face and killed him.

William D. Witten, Johnson County, August 7, 2009

Close Call

In 1950 in Lawrence County Vessie Workman was elected sheriff. That year he confiscated three gallons of moonshine whiskey when raiding his fifteenth still during his first year in office. Vessie's daughter is presently my office manager in Johnson County.

There was a robbery in Fort Gay, West Virginia, in some sort of a store's gas station. Sheriff Workman had gotten the details on this guy, who was actually from Paintsville, and the sheriff had thought that he saw this guy, so he approached him. They were having some sort of town celebration or something there in Louisa, Lawrence County. So the sheriff approached this guy, and when he got up close to him, this guy pulls a .32 pistol and shot him two times in the chest.

The sheriff then whirled around to try to get away from this guy, and this guy shoots him in the back. So he gets shot a total of three times, but the sheriff did not die.

There was a doctor there, and they got the sheriff to Huntington, West Virginia, and he stayed in the hospital for several months.

The fellow that shot him spent twenty-one years in prison.

William D. Witten, Johnson County, August 7, 2009

Santa Claus Makes an Arrest

There was a sheriff in Whitley County whose name was Dick Vermillion. He was a good friend of mine. I think we'd served on the board of directors of the Kentucky Sheriffs' Association a few times together.

Dick told me he had had a warrant for a fellow for about a year and was trying to find him. Dick said, "Fuzzy, I can't find that fellow, and the people are down on me, thinking I'm not looking."

Come to find out, Dick was a very innovative fellow. He heard this fellow's family was holding a Christmas party and the man was coming in. "Wonder how I can get him? I think I've decided to go there as Santa Claus," Dick said.

So he dressed up in a Santa Claus suit and went to the place where they were having the party, knocked on the door, and that fellow opened the door. Then the fellow said, "Why, here's old Santa Claus. Come right on in, Santa Claus."

Since they had all been drinking, Santa Claus was able to walk right in, put handcuffs on the man, tell him he was under arrest, and cart him off to jail.

Charles E. "Fuzzy" Keesee, Pike County, August 7, 2009

Sheriff Honored

Jim Hill was sheriff of Wayne County. He has passed away, and his son was sheriff after he was sheriff. When I first started being sheriff in 1990, I didn't know anything about the sheriff's office over there. I had been deputy sheriff about six months or a year, then I got elected as sheriff.

I called around, and Mr. Hill was really a very nice person. He sent his secretary over here to my office for one week to help me and my secretary out, showing her mostly what to do in the office and helping us get by in everything else. After that he also told me if I needed any help, or needed help for my secretary again, just let him know and he'd send his secretary back to us again.

Mr. Hill really helped me a bunch, and I couldn't do anything to repay him.

I think he had been shot and/or stabbed once or twice. He was widely recognized as a sheriff. At Pigeon Forge, Tennessee, where they've got Sheriff Buford Pusser down there in a museum, they've also got Mr. Jim Hill's autobiography information in there also.

Cathy [his girlfriend] and I stopped there one time and went in and read Hill's autobiography, and it tells that he had been shot once or twice, and stabbed, in the line of duty.

I don't know why they featured him at this museum in Tennessee, but he was a very good sheriff, and a very active sheriff. He was well known and appreciated.

James Pruitt, Cumberland County, August 10, 2009

Empty Office

When I left the sheriff's office the only thing I took out of that office was some plaques I had on the wall and my personal files. So I walked out of there and left everything else. But when I first took over as sheriff and went into the office, there was only one paperclip in there, and it was laying on the counter. That's the only thing that was in that office!

Well, I decided to keep that paperclip, and did keep it for a long time, but I put it in my pocket and kept it there for awhile, but now it's probably down at my house.

Harold E. Tingle, Shelby County, August 14, 2009

Gun Needed?

After I was sheriff here in Shelby County, one guy came to me and said, "Do you remember when so-and-so was there?"

I said, "Yeah, I remember him way back."

He said, "I called him one night and he said there was something going on at his place. A car had pulled in, but it wasn't a threat to us."

The sheriff asked him, "I guess you want me to come over there, so do I need to bring my gun?"

That was an outstanding citizen that told me this. But he didn't tell whether or not the sheriff brought his gun! [*Laughter*]

I thought kind of stuff like that was funny. These early sheriffs had some interesting stories.

Harold E. Tingle, Shelby County, August 14, 2009

Dead Squirrel

Sometime between 1989 and 1990, three lonely patrolmen were directing traffic where an accident had taken place. Officer Keith Broughton, now Sergeant Broughton with the Woodford County Sheriff's Office, noticed this poor dead squirrel that was as flat as a pancake. Ironically, its rigor mortis also resembled Sheriff Loren "Squirrel" Carl's squirrel mascot.

So the three amigos, which included myself, Broughton, and Ricky Vaught (now Sergeant Vaught with the WCSO) took the dead squirrel and placed it in the window of the sheriff's office. Of course, the three of us found this wildly humorous.

Later on, while working with Sheriff John "Bear" Coyle in 2005, we were all talking in the office about the practical jokes we used to play. Little did we know that the dead squirrel was assigned to then deputy

John Coyle to investigate the possibility of a death threat. Coyle took the dead animal, placed it in a can, and delivered it to the state crime lab in Frankfort. He did this to determine if the animal was poisoned or killed.

While talking, when we said something about the squirrel, Sheriff Coyle yelled, "What the hell, I still have an open case on that!"

Needless to say, the entire office burst into uncontrollable fits of laughter!

Wayne "Tiny" Wright, Woodford County, September 15, 2009

GOAT POOP

Back in 1996, a local farmer called Sheriff Coyle and complained that some goats of his neighbors had eaten three acres of tobacco. When I heard what had supposedly taken place, I said, "No way; I'll have to see this for myself."

The sheriff and I went to the farmer's property, and when we arrived, sure enough, some goats had eaten three acres of tobacco, row for row. You couldn't have mowed it better with a lawn mower. Well, the goats left little pellets of evidence there on the ground. Sheriff Coyle began collecting some of the evidence, and I asked him what he planned to do with it. He told me he was going to take it to the lab. I informed him that I didn't think he needed to take it to the lab in order to determine if it was poop.

Upon leaving the farm, I expelled gas in his vehicle. Not a word was uttered as I noticed Sheriff Coyle twitching his nose and smelling his hands. I opened the door of the moving vehicle and fell out, rolling with laughter. I asked him, "Does it smell like poop?"

He replied, "You son of a bitch!"

Wayne "Tiny" Wright, Woodford County, September 15, 2009

CORRUPT SHERIFF

We never had very much moonshine making in the Kenton County area, but a lot of it was bought here, as some people were making it in other places. When I was a kid in Ft. Mitchell, which is a very upper-middle-class area, there were three saloons in Ft. Mitchell. There was the Kentucky Tavern, Greyhound Grill, and across the street was my dad's shop and the Saddle Club.

Back in the 1940s nobody had air-conditioning, thus all windows and doors were open in the summer, and you could walk down the street and hear the tote board being called and so on. Gambling was wide open.

Another reason why my dad didn't want me to go into law enforcement was that he had so many of these guys that were on the take. During the war he bought recapped tires from a fellow by the name of Wop [a nickname] Berndt in Covington. So my dad goes down there to get some tires, and sees all these signs—"Wop Berndt for Sheriff" and all kinds of paraphernalia around it posted everywhere.

Dad says, "Wop, why are you spending so much money on a job that pays only about $4,000 a year?"

He looked at Dad and said, "Why, Charlie, it's worth $400,000 or $500,000 cash every year."

My dad was shocked. Wop won the election!

Wop never worked hard after that, except that he bought some saloons later. I'm sure it was profitable!

Charles Lee "Chuck" Korzenborn, Kenton County, September 17, 2009

Three Wise Thoughts

I hadn't been sheriff very long when this took place, just about one week. Sheriff Carl Meece of Casey County had been sheriff for something like four terms, and was county judge one term. He came over to see me, and we were sitting around talking. I said, "Well, Carl, you've been sheriff for a long time, so what advice would you have for me?"

He thought for a moment, then said, "First thing, don't make your county judge or fiscal court mad," then he said, "Don't make your newspapers and radio stations mad," and lastly he said, "Don't run over an innocent person getting to two drunks fighting."

Larry L. Bennett, Russell County, September 18, 2009

Three-Term Sheriff

I ran for the office of sheriff in Todd County primarily because I had been involved in law enforcement off and on through my adult life from age twenty-one. I served as special deputy or deputy, constable, city police officer, or in the sheriff's office in one way or another.

I saw things that I thought needed to be changed, and I don't like politics, but unfortunately they are the things you have to work with in order to try to make the change in the local government. The most significant thing that I've seen across the years with the many, many sheriffs that I have known—and I known all the sheriffs dating all the way back to Robert Miller Jr., who took office January 1, 1966, for his first term, and that was back when you couldn't succeed yourself. He had two sheriffs elected between him, so he was the only person elected as sheriff for three terms. He is the only person elected as sheriff for three terms in the history of the county, as far as I can research.

W. D. "Billy" Stokes, Todd County, September 17, 2009

OLD DAYS

We've had a law officer in the city of Elkton that got abducted, and he was injured pretty severely. Three people wound up serving time over what happened. There was a manhunt for him, and thank goodness I seen what was going on before I was old enough to be in law enforcement.

I don't think I've ever seen that many police officers in our county at one time working and looking for a police officer that had been abducted and injured severely. It took some time before they finally found him. But I don't think I've ever seen the Kentucky State Police and the Christian County Sheriff's Office, the Hopkinsville Police Department, Logan County Sheriff's Office, the Muhlenberg County Sheriff's Office, and even Montgomery County, Tennessee, sending people up to get him. That was in awe for me to see that many law enforcement officials come together.

So that shows the bond that police officers have for one another. We disagree frequently on a lot of items. Some of us may be Democrats, and some may be Republicans; and some of us may be all different races, all different creeds, all different genders, and everything, but when it comes down to it, you have to take care of your own. Doing that means a lot to another police officer. So what is needed is trying to take care of your own before something happens—in other words, trying to prevent something.

The police community in Todd County is economically struggling right now insofar as law enforcement is concerned. It has created some bitterness, especially with me having to refuse to take loans and having to lay off deputies. I can also see a rift between me and the state police. For example, our county is located in the corner of the Post Two District of the Kentucky State Police. Well, it takes them a long time to get down there when they have only one or two men out, and there is nobody in our county.

Another platform that I ran on dealt with certified officers. We've come a long way since the days of constables, deputies, and sheriffs—Earl Johnson, Carlos Abney, Doug Bouiseau, and Robert Miller Jr. One of the familiar statements that I remember since being knee high to a grasshopper was spoken by one of these men. If he could, he would go every time he was called, but would frequently say to the caller, "Have you got a gun?" Then his next words out of his mouth would be, "Well, shoot the son of a bitch."

Well, one time that sheriff got called in by the judge William S. Jones, judge in Todd and Logan County. Rumor has it that Judge Jones called the accused sheriff into court and said, "Sheriff, did you tell him to shoot him?"

The way I've heard it, the sheriff responded, "You're damn straight I did, Judge."

So the judge said to him, "Now, Sheriff, you can't be telling this to people."

In today's world, should something like that go on, I like to look at where we came from and where we're at now, and I like to have a vision as to where we're going to go.

W. D. "Billy" Stokes, Todd County, September 17, 2009

Inspiration

In Todd County we would have music parties when I was young, and my grandfather, Lucian Stokes, played the banjo. Street Butler would play, and so would Rob Shanklin from around Allegre. Earl Johnson played the guitar. Several of the others would get together from time to time, but those were the main ones that gathered to have music parties. These events were what inspired me to look at law enforcement. Earl Johnson was especially significant.

W. D. "Billy" Stokes, Todd County, September 17, 2009

Sheriff's Idol

Back when I took office they didn't have all these schools. My idol of a sheriff is Buford Pusser, a Tennessean. My mother knew him personally down in the Jackson area. He was filmed and got to be well known. Not because he was so mean, but because he wanted to see justice done in a fair and equal way. Following after him, I tried to treat everybody the way I'd want to be treated. I think that's the way he looked at it.

I'm in a Republican county, but I'm a Democrat. Nonetheless, I was elected four terms as sheriff—three four-year terms and one five-year term. So, I had to be doing something right for the people in this county in order for them to keep me as sheriff.

Qulin K. Escue, Grayson County, September 22, 2009

SHERIFF JUNE BUG

They used to tell a lot of stories about Junior Henderson, a sheriff who wasn't really law enforcement oriented. He was an old foxhunter, and he also had a college degree, but he never taught school because he didn't want to work. He was lazy!

His nickname was June Bug, and it was claimed that the way he got that name was when his dad sent him out to get the june bugs out of the potato garden. In a few minutes the father went out there and found him in the potato patch, asleep. So, that's how he came up with the name Junior "June Bug" Henderson.

Junior was sheriff, but I don't remember the year.

Kenneth Lee Morris, Butler County, October 11, 2009

EASYGOING SHERIFF

I remember Wallace Dockery when they told a story on him one time. He was bad about not carrying a gun. Well, on one occasion he was sent out to arrest this guy, and this guy had a gun when Wallace got there. The building was dark, and when Wallace walked in the guy made some kind of comment. Well, Wallace stuck his finger up against the man's chest and told him to put his hands up. Believe it or not, that fellow thought Wallace had a gun, but he didn't have a gun!

Wallace was a nice fellow. He knew people, he'd meet people, and I've heard him say a lot of times, "A drunk can cuss and call you names, but if you'll talk to him, treat him right to get him to jail, then most of the time he'll be laughing."

That's the kind of philosophy he had. He was sheriff from 1974 to '78. He was just a character, but he was a really good guy, easygoing when dealing with people.

His chief deputy, which I also worked for also, was James "Big Jim" Phelps. Big Jim was from Leonard Oak, and that's where he lives, even now.

Kenneth Lee Morris, Butler County, October 11, 2009

Turn on the Whooper—Sheriff's Coming

This is a story told to me by a guy that worked for one of the sheriffs years and years ago. He said they had gotten a call about a fight here in the county, so he jumped in the car with the sheriff and started to this community. Then the sheriff put his hand over on this guy and said, "Whoa, whoa, slow down."

So he slowed down and was trying to figure out why they were slowing down. The sheriff explained to him, said, "Look, they'll fight it out a little bit, so let them do it. By the time we get there they'll be worn out. So when we show up, we'll be able to take care of the situation."

Back in those days a fight was a fight, a fistfight. Today a fight is more than likely going to take place with some kind of weapon.

To continue the story, this guy that was a deputy sheriff at that time told me, said, "We slowed down, took our time getting there. About the time we got into the community out in the county, the sheriff told me, 'Now, you turn that whooper on over there. I want them to know the sheriff is coming.'" (It was a siren, but he called it a whooper.)

That was how they responded to that call. They expected these two men who were fighting would be totally worn out by the time the officers got there. The sheriff said, "When we get there they will be worn out, and they won't want to mess with us. They'll be shocked, and we'll deal with it and take care of it."

The fellow who was driving said, "When we finally got close to the community, the sheriff looked over at me and said, 'Turn that whooper on, because I want them to know the sheriff is coming.'" Then he said, "So we turned the siren on and let them know we were coming, then we rolled in and took care of the problem."

That sort of thing worked back then. When you got there somebody might be taken to jail, others might not. But the sheriff settled it.

Mike Armstrong, Shelby County, November 6, 2009

SHERIFF SHOOTS TIRES

A few years back we had a sheriff here in Crittenden County who went to make an arrest for a gentleman who was in a restaurant right in the middle of town. The restaurant was right across from the courthouse here on Main Street. The sheriff went in to arrest this gentleman, and this guy had his small son with him. The sheriff told him that he had a warrant for him and was going to take him to jail. This guy said he is not going to jail.

So the sheriff said again, "Yeah, you are going to have to go."

Well, that guy jumped up and grabbed his son and started running out the door. He ran on out to his car and jumped into his car, and the sheriff is right behind him. And about the time the sheriff came out the door, the guy was getting ready to pull out and take off. The sheriff pulled out his duty weapon and started shooting and shot all four of the tires out on that guy's car.

The guy takes off and basically was riding on its rims. He was going south on Main Street, so the sheriff gets on the old radio that he had. He called these city policemen on the other side of town and started telling them, "I shot them down, boys, I shot them down."

Well, those officers got to thinking that he shot somebody, and that got them all tore up. But come to find out, the sheriff had just shot the tires on the car right in the middle of town in front of everybody.

Luckily, nobody was hurt, but that's been talked about for many years since then.

Wayne Agent, Crittenden County, November 3, 2009

BIG, TOUGH SHERIFF

I wouldn't change anything at all about my career. I would listen to stories from other sheriffs who served back in the past as they told about things they did. What they described was totally different from the way things are now. They told me that if they got word about somebody doing something bad, the sheriff or deputies would go out and get him, take him up in the woods somewhere and just wear him out, then bring him on back. That was like the Buford Pusser days. They'd "whoop" them, and would never have to go back again. They could do stuff like that back then.

When he [name withheld] was a deputy for another sheriff he was a prankster, and one time he picked up someone and hung him up on a coatrack in the clerk's office and left him hanging. He was a prankster, and was so big and strong you couldn't do nothing with him!

Tommy Sims was a sheriff that I've heard many stories about. He was a big guy and the strongest human being I've ever met. They used to tell me stories about when they were interviewing somebody. Tommy would take them up on the elevator and by the time they'd come back, they'd spit out everything. He said that they'd tell the truth, even if he didn't ask them the questions. He had that claw grip. He'd just take them downstairs, put the claw to them, then back up they'd come, and they'd spill the beans on everybody. Sims was just a mountain of a man. Either one of his hands were as big as both of our hands put together. He was just a big, big man. He was sheriff probably from 1982 until around 1989.

I worked with him two or three years, then he passed away in 1993 or '94. He was a good fellow, but if one of the officers got into a fight with someone, they wanted him to be there. He could take care of anything that turned into a fight!

LeeRoy Hardin, Boyle County, January 11, 2010

"Drive Slow"

Back then this old sheriff, John Sawyers, told me that when I would be going to a place where a man and his wife was arguing and complaining, and she called the law, "Drive slow." Usually it would be over by the time you'd get there, and if it's not over the way I would do it is to tell them, "If you want to get a warrant to lock him up, this will cost you some money. Why don't you wait until in the morning to call me, then I'll come and get him and get a warrant to get him?" Or, "Why not let him leave tonight to go to his mama's and daddy's or somewhere?" Well, the next morning they'd probably never call.

But now they rush as hard as they can go, and maybe two or three of them goes to a domestic. And back then I went slow to a domestic because they were usually over. Of course, they are different now.

Glynn Mann, Clinton County, February 8, 2010

Changing Times

One of the sheriffs we had here in Monroe County, Joe Petett, was a great big man. I had very high respect for him. He was sheriff when I was assistant police in the Tompkinsville City Police Department. We called him Ole Joe, and if he would come after you, he got you! He was goodhearted, but would put you in jail, and then he might give you money to get you out of jail under bond.

At that time you could do things like that, but they have really changed things now. We aren't allowed to sign people's bonds, because you are bonded. Back in those days you could do things you can't do today. And back then there were whittlers who whittled pieces of wood out here on the courthouse square, and they would tell old wartime stories and do things like that. These days things are more professional. We have to do a lot of paperwork when making arrests or doing investigations. It takes longer to do the paperwork than it does to do drug busts and things like that. And all accident reports, cash reports, incident reports, and other things what we do today has got to be on computers.

Jerry "Slick" Gee, Monroe County, March 18, 2010

SHERIFF'S SPEECHES

Bev McClendon, a former sheriff here in Monroe County, is one of the best political speakers I've ever heard. He doesn't talk like a politician, he talks the crazy stuff! In one speech he made: "I'm going to dam up the Cumberland River and send law and order back to Jimtown, Fountain Run, Coon Foot, Light Oak, Sulphur Lick, Mud Lick, Sand Lick."

Every speaking he made, whether he was on the radio or out in public, he always closed with that old Irish saying, "May the sun set on your head; may the wind blow at your back; may the rain warm your crops . . ." I mean you've got to hear it. He would always end with that saying. I loved his speeches, and Bev was a good sheriff.

He also talked about the times he and one of his deputies, "Redbone," were called out to Earl Brown's. Some woman had pulled a gun on them, but they said that Earl grinned the woman down. Bev said that after they got done Earl was still grinning. Bev said, "We've done got her, Earl. Why are you still grinning?"

Earl said, "I've grinned so much my jaws are locked." [*Laughter*]

Jerry "Slick" Gee, Monroe County, March 18, 2010

PURSUIT WITH MILK

This is a somewhat humorous story about another Powell County sheriff, Steve Bennett, who was actually killed in the line of duty in 1992. That was a couple of years even before I became a police officer. I happened to be listening to the scanner and he was on his way home. He had worked that night and on his way home had stopped by the store to get a gallon of milk. So, on his way home from the store he got a call and became engaged in a pursuit. He got after this ole boy he'd had problems with before. He knew him.

So, he was pursuing this ole boy in his vehicle and he hollered at our dispatch and they asked him if he was okay, where he was located at that time, and other things.

He told them, "I'm alright but we're headed up Highway 15 and I don't know whether I'm going to be able to keep up with him or not because I just stopped and bought a gallon of milk, and this gallon of milk is about to beat me to death in this cruiser!" See, he was pursuing this ole boy, and the milk container was just bouncing around on him. He wasn't sure whether he could keep up with the ole boy.

I thought that was funny, because I could see that milk sliding everywhere and beating him to death.

He was a real good person. I first met him while me and others were out housing tobacco, and he was running for sheriff at that time. He came to the barn where fifteen or twenty of us were working. He was wearing a big white shirt and was just cleaned up. He asked all of us to vote for him. He had drove up out there and parked his car, then come in and worked with us there in the barn for eight hours straight with that big clean white shirt on. He stayed there until we got the tobacco housed. He didn't have to do that, but that left a good impression on us. He didn't have to do that. He could have just asked for our vote and left. His shirt was plumb filthy when we got through working!

Danny Rogers, Powell County, March 27, 2010

Chapter 9

DANGEROUS OR FATAL EVENTS

This gripping and penetrating chapter highlights the grave dangers often faced by law enforcement officers in the line of duty. Included are accounts of sheriffs and others killed or wounded as they attempted to apprehend criminals or save the lives of the innocent. In other stories fatalities were narrowly avoided, as the potential danger was averted through the officers' actions.

Not all stories herein describe sheriffs in direct danger; many focus on crimes of murder, sometimes gruesome (such as the victim with his head cut off), sometimes heartbreaking (such as the two young boys killed by their own mother in a murder/suicide), but always heinous.

Interspersed throughout the tales below are personal accounts that defy easy description—that of the deputy who, after a harrowing experience on that date, forever afterward refused to work on Friday the 13th; the state trooper who, haunted by thoughts of the victim of a tragic accident, thought he saw her ghost; the sheriff who, called to the scene of a fatal traffic accident, discovered that the victim was his own young daughter.

SHERIFF AT GUNPOINT

One Christmas Eve which was during my first term as sheriff, I got a call in my office. That was a different and very small office I had at that time, as it was eight by ten feet. I felt like Nelson Mandela, who had been locked up for twenty-two years.

The call I'm talking about is about a fellow that had tied his girl-friend up and was going to get a gun to kill her. It was raining, so me and Deputy W. C. Cooper went on Dye-Ford Road, and when we got out to the house a porch was across the road. The fellow was a former deputy jailer who lived in Glasgow. He was driving a red and white Blazer, and when we got there that Blazer was back, and I said, "Oh, my God."

I went to knock on the door of the house, and he stepped out of the screen door and pointed a .38 right between my eyes. It looked like a howitzer cannon it was so big. Well, the good Lord told me to get to talking to him, keep talking to him.

About two weeks before he'd given me one of them little dachshund dogs, but his niece wanted it. I took it home with me and kept it one day, and he wanted it, so I gave it back to him to give to his niece. Well, he liked me for doing that. I kept saying, "You don't shoot me."

But he was right there with his gun between my eyes, so he said, "I am going to kill myself," and put the gun to his head.

Then I put my gun on him and started backing up. There wasn't a gutter on that house, so that water was running off in my face. I was just backing up. He went on back inside the house, and I heard a gun go off, and I thought, "Well, he's killed her."

We were setting there, and she came out crying and said, "He's in there." He had just shot in the floor, and I went in there and he said, "Take me to jail."

He gave me his gun, and he rode in the front seat with me and I brought him to jail. He said, "I'm glad it was you, Peanuts, instead of somebody else, that come and got me."

I said, "Well, I'm glad so, too."

Well, the judge come in on Christmas Day and let him out since he thought it was just a little family dispute. He went home to Glasgow, but the next Saturday me and my wife was going to watch our son play basketball up at Elizabethtown, and I got a call on the radio telling me that he had committed suicide. He killed himself.

That was very sad. Just think now; if he killed himself, he'd shoot me, too.

Jerry "Peanuts" Gaines, Warren County, July 20, 2009

BULLET HOLE

This is a humorous story about something that happened a long time ago. One night it was raining, and I had two other police officers in the car with me, and we were going to get something to eat. As we started to pull in, this car pulled right out in front of me. It was raining, but

I could see the way he went across the line that something was wrong with him. I wanted to check him out, so I turned my blue lights on.

He started driving faster, and we got up to about ninety miles an hour with my blue lights on. We went on up the road quite a distance, then he turned off onto a road going back towards Larue County. We called ahead to get him stopped where the road we were on met Highway 357. We were on Highway 728, then got on another road they were building, and it was still muddy.

We wandered around back on this muddy road, and I had to keep my windshield washers on to see where I was going. Well, I was watching the road, and all of a sudden this guy that was riding with me leaned out the window, and he shot with his pistol. I said, "Put that gun up. What are you doing?"

He put his gun up, and we went on and finally got the guy stopped. I jumped out and reached and got the driver's door, reached into the car and got hold of the guy and pulled him out of the car. Then I put him in my car.

I went around to get the other passenger out, and he was drunk. When I started to put him into my car, the other guy tried to jump out over both of us. Well, I had a little slapjack, so I hit that guy that was trying to get out, and the slapjack busted, and the buckshots all went in this other guy's face. He said, "Don't shoot me again. I've already been shot."

I said, "What?"

He said, "Yeah, I've been shot in the back."

I thought, "Oh, my God, this guy has done shot him." It turned out, I looked and he had a bullet hole in his back.

It turns out that he had escaped from the jail, and the jailer had shot him in the back, but it wasn't a high-power weapon because it didn't really hurt him.

Everything turned out okay, but it scared me to death when I saw the bullet hole. I thought the guy riding with me had shot him.

I never did shoot at anybody like that.

Deputy James Veluzat, Hart County, July 30, 2009

Deputy versus Door

We had a call about a guy barricaded in his house. It was said that he had a young child in there, and he was under the influence of alcohol and drugs. He was threatening to shoot people, so we go down. We had called the state police, and they had come and pretty much had the house surrounded, and he wasn't visible.

We had looked in one of the windows, and he was periodically coming back and forth in the living room, cursing, fussing, and other things. I thought, "If we get him back in the living room we'll kick this door in and run in there and get him."

I had this one deputy who was not a tall guy, but he was really muscular. So I and one deputy stood on each side of the door. The porch on this house was about eight foot in length. So the deputy backs up, and when that guy comes through the door we'd give the deputy the signal to hit that door, and when he knocks the door in we'll rush to the guy and handcuff him.

He takes off with both feet, hits that door, and when that door sprung open it throws him plumb off the porch out into the yard. At that point we give him no mind, and I had another guy to hit the door and got it open. The door sprung, and it was just like somebody jumping off of a diving board. We went in there later to check on him. Of course, it knocked the breath out of him. That was a more dangerous situation then than having him laying out in the yard.

That was kind of a humorous thing we're always kidding him about.

William D. Witten, Johnson County, August 7, 2009

Deputy Sheriff Shot and Killed

Thirty-one-year-old Roby Fairchild was a part-time deputy sheriff in Johnson County. On August 23, 1975, Deputy Fairchild pulled into a store on Route 201 at Sitka, Johnson County, to purchase a pack of cigarettes. After being informed that the store was closed, he started back to his car when he noticed two men and a woman sitting on the back of a car drinking beer.

The two men were arrested for being drunk in public. Fairchild became the object of an argument by a man and his wife. As Deputy Fairchild placed the two men in his vehicle, one of those with whom he had the argument opened fire from an apartment window over the store, striking and fatally wounding Deputy Fairchild.

The husband and wife were arrested and charged with murder.

William D. Witten, Johnson County, August 7, 2009

Crisis Averted

The subject person of this story barricaded himself in a barn in the Wiley Branch area, located off Kentucky 3224. Allegedly he had a weapon and had made three threats to shoot himself and others. I responded, and when I was on the scene I called for assistance from the Kentucky State Police Special Response Team. The father of the man we were there to arrest arrived, and was able to talk his son into surrendering.

William D. Witten, Johnson County, August 7, 2009

Shots Fired

A deputy and I were on the scene at a trailer on Brown Fork off Kentucky 1559, where shots had been fired. As we were going around the residence to get a visual look at the shooter, a gunshot was fired. The bullet came approximately one foot between myself and a deputy. As two deputies were going behind the trailer, the person they were looking for had broken out a window and was attempting to climb out. The deputies apprehended him without further incidence.

William D. Witten, Johnson County, August 7, 2009

A Final Shot

I received a call from Brian Fork, located off Kentucky 3214 in the Elna community, telling me that a fellow had been shooting at kids riding on bicycles. Initially, two deputies responded to the residence, and both of their vehicles were struck by gunfire. Along with other deputies from my office, I responded for needed assistance.

After arriving I attempted to talk to the subject, and he began firing upon me. I immediately got down in a ditch, and the weeds where I had been standing were waving from gunshots being fired. He also fired at a building where a deputy was seeking cover, and bullets hit six inches above him.

We then called for Kentucky State Police Special Response Team assistance. After several hours of negotiations and pleas to talk him out, he turned music down and yelled, "One more shot and you can come in."

He turned music back up and a single shot rang out. Moments

later the State Police Response Team entered the house and found the subject had fatally shot himself.

William D. Witten, Johnson County, August 7, 2009

POTENTIAL DANGER

I had a friend who was having trouble with his family. I knew this gentleman very well. I responded to his house on Kentucky 3387 in the Chandlersville community to execute a warrant. He was in the bedroom when I went into the house. I yelled for him to come out of the house, but he wouldn't.

I then proceeded back to the bedroom, where he was sitting on the edge of the bed. I noticed his hands were creeping slowly down the side of the bed, so I directed a deputy to subdue him. After he was taken into custody we found a loaded .38-caliber pistol between the mattresses.

William D. Witten, Johnson County, August 7, 2009

FATAL ENCOUNTER WITH MOONSHINER

In August 1921, revenue agents with the U.S. Treasury Department responded to a call from Slate Branch, located off Kentucky 172, which was a notorious site for moonshiners. Federal agents and Paintsville policemen closed in on the location of a possible moonshine still. About twenty yards away from the operation, shots rang out, shooting and fatally wounding a federal agent and one of the Paintsville police officers. The other police officer was wounded but lived.

William D. Witten, Johnson County, August 7, 2009

FRIDAY THE 13TH

I had a deputy who was an intelligent young man, and he stayed with me several years. At one time he was my chief deputy and was a good, well-trained law enforcement officer. We received a call one day on a gentleman that had gotten out of prison at Eddyville on an appeal bond. As I understood it, a dentist in that area had put up an appeal bond for this fellow to get a new trial.

I don't know how he floated around and ended up in our area, but the inmate rented a motel room just right over the Virginia line, not very far from Elkhorn City, Kentucky state line. The motel clerk looked up one morning and saw this fellow carrying a TV out of his motel room and putting it in his car.

The motel clerk called the Elkhorn City Police Department, which was located close by the motel. So the chief of police went to investigate, and he obtained a description of the vehicle that the fellow was driving. The thief had gotten across the state line into Elkhorn City, and when the chief of police had found him, he had run his car into a ditch because he was intoxicated, probably on drugs.

When the chief of police got out of his cruiser, the inmate overpowered the chief, took his gun and his car. Somebody came along and picked the chief of police up, and hauled him to get back up to where he needed to go.

Soon after a young couple came by and saw the chief of police's car. "Well, that's the chief's car. We should stop to see if we could help him," they said.

At this point the inmate that had picked the chief of police up stepped out of the vehicle and took the young couple hostage. He jumped back in the back seat of their car and held the gun on the young lady, forcing them to drive him around to different places. They got here close to Pikeville, in a little area we call Shelbiana.

My deputy, who was Walter Petot, wasn't aware at this time that they were in our area. Petot had the headlight that had gone out on his cruiser, so he had pulled into a garage to get his headlight fixed. This young couple had pulled in there, and the inmate had passed out in the back seat of their car. He had held his gun on that young lady for a long time, so she was very eager to jump out of the car, and ran over to the deputy. The deputy asked her what happened, and she told him that she had been held hostage by this fellow. Deputy Sheriff Petot immediately went out to investigate since he was in sight of it.

The young boy that was with the young lady had gotten into a restroom there in the garage, and the inmate was trying to kick the door in so he could get to the boy. My deputy hollered at the fellow and told him to drop the gun, but that man then shot at him and missed him. Then the deputy shot in the air, trying to scare the inmate. Of course, it didn't, and the inmate shot at the deputy again, grazing the top of the cruiser. Then the deputy returned fire on the inmate and hit him in the lower groin. As the inmate went down the deputy ran to him, but the man still had a gun in his hand and tried to shoot at the deputy. But

Deputy Petot rushed over to him in time to set his foot on his hand and take his gun away from him.

The fellow wasn't killed at that time, so they loaded him up in an ambulance and took him to Pikeville Medical Center. And at that time we had not put a guard on duty because we didn't think it would be necessary, since we also thought he would be confined there for awhile. That same day the inmate was admitted, though, he had gotten a pair of scissors from the nurse and tried to stab her. After that we immediately put guards on him. He lived about ten days after the shootout, but because he would not accept medical treatment he later died.

That happened on April Fool Day of that year, Friday the 13th.

The deputy was really disturbed about it, so we asked the grand jury to investigate. I knew the deputy had done everything he was supposed to do by the law. So the grand jury ended up commending the deputy for probably saving the lives of those two young people.

When I got there on the scene the day that happened, the deputy was as white as a sheet. It had scared him, you know, so from then on he would never work on Friday the 13th. Just as sure as the Friday the 13th came on Friday, he was off duty. He worked with us a long time after that, and he is now working with the State Insurance Department as a fraud investigator and is doing a good job, but he still doesn't work on Friday the 13th.

Charles E. "Fuzzy" Keesee, Pike County, August 7, 2009

Fatal Shooting

I had this fellow I knew very well and we received a call, as well as did the state police, telling us that there was a domestic problem in a very remote area of the county at that time. The report states this fellow had shot his wife and that the state police had gotten on the scene before my deputy and I got there. I only had one deputy on duty that was close enough at the time to take with me, so we proceeded to go to the area.

The husband didn't kill his wife; he'd just shot her, maybe in the arm or shoulder. But they had two small children, and maybe other children as well.

The state police was already there, but when they arrived the perpetrator had barricaded himself in the house, so the state police were trying to get him to come out. When my deputy and I got there he was still in the house.

There were several police officers there that day, and at that time we had a county detective force, so one of the county detectives, Jack Banks, was there also. He had worked for me at one time or another, and was a good police officer. When we got up there in that area I told my deputy that was with me, "If we're not careful, someone will be killed here today." My deputy is deceased now, but he would tell you that as soon as I looked to see what was going on, I knew that there was a good possibility that someone would be killed there that day.

My deputy and I went over to the area of the house. There was a state police lieutenant there who had been on a loud speaker asking this fellow to come out of the house. Of course, the fellow didn't come out, so I asked the lieutenant if I could speak with him. He had always called me "Fuzzy" and he did know me.

The fellow did drink alcohol. I told him who I was, then called him by his nickname and asked him to come out. I told him, "You'll not be hurt. We'll take care of you."

Still he didn't come out. Well, a state police officer had walked up to the door and knocked on it, but he still didn't come out. I also walked up there, knocked on the door, and hollered at him, asking him to come out, but he wouldn't.

After that I walked around to the back of the house, and while doing that I could hear him firing shots there in that thin house. Bullets were coming through the house and even through one of the windows. The state police then decided it was time to use tear gas. When they did you could hear those kids crying in there, which was so sad to hear. To save his kids from a lot of problems, their father had probably covered them up with bed coverings. I didn't think it was a good idea that the state police put tear gas in there. I thought time would be better if we waited him out.

There was a constable that lived near that home, and the constable's brother had once shot this fellow that had barricaded. The constable's brother brought him in, and he turned himself in, then was sent to the penitentiary but didn't stay too long. The constable that brought him in was a good, honest person. I told them, "I think we ought to wait until the constable gets here. He knows this fellow, and maybe he can get him out."

When the constable couldn't get him out, one of the state police officers put on a gas mask, went up to the house and cracked open a door and looked in. At that moment the fellow shot the state policeman right through that gas mask into his mouth. We got him out of there, got him to the hospital, and he's probably still on duty.

My deputy and I walked back to our car, as I wanted to get on the radio. A state trooper came by. Butch was his nickname, and I knew him really well because I had worked with him. He had his bulletproof vest on, and as he walked by me I said, "Butch, be awful careful, because he's firing in the house."

Butch walked down into the same area from which I had just left just minutes before. He hadn't been there but fifteen minutes when I heard him holler and saw him fall. The bullet had hit Butch in the lower groin area. I had thought the other trooper would certainly die, as I didn't know he had recovered. But that wasn't the way it was. The other trooper, Butch, was taken to Kentucky University Hospital in Lexington, where he passed away a few days later.

Charles E. "Fuzzy" Keesee, Pike County, August 7, 2009

GRISLY MURDER

On December 13, 1995, Pike County sheriff's detective, Richard Ray, received information about a rumor of a missing man in the Virgie area of Pike County. The informant said that it is being told that Monkeytown resident Everett Lee Hall, known as T Hall, age forty-seven, had been missing for about nine months. The rumor also was that Hall had been killed and buried somewhere in the area. An inquiry at the Virgie post office found that Hall's Social Security and workmen's compensation checks were being picked up at the post office by Hall's ex-wife.

Copies of the cashed checks were obtained and the ex-wife was interviewed. She said that Hall had left back in March 1995 with a woman and told her that she could have his checks which she had been cashing. The checks amounted to $1,800 per month. She had also re-married. Relatives and neighbors of Hall were interviewed, and none knew where he was but suspected that he was dead.

Early in 1996 the ex-wife and her new husband were arrested for arson. The new husband had heard talk about Mr. Hall and where his body might be. With his information, and help from Mr. David Phillips and his mine inspectors, Hall's headless corpse was found fifteen hundred feet back in a coal mine on Caney Creek. The mine had been closed for fifty years, and Hall and his brother-in-law had been getting house coal from it to sell.

New information indicated that the ex-wife and her boyfriend killed Mr. Hall and put his body in the mine. During an interview she admitted that Hall was shot and killed in his home at Monkeytown and placed in the mine by the killer and her brother. Her sister helped her clean up the bloody crime scene. She gave information about the killer and his location in Florida. A warrant was obtained for him, and we contacted a detective in Titusville, Florida. They quickly arrested the killer there and he admitted to the murder.

He was brought back to Pikeville, Kentucky, and interviewed. He told of putting Hall's body in the mine and putting off dynamite to cave in the mine, with no success. He later went to cut off the head, hands, and feet, but became sick after cutting off the head, thus did not cut off the hands and feet. Later he went inside again to set the body on fire with oil and gasoline, but changed his mind and went back to Florida.

He said that he took the victim's head back to the victim's ex-wife in a bucket, but did not know what she did with it. We heard that she had burned it on the mountain above the victim's home, but we could not locate any trace of it. As to the recovery of the victim from the mine, I personally, along with Detective Richard Ray, Kentucky State Police detective Kenneth Slone, Coroner Morris, Dr. Emily Craig from Frankfort, and the mine inspectors recovered the body. The body was wrapped in a blanket and waterbed bladder with wire around it. We found where oil and gasoline, and old wooden mine timbers, had been piled on him.

The victim was identified by old X-rays and a partially missing foot from a mower accident. This was fifteen hundred feet inside the old mine, and we crawled over roof fall rocks to get in and out. If the killer had set this on fire, the mine might still be burning.

In Pike Circuit Court, both the killer and ex-wife were sentenced to life in prison for murder. The ex-wife's brother and sister were sentenced to several years in prison for tampering with physical evidence, but were probated.

Charles E. "Fuzzy" Keesee, Pike County, August 7, 2009

Don't Tell Nobody Nothing

There was a lady that lived right down below us there at home on Pea Ridge, and she had got out and was walking through the woods and found a moonshine still. What happened was told to me by Mom and Dad both. She reported it to the law, and law officers came out and got the still and blew it up like barrels and busted them, and everything.

They found out who told on her, and they found her out in the woods walking. Then they put her face down into the hot mash to kind of punish her. It didn't kill her, but it did disfigure her face for a long time.

Back then in those days, if you saw anything illegal you didn't say anything about it. You didn't tell anybody. And that lady that got her face burned didn't say anything about any other stills, or anything, after that happened.

I can remember a lot of times when people passing through there would stop to ask where someone lived, but very seldom you got anybody that told you where anybody lived back then, because they were afraid these strangers might be out there to do wrong things.

You didn't tell nobody nothing back in those days!

James Pruitt, Cumberland County, August 10, 2009

Domestic Shooting

I had two deals with people shooting at us. We were on west Highway 90 over in the Tooley subdivision, close to the Dutch Creek area. This man and his wife were having domestic problems, and we had been there a few times on domestic calls. This one time, the man had snapped and held her hostage and threatened to kill her.

So we went over there, and the guy shot at us two or three times, and he hit one of the city police cars once or twice. Of course, we got the state patrol officer and a SWAT team to come in. We were there with him probably three or four hours. His wife finally got a chance to get to the door, so she started out the door. He shot her sort of in the back there, then he shot at us a few times, and that was it. The SWAT team took him out. She was injured, but none of us were.

James Pruitt, Cumberland County, August 10, 2009

Quick-Draw Deputy

When I was a deputy, one time I went to arrest a guy under a warrant, and I knew the problem could be valid because he was aggravating. I had another officer with me, and I won't say what kind of officer he was. Anyway, we went to arrest this man and the other officer pulled his gun out and provoked him. That made me think that I'd probably have to shoot that guy. I pulled my gun out, and that was the first or second time I had ever done that, but I didn't shoot.

Why that officer pulled out his gun, I don't know. Things like that happen, and sometimes you don't have any control over it. Anyway, I finally got the other fellow calmed down, and I never did bring my gun up. He was the type of guy that both of us officers couldn't handle him, but he calmed himself down and never did shoot.

We did arrest that fellow after we got him calmed down, and there was no problem. In all honesty, I can't remember why we went to arrest him, but he had been in a little trouble, etc. His life ended up when he got killed in the penitentiary. However, he never did have any hard feelings against me, and I had none toward him.

Harold E. Tingle, Shelby County, August 14, 2009

PERCEIVED THREAT

An event that really scared me was the year when all the churches got together and had a religious thing at the fairgrounds. There was a really big crowd of people there. One of the preachers came to me and told me that his wife was at the church cleaning it, and there was another vehicle up there.

So I went up to that church, went back there and approached this man and woman, then got to looking at their license plate but couldn't figure it all out. It was a California plate on their car, and this was during the time when a lot of risks were going on through the whole country. I can't remember what year that was when I went to that church, but I kept looking at the license because I couldn't read some little letters on the bottom of the plate.

I called for a backup because I wanted somebody else there, because I was by myself. I had a bad feeling about the whole situation. Anyway, I asked them some questions, then I'd continue the conversation and was getting down to reading the little bitty number on a little sticker at the bottom of the license plate. If I stood up I couldn't read it. Well, that guy made a threatening move against me, so I reached and got my gun in my hand, but never did bring it out of the holster.

The lady who was there with him said, "That's enough." I figured she was talking to him, or maybe both of us! But I never did bring my gun out of the holster, because in your mind you knew it was something you couldn't go to court and say that he had threatened me. But in my mind he was making a threatening gesture to me.

Just as soon as this woman said that, this guy's personality changed completely. So everything was alright after that.

About that time another sheriff's car drove up. Anyway, we kept running and running the numbers on the plate, and finally got them all figured out. But there was something about that deal that was threatening, so I was probably lucky. I'll never forget that.

Harold E. Tingle, Shelby County, 2009

DEPUTIES BUSTED

During the 2009 ice storm, patrolling the rural areas of the county, delivering meals, checking on those without power, and ensuring that the roads were clear of falling limbs were major problems to deal with. Deputy Sutherland was en route to get Deputy Vaught, and on the way back a limb had fallen both behind and in front of them, thus blocking the road. They decided to try to drive around one of the limbs, but instead they drove over an embankment, went sliding down, and almost turned the vehicle over.

I was on my way toward them, cutting limbs as I traveled. Periodically I would ask them to describe their location, then I would tell them mine. Little did I know they had slid over the embankment, as neither of them wanted to tell me they had slid off the road.

They had called a local farmer that lives on the road and asked him to come and get them with a tractor and chain to pull them back on the road before I got to them and learned of their predicament. The farmer pulled them back onto the road, and they both agreed not to tell me what happened.

Little did they know I would be talking to this farmer later that day. He commented that they were lucky not to have gone through the fence and damaged the vehicle. The farmer is also a county magistrate, so he was glad the county didn't have to pay the expense of paying to fix the vehicle.

When I confronted the two deputies, they burst into laughter, knowing they had been busted.

Wayne "Tiny" Wright, Woodford County, September 15, 2009

CONTRACT ON INFORMANTS

The biggest life-threatening event really happened to me before I was sheriff. My grandfather and my dad opened up an automotive repair shop in 1934 in Ft. Mitchell. We'd been there for four generations. My son and I were running it later on, and we got to working on the Alcohol-Tobacco-Firearms agency's vehicles and some of their equipment. One day the ATF agent we dealt with most of the time came in to pick up a shotgun we had repaired for him. It was a pretty spring day, and we were standing around talking. Also, one of their motorcycles was parked out front and we were to do some work on it.

These two fellows came in on a couple of Harleys, and one was kind of clean cut; the other kind of rowdy and had a loud mouth. He came in and said, "I need a lid for my bag." He had lost the top of his saddlebag, and he saw our Harley setting there, so he figured we might have a way of getting something for him.

The agent that was standing by me—we were talking about something else—and he started picking up some clues that these were bad actors, so he started talking to the one that needed something and asked him, "Where are you all headed?"

The fellow said, "Oh, we're going down to Tennessee, and me and Mr. Smith and Wesson have got a bunch of dope we're going to sell down there to make a little money."

The agent was embarrassed enough, and his handgun was in his car located about a hundred feet away. My son said something like, "Well, you can probably get the top of that bag in Boone County," then gave him an address which was really not valid.

That got them out of there, then the agent got on his radio and had Boone County officers to pull these two cycles over on a traffic charge. They found $60,000 worth of marijuana in the two bikes and quite a large amount of cash. They were arrested and wound up in jail.

About two weeks went by, and the agent came in and said to my son and me, "I want you guys to carry weapons when you are out of your area. I just found out there is a $10,000 contract on each of you, because those two fellows knew where the information was from that got them arrested."

As far as I know, that contract is still out!

Charles Lee "Chuck" Korzenborn, Kenton County, September 17, 2009

Case Solved Sixty Years Later

Newport, Kentucky, of course, was wide open to gambling, and an interesting case comes out of that. In 1948, when I was about ten years old, there was a black man found dead on Kyles Lane. He was stretched out with his hands crossed like he had been hit and had two or three .45-caliber bullet holes in him. Nothing much was done about it. He was a black man, and people didn't give a darn in those days. I don't remember anything coming out of what happened, except there was an article in the newspaper.

A few years ago I got a letter from a New York attorney and he said he had a Mafia hit man and wanted to go for state's evidence to get time off for being a good witness. He claimed he had been in on some murders in northern Kentucky in the 1940s. And he described this murder that he had committed on this black man that was involved in gambling operations in northern Kentucky. He asked if there was any way we could corroborate what he was saying.

I turned the case over to Sergeant Damien Stanton, who is an excellent deputy. I also played taps for veterans' funerals. And a black man, whom I'd gotten to know very well and was his friend, was brother to the woman that was married to this man who was murdered. My deputy was able to get some interviews from her, and he did some research in newspaper articles and other reports and sources. So, we were able to solve that sixty-year-old murder. That took place in my office about five years ago.

That was a very interesting thing. I can remember the murder, and that nothing was done about it. I recall all that as it was happening, as I was very interested in it. That was a cold case file, which is a term used when a case is closed unsolved.

Charles Lee "Chuck" Korzenborn, Kenton County, September 17, 2009

SHERIFF'S NEIGHBOR CONVICTED FOR MURDER

We had what turned out to be one of the most expensive murder trials in the state, and it happened about three doors from where I lived at the time in Edgewood. A woman had been cheating on her husband, but she didn't want to change her lifestyle, so she and the guy she was running around with and a friend of his shot and bludgeoned the husband to death.

As sheriff I walked down there to get her in a neighbor's house [for] questioning, and she was arrested for the murder, and also the two guys were arrested. Well, as the trial was coming up, they decided they were going to have to change the venue, so they changed it to Fayette

County. The Fayette County sheriff said she could not afford to provide security for the woman on trial. So I had to send my bailiffs down for the proceedings.

They tried the case, and it did wind up in a hung jury. They had to go to trial again, but finally the woman confessed to the crime before we had to go into that second trial.

I never did get paid for my extra expenses there, and I was told by the finance administration that it was the most expensive trial in the history of the state.

The woman was convicted, and I think she got a life sentence. By that time, I believe, you could get life without parole. But unfortunately, in times past you either got the death penalty or twenty years. At that time some people wanted to do away with the death penalty, so a guy could get away with serving twenty years. If he was lucky he got paroled in less time than that.

Charles Lee "Chuck" Korzenborn, Kenton County, September 17, 2009

Gangsters

This took place back in the 1950s or early 1960s. Charlie Drahmann and Jimmy Brink owned the Lookout House, which was a pretty classy gambling joint in Kenton County. And the FBI was always looking for the local gangster. I got into the business of working on Jimmy Brink's and Charlie Drahmann's cars, and I got to working on Jimmy Brink's secretary's mistress's car.

She was an interesting, well-read lady. I guess I must have worked on her cars thirty or thirty-five years, maybe even longer. She told me one story when the FBI was looking for Jimmy Brink. They have a beautiful mansion that was built at the turn of the century, big high ceilings and things. Her desk was in the foyer, and the FBI was questioning her, and little did they know Jimmy was in a secret compartment right above her head.

Brink and Charlie Drahmann were murdered, in my view, by the Mafia, which is the Cleveland Gang. Jimmy Brink was a single-engine pilot, and his plane crashed with Charlie Drahmann. There was something like $40,000 or $50,000 cash in the plane when it came down. I suspect they were not out of gas.

Being a widow, Mrs. Drahmann lived on Dixie Highway in another fancy house right across the highway from Jimmy Brink. She wound up being courted and married by a fellow, Mike Coppola, who was a New York gangster.

The point of the story was that she got into a big fight with him at what is now called Barley Corns and used to be Retschulte's Restaurant on Dixie Highway at Lakeside. She chased him to the airport and they get into a fight there at the airport. He threw her into this one car, and they go down Route 8 toward Ludlow-Bromley area. He beat the heck out of her, threw her out. A car happened to be in this deserted area, and the driver saw what was going on, then reported the license number. The license number was put on all points bulletin by the dispatch, and as the car was going through Dixie Highway to Ft. Mitchell a local officer saw it, pulled it over and recognized Coppola, and let him go!

That's the way things were done in the old days, unfortunately. Too many law enforcement officers just turned their heads. Now, since I became county sheriff, it has been rather interesting to the local people to have a county sheriff that does his job.

Charles Lee "Chuck" Korzenborn, Kenton County, September 17, 2009

DRUNK WITNESSES

A lady called me one morning and told that this man had been killed, then she told me who she thought shot him and where it had happened. So I went to the residence, which was actually a mobile home, and when I pulled up I didn't see any vehicles. Then I did see blood in the driveway that led all the way to the trailer. I also looked inside the trailer and saw blood on the floor. It appeared that somebody had tried to mop it up, but hadn't done a very good job, only smeared it.

A little later in the morning I got a call that a body had been found down near the lake. What happened was, the body had been shot there at the trailer and then the body was taken down to the lake and dumped beside the lake.

During the day we rounded up some witnesses in the case and arrested the guy that did the murder. We brought them down to the sheriff's office and took them back in the back office and questioned them, one at a time apart from each other to see what their stories were. Well, each one we would bring back to question would be more intoxicated than the one before, and by the time the last one was in there they said, "We're just going to tell you everything." They were really good witnesses, and we couldn't figure out why they were intoxicated.

Well, the night before, me and my deputy had been out working on trying to catch a bootlegger. And we had an informant to buy a fifth of vodka from this bootlegger, and we hadn't had time to tag it or anything, so we just stuck it in the desk drawer and had forgotten about it.

Well, the witnesses had drunk that vodka while we were questioning them. We opened the door in the desk, and the vodka bottle was empty!

Larry L. Bennett, Russell County, September 18, 2009

GHOST SCARED

Back when I was a state trooper over in Monroe County in the mid-1970s, I got a call telling me about a fatal accident in the Mt. Herman community on Highway 63. On this road that turned left out there, there was a pop-up rise, and this one car that had some teenagers in it popped over the rise and came down onto the top of this other car and killed the lady that was driving that other car.

She was a young lady, and the accident happened right near her house. I can't remember if it killed one of the teenagers in the other car, but it overturned. I went out there and worked this accident, then later charged the driver of the second vehicle with manslaughter for driving recklessly and causing death of this young lady.

The young lady that was killed was pretty, and had a small child. We thought for awhile the child might have been in the car with her, but it wasn't. She had dropped it off at a family member's house and was almost home when this wreck happened.

Well, I was young, and this wreck really bothered me. I was working the criminal case, and I had some questions I had to ask her husband. However, I didn't want to bother him at this time, so I waited a week or so after the funeral before going out to talk to him about it in order to get my information for the case report. It was late in the afternoon and I was going out to the residence, and the sun was almost ready to set. While driving out there I had to drive right by where the wreck was, and I was really sad about what had happened there. I went on to the house, and when I pulled up into the driveway the house looked sad and lonely because this young lady, her child, and husband lived there when she got killed.

I parked in the driveway, then went and pecked on the door, but nobody comes to the door. I pecked again but nobody comes to the door, so I looked up through the window there but didn't see anybody,

234   *Tales from Kentucky Sheriffs*

so I started to walk away. Suddenly I hear the door open, so I turned around and walked back up on the porch, and started looking through the screen at this woman that was there. She looked exactly just like the woman that got killed. I looked back to see just how far it was to my car, as I thought I was looking at a ghost. Her husband, I don't recall what his name was, but I asked her if he was here. She said, "No, he's not here." She looked real bad; her eyes were really sunk in, and she just felt bad.

At that time I'm still thinking that I'm seeing a ghost. Then she speaks up and says, "I'm her identical twin sister." So I breathed a sigh of relief. I did not know that the young woman that got killed had an identical twin sister.

Larry L. Bennett, Russell County, September 18, 2009

CHASING BANK ROBBERS

When I was a deputy a lot of things occurred, but those things prepared me for who I was to be, a sheriff. Back in 2003 or 2004 we had a bank robbery in Maysville around 9:00 a.m., just after the bank had opened up for the day.

The chief of police and the assistant chief of police of Maysville would always go out, get their coffee, then take a tour of the town. They were the first ones to get in the chase for the robbers.

I wasn't too far behind, and was driving. We were engaged in a high-speed pursuit, and they had brandished weapons and were firing out the window, shooting their firearms in our direction. We were on Highway 11, going towards Fleming County. We radioed ahead to Jerry Wagner, the Fleming County sheriff at that time. He took care of the roadblock, and he had pulled a tractor-trailer across the road. Even though that truck had the road blocked, they did not stop one bit, thus ran head on into it.

Fireballs and shots were being fired after the collision. It turned out that the robbers were shooting and trying to kill themselves, and were not shooting at us. We got two of the robbers out, and they are in the penitentiary now, a male and a female. There were two males and a female that committed the robbery. One of the men died, but the other two lived and were sent to prison.

That was definitely the most dangerous work that I had as a deputy. It was the second bank robbery investigation I had been involved in.

Patrick Boggs, Mason County, September 15, 2009

Biggest and Baddest Outlaw

We also had another sheriff in Todd County, Doug Bouiseau, who was a well-known person. He ran and served as sheriff in one of the terms when Robert Miller Jr. had to set out. Doug was a very, very good sheriff. I wasn't really old enough to remember him, but everybody I talked with when I went through the county praised him. Doug is still alive, and he is a very, very good man, and made us one of the very best sheriffs we ever had. When I went out campaigning for office, people would talk about Doug. He just had one of those personalities you just can't forget. He lives in Guthrie, located in the extreme southern part of the county.

Many people have told me a story about him, but I haven't talked with him personally about it. The story claims that at one time we had somebody that was bad, and had the reputation of being the biggest and baddest. He wound up out at our high school, not as a teacher but as an outlaw at the function, and as I understand it, the city police wouldn't bother him, and nobody else would bother him, because he was big and bad, and he'd done told people, "There ain't nobody going to mess with me."

While there at the high school he was causing some sort of ruckus. Sheriff Doug heard about that fellow being there at school, so he goes out there, walks up behind the man, and calls his name. The story has it that the sheriff had a little sawed-off shotgun, pulled it up in the back of the outlaw's ribs, and said, "Let's go."

The outlaw said, "Yes, sir."

In a small, small town, everything spreads around by word of mouth. They tell the story rather consistently, saying that later on in this outlaw's life we had another constable, Carlos Abney, who was very diligent. He was the only man I know who served in two different counties: in Kentucky and the other in Tennessee. I don't know how the constable got by with it, but he was in Allensville. Well, he met up with this outlaw one night who tried to shoot Abney in a standoff they had there beside the road. The outlaw had a semiautomatic pistol, and Mr. Abney thought he had no choice but to put his hands around the top of the pistol and try to duck the bullet, but the bullet went across the top of his head. I went to Mr. Abney's funeral and saw this scar he still had there on top of his head. I could see it because his head was pretty bald.

The outlaw tried using the semiautomatic pistol again to shoot Mr. Abney. I don't think Abney had the training to let him know he needed to jam that automatic pistol up. I think he was just trying to dodge that first bullet.

Nowadays we are trained with a semiautomatic pistol, and we have to defend ourselves by trying to get our hand over the eject so the fired round can't come out and it jams up the gun.

W. D. "Billy" Stokes, Todd County, September 17, 2009

Proactive Bank Teller

We had a branch bank of the Clarkson Bank in Clarkson. These both happened within two years, I think, but I did go to both cases. We got an alarm in that the bank was being robbed. In both cases the same teller was working, and the teller shot and killed both bank robbers. That happened about a year apart, then they eventually closed the bank.

That bank teller was never charged with anything. He was interviewed, but never was arrested. However, those were probably the worst cases I ever worked with.

Qulin K. Escue, Grayson County, September 22, 2009

The Bus People

One time we had what they called Bus people. They were kind of a religious group that came in to the Millerstown area and bought this big farm, stayed by themselves, and educated their own kids. This took place probably just after the deal that took place in Waco. So I guess the federal government was getting a little worried about these groups, so they were kind of investigating them. And they also investigated this group that we had down here.

We would fly over and photograph their farm from aircraft. An FBI agent came down there one time, and he was asking me about them. Of course, I knew those people and dealt with them on different occasions. The agent said he was having to do a little investigation, that he would like to know a little something about them. I said, "Well, I'll tell you what," to that young FBI agent, "we'll just drive up there."

He said, "Oh, no, we can't just drive up there."

I said, "Sure we can," so I just tore out up the driveway. They lived a pretty good distance off the road, but this one young boy tried to stop us down at the end of the road. He had a water tank on a trailer, hooked behind a tractor, and he was filling up that water tank.

Since I didn't stop for him, since I knew the main guy up there, he just stole the hose out of the water and got on that tractor and almost beat me to the top of the hill. So when we got up there, I don't remember what all we told them, but that we were just looking around.

The funniest thing about that was what we found out later on during the investigation—that they thought about taking us hostage while we was up there! I told the FBI agent later on during the investigation that they thought about taking us hostage while we was up there. When I told that to him, he said, "Oh, my God, I can't believe that." That just scared him to death because I drove him all the way up to the top of that hill where they lived. They called them Bus people because every time you saw them they were in a bus. The first time I ever run into them they had their own leader and had their own law enforcement person and he wore a little ole badge and everything. When they would come into Leitchfield they would pack guns with them, long-barrel guns, to protect their leader. Finally, we just had to get together and tell them, "You can't pack guns here in this town. It's fine for you to come to town, but you're not going to bring any guns with you."

They are no longer here. The leader was in the process of being accused for sexually abusing a child. During court one day in Leitchfield, he came up there and brought a gun with him. Accidentally or on purpose, he shot and killed himself while in the car while he was there at the courthouse. That was after my tenure when he killed himself. After that happened those people just dismantled and sold, and most of them moved away. I think some are still living around here, but they're not still into the things that they were.

Qulin K. Escue, Grayson County, September 22, 2009

Son Killed His Parents

One of the saddest cases we had during my tenure in office was when a young sixteen-year-old boy killed his parents in the Sadler community. He shot his father in the head, then beat his mother to death with the butt of the rifle.

Their son had run away from home and went to Florida, and his parents went down and picked him up. The lady who took care of the juveniles at the time wanted them to bring him to her and turn him over to her. That was late during the afternoon, or night, when they arrived home with him, so they said, "No, we'll just keep him tonight, then bring him up and drop him off tomorrow."

The son killed them both that night, took their car and went to Bowling Green, rented a motel room, and watched movies. If I'm not mistaken, the police officers caught him over pretty close to the Mexican border. He had taken his parents' jewelry, and he was going to pawn it. It is said that he kept circling the pawn shop over there, so the guy that ran the pawn shop got a little nervous, so he called the police and gave them the tag number. Of course, they already had the tag number, as they were suspecting a double murder case.

He was sentenced to prison, and is still in the pen.

Qulin K. Escue, Grayson County, September 22, 2009

Dangerous Schoolmate

This took place just outside the city of Leitchfield one summer night. I was called at home by a police dispatch who advised me that there was a drunk man going door-to-door threatening the occupants with a gun if they didn't go pull his car out of the mud in which he had hung it up early that night.

I tried to get a city police officer to take care of it, because it was in seeing distance of the city limits, but he didn't do it. So when I arrived city police officer Tim Moutardier did go with me. We saw a car stuck in the woods, and I approached it and looked inside, but didn't see a gun. I assumed he had passed out.

I told Tim that I know the fellow because I went to school with him. When we got to the car I opened the door real quickly, reached in, and got hold of the fellow before he came to. That fellow was laying in the front seat with his hands behind his head. Well, when I opened the door he comes up with a pistol and had its hammer back ready to fire. We stepped back with our guns drawn, looking eye to eye trying to get him to put his down.

After what seemed like thirty minutes but actually only seconds, he finally put his gun down. By all rights, one of us should have been shot. Truth of the matter is if I had not attended school with him and knew him well, I would have fired my gun at him.

The judge gave him a choice to go to jail or leave town. So he moved to Florida, and has never returned, and that took place back in the 1980s.

Qulin K. Escue, Grayson County, September 22, 2009

SHERIFF'S LOSS OF PRECIOUS DAUGHTER

The worst thing I ever experienced while in office took place on January 18, 1993. I was called to a wreck that had taken place, and it was my only daughter that was killed in this accident.

I never will forget that it was 4:00 and time for me to go home, and I got a call from an officer in Clarkson, here in Grayson County, to come to a wreck up on the interstate.

Of course, it was quitting time and I didn't want to go, but he insisted that I come. When I got up there it was my only daughter, and she had been killed in a traffic accident. She was seventeen years old. I didn't know about it until I got there. She was driving, and there was a little skiff of snow on the road. She passed a vehicle, then when she cut back in, she lost control of her vehicle and ran into a rock ledge shoulder.

Qulin K. Escue, Grayson County, September 22, 2009

TRAGIC DEATHS

This profession allows you to see the best and the very worst of society. I've seen the very best and the very worst in people. There have been countless heart-wrenching things that I've seen. I tell people all the time that I've waded through more blood in my career than any person really should have to. One thing that has always struck me is the senselessness of events that are heartbreaking and filled with misery. But on the other side, I've seen a lot of really good things, too.

Here's a story in which I was called as detective to work in what was an apparent double homicide/suicide case. A young mother was so distraught with life that she elected not only to take her own life but also the lives of her two small children. She went out here on the south side of Daviess County, parked outside of a tobacco barn and rigged a hose in the vehicle they were in, and asphyxiated herself and her two small boys. Of course, they died from carbon monoxide poison.

I remember that when I went out there to work that scene that morning, I'll never forget it as long as I live. When I viewed the bodies in that vehicle, the mother was up front, and the two little boys were in the back seat. It was cold, so she had covered the little boys up. Apparently she had concern as to whether or not they were warm, but she still took their lives. Their ages were like maybe four and six years old. I remember that as one of the boys died, his hands were outstretched like he was reaching out to his mother for help. That's the way he died, so that has stuck with me all these years. It was as if the little boy was looking up to his mother, asking, "Why, Mama?"

Keith Cain, Daviess County, October 1, 2009

COMMON SENSE AND PARANOIA SAVE THE DAY

This is a story about something that, if it had occurred five years after it occurred, I probably wouldn't be here today. I had virtually no training in law enforcement, and just let common sense dictate a lot of what I did.

When that happened, I was on the road as patrol deputy early one morning, and a call came out about a stolen 1966 Buick Skylark. There is a location in western Daviess County, actually on the western city limits of Owensboro, that is now all houses in a very affluent neighborhood. Back then it was called Bon Harbor Hills; it was an area on which abandoned coal-mining properties were located. Back then, in the 1970s, it was what I refer to as Indian country, because that's what we referred to as enemy territory in Vietnam. Bon Harbor Hills is where a lot of people took stolen cars, where we found dead bodies, where we found stolen property and dope fields. It was a secluded area where a lot of criminal activity took place. It's not like that at all now.

When that call came out that morning I thought to myself, "If I were the person that had stolen this car, that's where I would take it." So I got in my patrol car and drove out to Bon Harbor and just started driving around out there. It was a very secluded, remote area. Sure enough, I drove right up on a 1966 Buick Skylark that was hung up off the side of the road, up a little incline, and there were two people there trying to get it out. I could tell by their looks that they were undesirable types. That was a little more easily detected back in the early 1970s than it is now.

But I can recall as I drove by and looked at them, they looked at me. Well, I thought that I wasn't prepared to deal with this right now, so I just drove on past them. So I drove up over a hill, got out of sight, turned back around, and then I got on the radio. I identified myself, gave them my location, and told them I thought I had the stolen car as well as two suspects. I then approached the stolen vehicle and requested backup. I got my pistol out and sat it next to me so I would have it right there in my hand.

This time when I drove back over the top of the hill, knowing where they were at, I was able to wheel in, jump out of the vehicle, and take them into custody before they really realized what was really happening.

After my backup officers arrived we put these two men in our vehicle then went over and searched the vehicle. Sure enough, it was a stolen vehicle and had a lot of stolen tools in it that they had stolen during a burglary that night. And also in the vehicle right under the driver's seat was a Webley [British military issue] .45 revolver fully loaded. So I asked one of the individuals I had taken into custody, "What do you have that pistol for?"

He said, "I was getting it to kill you with, just as soon as you came by."

Now, had I stopped there when I first saw them, he would have had ample time to retrieve that gun and shoot me. And he told me that's what he was going to do.

Although I didn't have any training at that time, the common sense and somewhat paranoid demeanor probably saved my life that day.

Both of those individuals were convicted and went on to the penitentiary, then about five years later, when they got out of the penitentiary, one of those two individuals abducted, raped, and murdered a young lady on that same end of town.

What I'm saying is that this individual told me he was going to kill me, and I know he could do that, because five years later after he got out of the penitentiary he perpetrated a murder. Ten years later in my career, if that had happened I might have just jumped out to take care of business, and if I had done it, I wouldn't be here today.

God has a plan for us, and his plan that day was for Keith Cain to continue on with his career, instead of just being a name engraved on a wall.

Keith Cain, Daviess County, October 1, 2009

RIOT DURING COAL MINERS' STRIKE

Back on December 7, 1977, when there was a nationwide coal strike going on, it got extremely violent throughout Kentucky. A lot of people were shot, some were killed around the coal mines in eastern Kentucky, and that bled over into western Kentucky. What happened was that the union miners were attempting to shut the mines down that were located in our county.

There were about four deputy sheriffs and about three or four or five state police officers who were called upon to enforce a restraining order at the entrance of one of those mines. That resulted in a riot in which there were about seven hundred plus miners and about twenty police officers. Well, back then we didn't have riot gear like we have now: no body armor, helmets, etc.

I sustained injuries out there that day that resulted in two facial reconstruction surgeries. I was beaten with a baseball bat and my jaw broken, and several bones in my face were shattered. I was beat so severely that when taken to the hospital, my family doctor didn't recognize me because of all those injuries.

What I'm saying is that there have been instances that occurred that probably could have, and likely should have, ended my career. But I've got to believe that the Lord had a purpose for Keith Cain, because I'm still here today.

Keith Cain, Daviess County, October 1, 2009

Heartbreaking Note at Crime Scene

I had arrived at the scene of a domestic disturbance that, tragically, resulted in the death of the wife. As she lay prone on the floor, all life having left her, I set to the task of processing the scene by fingerprinting, sketching, measuring, photographing, etc. I had no thought to the tragic loss of life that was evidenced before me, at least not before my camera lens focused on a bloody thumbprint on the refrigerator door. The viewfinder settled on a handwritten note affixed there. I lowered my camera and with some curiosity read the note, obviously written by a very small child. I recall those words to this day, as they are etched in my mind forever. They reminded me then, as they do now, of the senselessness of violent acts.

This is what the note said: "Dear Mommy, today in schol we lerned about turtles. We lerned the mommy turtle comes to land to lay her eggs. Then she goes away. Mommy, please don't ever go away."

Her mommy was on the floor and was never coming back. That

note, scrawled in the innocence of a small child, had a profound impact on the way I have since viewed crime victims.

Keith Cain, Daviess County, October 1, 2009

Almost Shot

Tommy Loving was a Drug Task Force coordinator in Warren County. Together we went out to arrest a bootlegger, and that fellow came out with a .38 pistol. Tommy grabbed him and was holding onto the pistol, and I had to bring my .357 Magnum out and put it beside his head to get him to drop it. But they were wrestling with a gun, and it was right in front of my belly. Well, Tommy had an imprint of the hammer where he had tried to fire it, and Tommy's finger had caught it and kept it from firing. If it had fired, it probably would have shot me in the stomach.

Kenneth Lee Morris, Butler County, October 11, 2009

Preachers Murdered

There was a preacher in the Jetson area, here in Butler County, and there was a guy that had a mental problem. He told this preacher, Brother Blounk, that the Lord told him to kill him [the preacher]. He then went to the preacher's house and killed him. Well, he was truly in bad shape. As far as I know, he's still in the asylum up in Louisville.

That happened back when I was a deputy, probably in the 1970s.

We also had a preacher killed back in the late 1930s or early 1940s down in Leonard Oak. It was always said that some persons thought he was a revenue agent because he would ask a lot of questions and make a lot of comments about moonshiners.

The story about his death claims he was shot while up in the pulpit. It is also said that some guys stood outside the church building and drew straws as to who was to kill him. Anyway, he got shot. I think it was someone in the Gary family [Gary Brothers Crushed Stone], Bowling Green, that got convicted for shooting the preacher. It was some member of the Gary family that did it, because they were originally from Leonard Oak.

Kenneth Lee Morris, Butler County, October 11, 2009

Dangerous Domestic Situation

This is about something I dealt with back in the early 1990s. Back then we had to work different day shifts and had to work hours later on during the night. One night I was working, and was the only deputy on duty here in Shelby County. I got a domestic call in a community, so I proceeded to go out there. When I arrived I knocked on the door and a woman came to the door. She had a big bump on the side of her head where she had been hit by her husband. I think it turned out that the families that were there included two sisters involved in this situation. But the two husbands were not related.

As I talked to the injured lady, she informed me that both of the men had been drinking, but only her husband hit her. The other guy hadn't done anything. So I informed her to go to the room with her family of three kids and the other lady and her three kids. I told her to go to that room and sit down and lock the door. Then I said to her, "If you hear something scuffling out here like a bad thing, you get back on the phone and call that dispatcher you just talked to and tell him I need help out here."

During those days my radio wouldn't reach my dispatcher. If you were far out in this county and away from here, then you may have to relay yourself through somebody else to get the dispatcher, especially if he's on a portable. You may have to call another deputy to get him to relay for you. The radio systems weren't like they are today.

Anyway, they went and locked themselves in the room, and I came on into the house and walked over to the room. When I got there two men were standing there, and fortunately for me I assumed that both of them knew who I was. They knew I was calling them by name, and I proceeded to talk to them by explaining to them the law and how it was.

They were both drinking. One wasn't too upset, but the one that was doing all the whipping and hitting was pretty much agitated. We got to the point to where I informed him as to how the law was involved in domestic violence, and that the law said, " . . . shall go to jail." It didn't say *may*, or *could*, but it said *shall* go to jail.

When I explained that to him, he looked at me and said, "I'm not going anywhere."

So there was just me and those two guys standing there. I knew there wasn't a trooper in the county, and I also knew that the only other law enforcement officer that might be in this county would be a city police officer or two. I also told myself that it would take somebody about fifteen minutes to get there. In the process of going through this, about that time the dispatch got to me on the radio, and they asked me if I was okay. I indicated I was okay, but they asked if I needed any backup.

Like I said, this guy looked at me and told me he was not going anywhere. I said to him, "Hold on a minute." Well, at that point in time they were sort of standing off in another room. I was kindly verbally trying to talk to them to keep them calm. There wasn't any use in pushing this thing into a situation I didn't need. There was a big rocking chair setting there, and I kinda sat back down in that rocker. They were ten or fifteen feet away from me, standing over there on the floor.

I looked at that guy that had hit his spouse and said, "You tell me, do I need any backup?"

He stood there a minute, then I said, "I'll tell you what. There's no doubt that you two guys can fight if that's what you want, but I don't know if both you guys can whip me. And you don't know if you can either. But I'm going to do what I can do, to get out of here and do something with you."

They both just stared, looking at me. I said, "You've got two options. You can go with me and we'll go down here to get in this car and go to Shelbyville, where you can be a man, confess up to what you have done here, then tomorrow get yourself bonded out and come home. Or you can start something here, and I can guarantee you one thing—it may take my army ten or fifteen minutes to get here, but when my army gets here they will clean up this mess, including you."

I was sitting down, something I should have never done, but I was trying to de-escalate this thing and make them feel comfortable. The old boy that done all the hitting stared at me and said, "Mike, I'll go with you." When he said that I told the dispatch that I didn't need any backup. We went down, put him in the car, and went to Shelbyville.

But I'll bet we were fifty-fifty—we were either going to have a fight there, or he was going to go with me. I didn't know which way he was going to go until I looked at him and asked, "You tell me if I need somebody to show up, or are you going with me?" At that point he decided he was going with me. He was charged with domestic violence, and I'm sure he was convicted somewhere along the way.

Mike Armstrong, Shelby County, November 6, 2009

Sheriff Pulls Gun

I've been involved in dangerous activities several times, such as feuding and fighting, and I've been hit a few times myself by someone's fists and other things. When I get socked by a fist I usually fly right back at them and hit them with my fist, or with a club or whatever I can grab hold of right quick.

I had to pull a gun one time when these two guys came to tell me that a guy had been stabbed and everything. I got in a car and went to him. These two other guys came up pretty fast. So I pulled my gun out and made them both lay down right in the middle of the road with their hands over their heads.

As to how they reacted, when they saw the end of my gun barrel they acted pretty good. They stayed there face down until I handcuffed them, then I took them to jail. They were tried in court, and are still in court right now.

John "Tuffy" Snedegar, Bath County, December 11, 2009

Resisting Arrest

Awhile back, me and a state policeman went on a call about a man and woman fussing and fighting. The dispatcher couldn't tell us exactly what their address was. All they could tell us was what road this couple lived on. So I said, "Well, we'll go to the place I usually have to go to all the time."

We went there, but it wasn't where they lived. While we were there we heard him over on another hill cussing us. He saw us over there, and he was cussing and everything. He yelled to his wife, "There's that goddamned sheriff over there."

I told the state policeman, "Well, let's go down here, then we'll go over there."

So we went over there and talked to him. He kind of got aggravated when we told him he was under arrest, and he told us he wasn't going with us. Then he started toward the state police, so the state policeman shot him with a taper gun. That's the kind of gun that all state policemen carry these days. These guns have two proms [wires] that sticks in you. Every time you pull the trigger, they'll stick in you, just like when you shoot and stick them in a cow.

I thought that guy was going to fall, so I backed off just a little bit from him. But instead of him falling, he took off running. That taper gun didn't bring him down. Of course, he was all "pilled" up and drinking, too. The state policeman shot him three or four times, but that didn't do a bit of good. Those shot items would not kill anyone, but they'd make you think you were being killed. If a person is really "pilled" up on drugs and things, that makes that person meaner.

What I said was, "Oh, Lord, the fight's on now." We had to take off running trying to catch him and put him on the ground. But we like to have never caught him. When we caught him, it took us forever, but we finally got him handcuffed. It took two of us to do that, because he was fighting us. That trooper kept pulling his gun trigger, and that guy would yell, "Ur, ur, ur."

I finally told the trooper, "I wouldn't carry one of those guns. Here's what's going to be my stun gun." Troopers have to be shot by one of those guns to know what it feels like to the person they shoot with one of them.

John "Tuffy" Snedegar, Bath County, December 11, 2009

Sheriff Lays Down Gun

I got a call late one afternoon during the fall season, likely in September, telling me that a man had a woman held hostage in their house. I went out there to see what the situation was. That was several years ago when we had only a small sheriff's department, thus typically responded to calls by ourselves. We had maybe one person on a shift, or whatever.

That was just a routine call, but when I got to their house just at darkness, the lady was screaming. I was standing outside in the yard, close to a porch that was about on ground level. She was still up there in the house at the front door. She was screaming and yelling, "He's threatened to burn me and the house up."

I said, "Where is he?"

She said, "Well, he's not here. He's done took off." Then she went to say, "Don't you smell that gas in this house?"

He had thrown gas all through the house and had left. I was taking the information from her, and it had probably gone on for four or five minutes. Well, all of a sudden he comes around the side of the house and stopped twelve or fifteen feet from me. He had a gun pointed at me, and told me he was going to kill me. All the time she was screaming and yelling. I tried to get her calmed down, and she was yelling to him, "Don't shoot him! Don't shoot him; don't kill him!"

I started talking to him, trying to reason with him, but he was severely intoxicated, very emotional, and very nervous. His gun was shaking in his hand. When I started talking to him, trying to calm him down and telling him to lay his weapon down, he wasn't interested at all in what I was trying to tell him.

In the meantime, the dispatcher was calling routinely to find out if everything was alright, but that fellow wouldn't let me answer my radio. So I'd keep talking to him, and he was telling me to lay my weapon down, and I'd say, "No, I'm not going to do that."

I started backing away from him, but there wasn't a tree to get behind, not a ditch to get in, and there was nowhere to go in the level yard there. Well, he started walking a little closer to me and got within approximately six feet of me, and then he was telling me he was going to kill me.

I think it was a .38 pistol that he had. If you have never looked down the barrel of a gun pointed at you, let me say that they get rather large at the end of those barrels when you are looking at them!

Anyway, I kept talking to him, and the dispatcher keeps calling for me, but I can't answer. So, this man's wife started yelling back up on the porch, and he tells me to lay the weapon down.

I told him, "No, I'm not going to do that. Come on up here and I'll talk to you after you get in the light so I can see you." I knew if I could get close enough to him, I was going to take care of him, or at least was planning on it.

He came up real close to me and said, "Oh, you are a smart SOB, aren't you. So, I'm not getting any closer to you."

At that point in time he was really nervous and agitated, and his wife was screaming continuously, "Don't kill him; don't kill him!"

I finally decided that due to the condition he was in, and the frame of mind he was in, that he was really going to shoot me. He told me to lay my weapon down, and doing that is a no-no if you are in law enforcement. You don't ever say what you're not going to do unless you are there when you say it. So I laid my weapon down right there on that front porch, which was about waist high. I was standing there and was thinking, "When he gets on up here and starts to pick that weapon up, that's when I'll get him." I was going to grab him, grab his gun, and get him. When he got up there within four feet of me, I was standing right there, but never did back up to lay the weapon down. He told me again how smart I was, told me to back up, and I did.

He grabbed my weapon and took off running. About that time other people were getting there, and I could talk with the dispatcher and others.

Within thirty to forty-five minutes we had him apprehended and took him to jail. Not long thereafter we went to court, and his wife testified in his behalf, saying that he didn't know what he was doing and blah, blah, blah, she went on. She even said there wasn't any gas in the house, and he hadn't threatened to do anything to his family. Anyway, we had him charged with robbery because he stole a weapon, and that was the most serious offense we could charge him with. So the jury either had to find him not guilty or guilty. If they found him guilty of robbery, the sentence was a minimum of ten years. He could have been charged with other things, but they found him guilty of robbery and sentenced him for ten years.

I think he appealed it, but did serve two or three years. His girl-friend went to visit him in jail all along. He is deceased now, died as a rather young man.

Barney Jones, Barren County, December 21, 2009

Culprit Lays Down Gun

We had another gun situation that deals with this guy that held his wife against her will in their house, and she had gotten away from him and gone to a neighbor's house to call 911. We responded to the call; he was intoxicated and threatening to kill her. Two or three of my deputies got there, and this guy was holing himself up inside the house.

I had also decided I had better get on out there, so when I got there the deputies had been there five or ten minutes and were trying to block off the road to the house. The guy was screaming and yelling from inside the house. I knew him so I hollered at him, and he said, "Is that you, Barney?"

I said, "Yeah, how are you doing?"

He said, "Well, not too good at the moment."

I said, "Come on out here on this porch and let me talk to you." I was not on the porch at that time. I was still out there in the road, perhaps one hundred yards away from the house.

He came on out onto the porch, and then I said, "Lay that gun down. I want to come on up there and talk to you."

He said, "You keep them others away from me."

I said, "I'll keep them away, so don't worry about it."

So he laid his gun down, and I just walked on up there, picked his gun up, and arrested him without any problems.

Some days are good ones, and some are bad days.

Barney Jones, Barren County, December 21, 2009

Hostage Situation

I had a situation that started in the city. This fellow killed his girlfriend, and I think it took place in the vehicle. She had been seeing another fellow, so he killed her, then takes off with her. This other fellow that he did not kill, and this girl, were in a car. He killed her, and the other fellow ran off. The fellow that shot her jumped in this vehicle and starts driving the vehicle out into the county.

We were all there looking for him, and he runs into this house where this elderly lady lived. The car was still running out there, and the woman is dead in the car, cold. Then he takes this elderly woman hostage and takes her to a bedroom and barricades himself in this room.

We were going into the house, gradually moving in. He shouted at us through the walls, and this standoff lasted for a long time. That fellow was a good friend of a state trooper that was assigned to Frankfort at that time. That state trooper was the only person he wanted to talk to. They got in touch with the trooper, then flew him to Glasgow. When he arrived they took the man that did the killing and negotiated with him. After six or seven hours they finally persuaded him to release the elderly lady.

Of course, the SWAT team was there, and this went on all night long. That fellow would not give himself up, thus the decision was made on over in the next morning to shoot tear gas into the house in order to take control of the situation. When they shot gas right into that room, they went in and got him.

I was at his trial and his mother testified he was just irate at everybody. He did listen to me then, as I was trying to explain to him that his mother was trying to explain his childhood, and how he was raised. The jury convicted him, and gave him a life sentence.

That was a stressful situation.

Barney Jones, Barren County, December 21, 2009

Career-Threatening Event

I was the kind of sheriff that got along with everybody, and I never got into situations that were extremely dangerous. The most dangerous event I ever got into was when I was a deputy, not a sheriff. I never had to use force on anybody; never had anybody with a knife-sticking threat or slapjack. I was always able to talk to them and communicate to them. I grew up in this area and knew everybody around here.

However, one night I had a drunk, when we pretty much took calls by ourselves back then. His mom and dad called me to tell me that he had locked himself in the bathroom with a razor in his hand, and he wouldn't come out. I went out there and went into the house to try to get him to come out, and I set there and talked to him. He had been on some drugs and alcohol and whiskey, and finally he knew who I was.

He came out and had the razor in his hand. We were looking straight at each other. Since he had the razor in his hand I stepped back a little bit and sort of reached for my gun. I never had to do that before. Well, he kept making one step closer and closer toward me. Finally I said to him, "Back up. Don't get any closer to me with that razor blade."

He was kind of swerving it around, so finally I drew back on him. Many thoughts were going through my mind about things like, "What will I do if I have to shoot this guy? Here he is, and here his parents are, and I'm here all by myself, with no backup." Then I thought, "It's going to be them against me. I'm not going to win this case." Then I said to myself that it's better to be tried by twelve [jurors] than to be carried by six [pallbearers]." So I took out my gun, thinking that I'm going to take my chances. But I didn't cock the gun, just pointed it at him and said, "Now, drop your blade."

Well, he made one more step towards us, so I then pulled back the hammer on my gun, pointed it at him and said, "If you make one more step, I'm going to let the hammer go." When I did, I said, "Lord, if I ever needed your help, I need it now." By the time I raised my hand up, pointed my gun at him, and pulled the hammer back, he dropped the blade.

Now, you talk about somebody setting there shaking—I was doing it. I was thinking that if I have to kill this guy, my career is over. I'll be sued, and I'll be sent to prison. I went on and thought to myself, "There ain't nobody going to be here but me and his mom and dad, and they'll swear up and down while testifying that I shot him and he had no razor blade." But they were just setting there; didn't try to intervene or anything. It just so happened that when I pulled the hammer back, he dropped the blade.

When all that was said, cleared, and done, I took him on to jail and never had a bit of trouble from him from then on out. That's one of the scariest situations I've ever been in. He'd had a bad problem with alcohol and drugs, and his dad and mom had problems with him.

He came to me two or three weeks later, shook my hand, apologized, and then moved to the state of Virginia. Since then he's come back to visit and come up here to talk to me, just as nice as he could be.

LeeRoy Hardin, Boyle County, January 11, 2010

MERITORIOUS SERVICE

Before I was sheriff in Lewis County I served twenty-five years with the Kentucky State Police. I had a successful career with the state police, rising from the rank of trooper to the rank of lieutenant colonel, the highest rank attainable.

In August of 1980 I was a sergeant assigned to Post 8 in Morehead, Kentucky. While at the post one day the dispatcher received a call from one of the small cities within the Post 8 district. The call was about an attempted murder on the middle-aged police chief of that city. The chief went to the location where the man was working and informed him about the warrant. The suspect then went to a vehicle, obtained a shotgun, put it to the chief's head and threatened to kill the chief if he didn't immediately leave the area.

The chief left and called the KSP post for assistance. A lieutenant and another sergeant were on post. I informed them that although a trooper was on duty in that county, we as supervisors should handle the situation. After informing the chief to obtain a warrant for attempted murder, we traveled to that city. We got the warrant and traveled to the location where the man was working. As we approached the area the man observed us and ran to the vehicle and immediately got the shotgun and brought it with him so he could shoot us. I was in the front passenger seat leaning out and yelling at the man to stop as he ran to the vehicle to get his gun.

When he raised the weapon to shoot I fired six rounds from my issued .357-caliber Smith and Wesson revolver. I then started to reload the revolver (during all this time the cruiser was still in motion), and I felt and heard a loud noise and concussion to the side of my left ear and face. Glass was flying from the front windshield and smoke was inside the vehicle. My thoughts were that the suspect had shot me in the head, because when I fired my weapon he was firing on me.

We were trained when firing a revolver at that time you shoot empty and you only reload two rounds to save time. I remember having difficulty getting the cylinder open, but I did, then loaded it with two rounds and exited the vehicle, which had stopped by that time.

The suspect was lying on the ground with the shotgun across his legs. I kicked the gun away and the suspect died. The lieutenant observed blood running down my left leg from my knee and told me I had been shot. I was taken to the hospital five minutes away, and a doctor removed a bullet fragment from my left knee area. I returned to the scene, which was being processed. I gave my weapon, as protocol, to the investigator, and that is when I observed the barrel was crooked and the trigger did not work.

What had occurred was when I was reloading, the officer in the rear seat had fired five rounds from a mini caliber next to my left ear through the windshield, and that was what caused the glass and smoke. One round had struck my revolver, shooting a hole in the barrel and housing of the cylinder, destroying my revolver. A fragment from that round then entered my left knee.

I was awarded the Kentucky State Police Citation for Meritorious Service for my actions that day.

William D. Lewis, Lewis County, January 13, 2010

Successful Investigative Techniques

Approximately nine months before I became sheriff of Lewis County, a Lewis County man had disappeared on or about April 11, 1998. The suspicion was the man had been murdered. He had last been seen in the company of a transient white male and female. The previous sheriff and his deputies had conducted searches for the missing male, but very little in the way of investigative techniques.

When I was elected sheriff of Lewis County, I initiated an aggressive investigation into the disappearance of the missing person. I learned through leads that the couple had and was traveling west in the United States.

There is a statute, KRS 421.250, in the state of Kentucky that sets out the procedures for procuring attendance as witnesses of persons who are in other states. I requested the commonwealth attorney empanel a grand jury to issue an order for the transient couple to be taken into custody as material witnesses in this case. The grand jury returned the order and it was signed by the Lewis County circuit judge. I had the order entered in the National Crime Information Center. A few days later the couple was taken into custody by Bisbee Police Department in Arizona. The couple was just a few miles from the Mexican border, heading toward Mexico.

The transient couple was brought back to Lewis County, Kentucky. After interviewing them and also subsequent interrogations, they confessed to murdering the Lewis County missing person. They had buried him in a shallow grave next to a creek.

William D. Lewis, Lewis County, January 23, 2010

USE OF NEWS MEDIA HELPS SOLVE CRIME

On Friday, January 15, 2010, my office received a call around 9:00 a.m. telling us that a shooting had occurred in a private residence on Montgomery Creek in Lewis County. The initial information told that a black male had gone to the residence and knocked on the front door. The wife at the residence answered the door and the black male asked to speak to the man of the house. The wife went into another room and told her husband that a black man was at the door requesting to speak to him. She told her husband that the black man looked suspicious, and that he should take a gun with him.

The husband took a .357 Colt revolver and went to the door. As soon as he approached the door the black man opened fire from a .40-caliber semiautomatic pistol. The man, from inside the front door, returned fire. That man and the black man on the front porch were approximately three feet apart when the firing began. The black man shot the man inside the house seven out of ten shots, and the man inside shot at the black man five shots and one round had struck him in the left side of his face. We later learned that he was hit.

The black man ran to his vehicle, which was white in color, and fled from the scene. Although seriously wounded, the white male resident made it to his vehicle, and his wife drove him to Garrison, where they met an ambulance. He was transported to a Portsmouth, Ohio, hospital, where he underwent emergency surgery to save his life. He was stabilized and then was airlifted to Columbus, Ohio, for additional surgery.

Due to our investigation, we learned that a man who had a previous relationship with the victim's wife prior to her marriage to the victim had been observed talking with a black man at a convenience store in an adjacent county prior to the shooting. I dispatched a deputy sheriff to the convenience store to determine if videotape tape existed of the two men meeting at the store. Luckily there was a videotape showing a white male and a black male, the shooter, meeting and exchanging money thirty minutes prior to the shooting. In addition to this video, another video was discovered in another convenience store just before traveling west into Lewis County from the adjacent county that is east of Lewis County. The video shows the white male in his vehicle, and the black male in his, traveling to Lewis County.

I located a witness who observed the white male driving in a location that was close to the shooting incident fifteen minutes prior to the shooting. One of my deputies located a witness who also saw the white male driving his vehicle, a 2010 Camaro, maroon color, about two miles from the shooting at about the time of the shooting. The same witness said about five minutes after the shooting, he saw the white male and met a white vehicle being driven by a black male that was going at a high rate of speed.

Through our investigation we gathered enough evidence to arrest the white male the same day of the shooting. The white male had had a relationship with the victim's wife several years ago, and she had a child by him. A week before the shooting the white male had a heated argument with the shooting victim.

No one knew the black male or where he was from. A couple of days after the shooting I decided to release part of the video showing the white male and the black male interacting to a local television station. I requested they release the video and ask the viewing public to contact my office if anyone could identify the black male. Approximately thirty minutes after the video was broadcast on television, my office received three phone calls identifying the shooter. They gave us the name of the shooter and that he resided in the Raleigh/Durham area of North Carolina. They also said the shooter worked for the white male for a construction company based in Virginia.

My deputy, who is the case officer, contacted North Carolina authorities and discovered the shooter had a lengthy criminal history. Armed with this information, a warrant was obtained for attempted murder. The victim was still barely alive. The suspect was entered into NCIC (National Crime Information Center), and North Carolina authorities were notified of the warrant.

On Sunday, January 24, 2010, Durham County, North Carolina deputies arrested the suspect. Extradition proceedings will be conducted in returning the suspect to Kentucky. The suspect had been shot in the nose and on the left side of his face. Blood samples collected at the scene will be compared to the suspect.

The news media was essential in helping us solve the case.

William D. Lewis, Lewis County, January 23, 2010

Closest Sheriff Came to Shooting a Man

We've had standoffs involving people shooting out of trailers, persons who are mentally insane. We had a major event that took place up on Highway 206 back when Bobby Willis was sheriff. We had to call a state SWAT team in, and they went in after dark and shot tear gas into the trailer. This fellow came running out through the front door, but they did save his life.

We've had other incidents like that, and I've had a few things that happened, and I'd rather have been somewhere else, but you can't back off. You've got to stay with it.

The closest I ever came to killing a man, and it was really close, happened about seventeen miles up here in the county one Sunday night about 9:00. A guy stepped out from behind his trailer with a full-sized gun, which turned out to be a rifle with eighteen rounds in it. He had been drinking, and broke a broom handle on his wife and choked her, and had been shooting around there.

I didn't know him, and I'm not going to forget him either, but he straightened up after that. It happened when I was headed down through there with my spotlight on, and the state trooper was also coming. We had both been there once, but he wasn't there. He'd come back by the time we got almost back to town, so we had to turn around and go back. I beat the trooper back up there a little bit, so I guess I drove fast.

When I got there this fellow come out from behind that trailer, and I stood there for five or ten minutes talking to him. When he stepped out I had my headlights right on him. We began talking and were twenty to twenty-five feet from each other. Anyway, I shot outside of that car with my gun and went over to the passenger's side by the trunk. I had the bead on him, so I said to him, "If you raise that gun up, I will kill you, but I'd rather not kill you; I'd rather for you to drop that gun."

"Walk on around here and I'll surrender," he said. Well, he did drop his gun before the state trooper got there. This lady said something about the fact he always had a little automatic in his pocket sometimes. I asked him if he had one, and he said, "No."

Then I said, "You walk on around here to my door," then went to the driver's side to wait for him to come around. I still had a gun pointed at him.

He walked around there, and about the time he got to the end of the door where I was going to get hold of him, the state boys had got there and they were walking around behind him. He turned around and started cussing them, so I grabbed him and pushed him up against the car. He didn't have a gun on, and I arrested him right there.

That was the closest I ever got to where I was going to shoot somebody.

James Ralph Curry, Adair County, January 11, 2010

Man Intended to Shoot

Bobby Willis, John Ballou, and I were down at a place one night, and this boy was in the bedroom with this kid. I stepped up, and this child was in there asleep. This guy was dangerous, and the woman there said he had a gun on us all the time he was there. We didn't know he was there, but she said he went out the back door and ran off.

Actually, he didn't run off, because he was in that bedroom where the child was sleeping. That's where he saw us, expecting to shoot us.

We've had some pretty close calls, and I'm lucky to be here.

James Ralph Curry, Adair County, January 11, 2010

Husband Kills Wife

This one boy that was charged with a murder was my friend. We had worked together because he was a backhoe operator and other things. He was a good ole boy until he started drinking, and he went wild when that took place. They called and told me to go down there, as he had killed his wife.

Before I got there I met his son on the road, and the son told me that his father had hit him. Also, his neighbor said to me, "You'd better wait for the state police."

I said, "Well, I work with him, so I'll go on down there." I thought I might save his wife's life. Then I said to his son, "You go with me, but you get down behind the brick wall and reach around and peck on the door, and I'll stand out here with a weapon in case he comes out shooting."

I knew he had a lot of weapons inside the house. So the son pecked and pecked, but his father didn't come to the door. So I said to him, "You lay down and let me knock on the door." So I got around behind the brick and knocked real hard on the door, then said, "I'm Glynn Mann; come out."

He said, "Come on in."

So I went in but had no problem with him. He had done a real bad murder. When I went into the house I saw a bottle of whiskey and a weapon and quite a bit of ammunition laying there on the table. I asked him, "Where is she?"

He said, "Right in there."

I said, "Have you hurt her bad?"

He said, "I think I've killed her."

Then I said, "Let me feel of her pulse." She was really bloody, lying up against the bed. I felt of her pulse and then I knew she was dead. There was a wet towel laying there that he had been using in trying to wipe the blood off of the girl. And there was a shotgun there on the floor, and it was broken where she'd been hit on the head. She also had been stabbed and shot in the back of the head with a .22 rifle. He didn't know it, but it was bird shots, and I don't think that gun would have killed her. Also, the state police said she was stabbed with scissors.

I told him I had to arrest him. I said, "You're my buddy, but I'm going to have to put the handcuffs on." So I arrested him and put him in a vehicle.

He had been working out of town, and people had told tales to him about what his wife had been doing incorrectly. When I put him in a car and handcuffed him he said, "I've got a good roll of money here, and I want you to give it to my boy."

I said, "Your son don't need that, so let me give him a couple of hundred dollars." Well, the boy had come up by that time, so he took what I gave him, then I took the rest of the money and gave it to his brother.

The fellow who had killed his wife spent his time in prison, is out now and doing really good. He is working every day, but it still bothers him. In conclusion, let me say he was going after his wife for what she was doing, and was also looking for a male friend and his girlfriend. He didn't find them, but we interrogated them later on, and a little bit of what they told about her was true, but most of it was false.

Glynn Mann, Clinton County, February 8, 2010

"Everyone Lived by the Gun"

I can't tell you much about revenue agent Big Six Henderson, but I do know he would come over here when Odell Cummings was sheriff, who is former sheriff Johnny Cummings's father. Big Six came over here a lot, and he would get the moonshine whiskey stills. When I was sheriff they made whiskey in a different way. I found one man who was cooking and making whiskey on his stove. But they told me that was not against the law, since he was just making it for himself. That was taking place down near Seventy Six Falls.

But Big Six would come in here and get them stills. Back during the time I was on that walking mail route as a job, Odell Cummings would tell me big tales about when he was sheriff. Back then he rode a horse part of the time and drove a car part of the time. And back then everyone lived by the gun. My father, who was a constable in Russell County, got killed. Four fellows over there went to a ballgame on Indian Creek and got into a fight and killed one another. Although my daddy was a constable, these four men had had trouble once before. When they shot each other three of them died right then, and my daddy died the next day.

They were going to have a ballgame with the blacks from Burkesville. Back then everyone went to these baseball games—big crowds. The black players didn't show up, so the Russell Countians organized a team down there on Indian Creek. A lot of tales were told about what happened, but my mother never would talk about it very much.

Glynn Mann, Clinton County, February 8, 2010

"Just Don't Shoot at Me Anymore"

Well, I've been shot at in past times. We were in the Mural community at the time this took place looking for the subject about whom we had been called. We were coming back out of Mural toward Monticello and we got behind this old car, then attempted to stop it. We turned off the lights. We kept trying to get that car to stop, but the driver wouldn't stop. He wasn't going real fast, but just kept driving at a speed of thirty to forty miles an hour. There was another deputy with me, so we followed the car for a long time. I was driving.

We may have followed the car a mile or more, then the other deputy said, "Pass that old car, then stop in front of it."

I said, "Okay." The road was pretty straight there, so I just pulled over and started to pass. But when we were just up beside them, that fellow in that old car emptied his old pistol when he shot nine shots at us right through the side window and windshield. The shots didn't hit either of us.

That's about as close to being shot as I can remember. We went on to arrest three people who were in that old car. One guy took all the blame for the shooting, and then served some time in the penitentiary. But he is back home now, and he comes by and visits me and is as nice as he can be while we talk. He told me several times he is sorry that shooting ever happened. When I was elected as sheriff, he came by and asked me if I held a grudge against him, and I said, "No, but just don't shoot at me anymore." He said he wouldn't. [*Laughter*]

Charles L. Boston, Wayne County, February 13, 2010

FAMILY FEUDS AND KILLINGS

Charles L. Boston: I was off on a Sunday afternoon when I was deputy, and a shooting occurred on Highway 167 about a mile or two out of town. This guy shot and killed two, and when Sheriff Joe got a call, I heard it or they called me, and I went out to where it happened. The guy that did the shooting wound up being killed also. He died from two different gunshots. Let's let Joe Conn, who was sheriff at that time and I was his deputy, tell the rest of the story.

Joseph Conn: Okay, I'll tell it, and this is the way I remember what happened. These fellows who were involved in the shooting were ex-brother-in-laws, and they had feuded for years. Their houses were about thirty feet apart. This one guy, whose son was school principal in Wayne County, went out to pick his daddy up out on a little farm he had. When he pulled up there were so many vehicles there he couldn't get out of the road, so when he pulled up he didn't see his daddy. He'd already called him to tell him he was coming.

When a neighbor pulls up he asked the neighbor, "Have you seen Daddy?"

"Yeah, he's coming up the walk right now."

Well, his ex-brother-in-law was hunkered down over behind a bush and shot the school superintendent's daddy's head off with a shotgun.

The school superintendent was backing back up the road and he saw what happened. He jumped out of his truck with a pistol, shot one time, cocked it again. Then a fellow shoots him in the face, and he runs around and jumps in his truck. He shoots through the window, and as he dives in the next load of shots hits him right in the back of his neck. He shot him five times, then the other man shot him a total of seven times.

I was in the office at that time working on a stolen boat theft case. The fellow that called said, "Get out here quick! So-and-so is going to kill the whole neighborhood." While he was telling me that I hear four shots over the telephone.

I immediately headed out there, but when I got out there I had to go on up to park. Nobody was making any noise. It was just eerie still. When I got out and walked toward the house, I saw the man laying face down in the yard. Then I went by his son's truck, and he's laying in the seat.

I called for some backup help, like coroners and policemen. Well, two policemen come out there, and I held up my hand at them. I said, "Stop, I don't know where he's at if we are looking for so-and-so."

I took a shotgun out of my car, and one of them said, "Here goes a man with a shotgun."

I said, "If that's so-and-so, stop him."

Well, he hollered something at him, and the man that was running yelled back and told him to go to hell. The man was headed for the woods, and I get there and hollered at him, "Stop and lay that shotgun down!" Then as he turns around, I shot him. That was about one hundred feet, and I hit him in the left-hand portion of his stomach. I broke him in two, and when he goes down and picks up his shotgun, I shot him again. Of course, my gun was out of range, and he was shooting at me with a .32 full-choke Ithaca and making flashy noises.

Well, me and one of the policemen went over the fence after him. Then he goes over the fence and we start shooting at him again. Everything gets real quiet, and then we hear this "pop."

He took a .38 out of his pocket and put it right there behind his ear. This one policeman went over the hill with me, and he sticks. Well, we can't find the other one. Well, I start back and go over the fence and he is dead.

I took up my hand radio and started calling to tell them to send a coroner and a detective. Well, Deputy Boston is on his way there. Well, this city policeman comes on and starts going "Blah, blah, blah," and I said, "You shut your so-and-so mouth; I'm running this carnival. And just where in the hell have you been?"

He said, "I was going out yonder to head him off."

I said, "How are you going to head him off out there with him going that way?"

He was running as hard as he could go, and I went and asked a man standing there, "Where did he go?"

"He's hiding behind my house."

The pathologist said, "If shot here, he wouldn't live very long."

Well, he knew it and he used that .38. All he had was a bottle of Valium, his car keys, a pint of Four Roses with a small amount still left in it, maybe three inches. I've still got it.

Charles L. Boston and Joseph Conn, Wayne County, February 13, 2010

Dangerous Chase

Everyday when you make an arrest you are involved in a dangerous situation. A lot of times we are called about a domestic violence situation, or a very volatile situation, and you get there and everybody is against you. All of a sudden they are fighting, and you are in the middle of it, so both of them end up fighting you. In other words, before it is over with they are both mad at you.

I'm in my thirty-eighth year in law service and I've never shot anybody. But I've been in a situation where a guy pulled a gun, then I shot and missed him. I really tried to hit him! But I was glad I didn't hit him because I got so close to him and he threw his gun down in order to surrender to me. I was actually trying to hit him, but I was falling backwards.

I guess the most dangerous situation that I ever got involved in personally was a sort of weird situation. I'm on duty twenty-four hours a day, so everybody has got my phone number. I give my cell phone number out to citizens so that if anybody needs to get in touch with the sheriff, they can call me. Just last night I got called in on a burglary that was in progress. The person that called said he saw this side-by-side ATV, and two boys were trying to break into a building. So I jumped up and ran outside to get in my Tahoe, then started hollering at my deputy, but he was already pulling in right then. See, they'd already called the police, but they still called me.

I had been at the house for a couple of hours, then at 8:00 I decided to go get me a cup of coffee at the Marathon, which is a little Quik Market. I went in there and called the deputies if there was anything going on. Well, I used to go to the Quik Market that was down at Dry Fork which is located on Highway 15 just before you get into Whitesburg. When I started to go there I got to the bypass and then decided I'd just run up to a Quik Market close to Arby's.

Just as I was driving on the bypass, just before closing time at the market, they called and said, "There's a robbery. Somebody has just broken the window out of the Quik Market. They went in and got the cash register."

Well, I went zooming up there and pulled in at the one up here in town. When I pulled in this guy was standing on the outside and was locking the door. I pulled in and said, "You didn't have a robbery?"

He said, "No."

I called and they said, "No, it's the one at Dry Fork."

So if I turned around and had gone to Dry Fork, I'd have pulled up while it was going on. Well, when I got there the police, deputies, and state troopers were there. We were trying to figure out who this guy is, and we go in and got the video. We were watching this video, and this guy goes back toward Isom and Hazard. We could see the car pull out, so we were trying to see the license number and everything, but we couldn't get the license number because it was blurred.

The deputies said, "Well, we'll go down toward Isom and check around."

Everybody was spread out and we were in there trying to get a copy. We had the guy to come, and he was making us a copy of the action. We could see the guy breaking the window out, then go in and begin grabbing stuff. It was a good picture of him, so everybody was trying to figure out who he is. All of a sudden, the other market that I went to, while we were there the guy had drove back by us and goes on up there to the same store that I was at the first time.

We went back up there and we had some deputies still there here in Whitesburg at the other one. So we were out there talking, and I'm standing there beside my Tahoe with the motor running. We were saying, "Well, this guy went by Isom, so he had to come back by while we were standing there."

About that time this car passed by, and it was his car. I said, "There he goes," then jumped in the Tahoe. Well, by the time these policemen all get their cars started, I'm already chasing the robbery suspect. I got up there to Mayking and was trying to catch up with him. I told the others, "I can't tell if he's turning off the road or not." I saw taillights going up, then saw taillights going this way and turning off. I didn't know which car it is, and by the time I caught up with him I could just see the taillights.

The city police officer was driving up behind me, so I said, "You take the one that turned off, and I'm going to get this one going this way."

I went straight ahead to try to catch up with that car, but I was right behind the city policeman's car in pursuit. Well, I turned around since I knew that the city policeman has got him. Well, the way the road goes you've got Pine Creek and Cram Creek that have a crossover road in the hollow. All of us that know the road, you can go up Pine Creek and cross over, then come back out on Cram Creek.

Well, the city policeman was chasing him at Pine Creek, so the first thing I thought about was that I'd go up Cram Creek and try to get up there and block the road at the crossover. While I was going up through there I could hear the pursuit going on. The city policeman called to tell me that the fellow had wrecked and run into the ditch line at the crossover road. So I go on up there and found a place to park my Tahoe to block the road. I didn't block it completely, but the part that I left was right beside a culvert and a rock cut ditch. I said, "If he don't stop and he hits my Tahoe, as he goes around he's going to wreck over here."

So I had my vehicle in position, and when I opened the door and got out with my weapon, here the guy comes. I was standing behind the door, and when he comes up there I am standing beside the police car on the left side. He slows down and began going around the way I wanted him to. He comes back and headed straight at me. I tried to get out of the way, and that car hits the culvert right in front of me, then it stands straight up. I thought it was going to land on me, so I tried to get out of the way and then shoot my weapon, and the shots hit in the bottom of the car that was standing up in front of me.

It turned out that the guy just wrecked and wasn't hurt. I was in a real dangerous situation, but I didn't shoot him because I thought I had everything all figured out. But here comes the guy straight toward me. Anyway, he was on drugs, and was just out of control. He'd go and break in, then just grab stuff. You just never know how dangerous a person is when they are in the condition he was in.

We arrested him, and he is now in the penitentiary.

Danny R. Webb, Letcher County, February 27, 2010

DEVASTATING MULTIPLE MURDERS

The worst death I have dealt with was that of a black boy when I was assistant city police officer. I won't call his name, but he shot his girl-friend, shot her boyfriend, shot and killed her mother, and also killed the fifteen-month-old baby that was the daughter of his girlfriend and her other boyfriend. The state police arrested him, so they tried him in Columbia, not here, for capital murder and asked for the death penalty. Two women had him tried in court, and he got double-life sentence. He is still in the penitentiary, and may be paroled in 2020. He was the girl's boyfriend, but she'd already had a child by someone else. Those killings took place here in Tompkinsville.

That was probably the worst thing I ever had to deal with. It is of interest to say that I went to school with him and we were friends and played ball together. I was coming through the stockyard one day and he flagged me down and said, "Slick, something bad is going to go down here in a few days, but I promise you that you won't be working when it does take place."

At that time I was off on Wednesdays and Thursdays, and that happened on Thursday. However, I got called at home and I went there to the scene. When I got there the trooper had taken him out of the house. The trooper had a machine gun that Sheriff Bev McClendon had laid down. One of the black residents stole it. I get along good with the black people, so the guy that called me told who had the machine gun. I got it and took it back to Bev.

Jerry "Slick" Gee, Monroe County, March 18, 2010

RECENT MURDERS AND SUICIDES IN MONROE COUNTY

The worst murder since I've been sheriff was a double murder. They are to be tried the first of April. This was a queer's murder. The guy accused of doing it was with another man, and that man had taken up

with another man. In my opinion, the suspect they captured went in
and caught them together, then killed both of them.

A month before that we had a killing down here on Second Street where
they were fighting over a bottle of whiskey. One guy took out a knife,
but this other guy took the knife away from him and stabbed him in
the heart.

While me and this state police officer were interviewing him, he
claimed self-defense. That could have been true, but he actually stabbed
the other fellow eight times. He is to be tried for murder.

Two other murders that took place dealt with gunshots. One guy was
a pedestile [pedophile], and that was before they had to release names
of the pedestiles to the sheriff's department. There was this guy from
Burkesville who moved over here and raped a fifteen-year-old girl and
give her drugs. She overdosed and they tried and convicted him of
murder, so he got a life sentence.

I am told that a pedestile cannot be cured. In times past, when a
child molester went to the pen, the prison inmates killed them. They
thought they were perverse and didn't want a perverse around or near
them.

We had a guy that molested this four-year-old girl, who was his niece.
He went to the pen while Joe Petett was sheriff. He was in the pen thirty
days, then went up to the third floor where he was pushed and killed.

So many child molesters have been killed by inmates within recent years. These inmates don't care if you stole your grandma's Social
Security check, murdered somebody, or raped some woman, but if it
comes to molesting a kid they've got this code among themselves that
says child molesters are perverted and should not be around them, so
they killed them. But since they killed so many sex offenders, the latter
are now put in separate wards with other child molesters.

In 2004 Monroe County had the highest rate of suicide among all counties in Kentucky. Most of these people hanged themselves. In one OD
[overdose] instance, me and my deputy Roger Barlow went out to check
out a situation in which a mother had OD'd. When we got there, her
little two-year-old child was lying right up against her. She didn't even

know her mother was dead. Her mother had committed suicide. That was pretty rough for us to deal with.

These suicide victims ranged from seventeen to seventy years old. There was a girl at Fountain Run, a registered nurse, who killed herself. She was twenty-two years old. She wrote a suicide note and put it right by her head. The note said, "I can't live any longer. Forgive me. I love you all, Mom and Daddy."

We had one guy that committed suicide by shooting himself twice. He had a revolver and shot himself, but didn't die right then, so he shot himself again, then had the hammer drawn back in his hand so he could shoot himself again. But he died after the second shot.

Jerry "Slick" Gee, Monroe County, March 18, 2010

Kettle Creek's Dogs

Over in Turkey Neck Bend, "Kettle Creek" Jack had a store that was robbed and took a lot of money off of him. He had the dogs, and if you pulled up to investigate they'd eat you up, so Kettle Creek Jack would come out to calm them down.

I think the robbers got about $20,000 he had hid in his refrigerator, but they didn't get it all. He had about $50,000 hid around the house, according to what his sister told me.

I don't know how they got in the store because of the dogs, but whoever did it had to be somebody that knew had been there before and knew those dogs. A stranger could not get by those dogs, because when I or my deputy pulled up, we'd have to blow our horns. Those dogs would follow us to the doors, bite our tires, and just do everything. I wouldn't get out for nothing. You'd have to shoot them.

Jerry "Slick" Gee, Monroe County, March 18, 2010

Sheriff and Deputy Both Killed

Steve Bennett and a deputy sheriff were killed in the line of duty in 1992. They were serving a warrant probably about six miles from Clay City, Powell County. They had gone to serve a theft warrant on a guy who was from Ohio. The deputy went up to the residence and attempted to arrest this guy. We're not for sure what happened, but the deputy didn't arrest him and came back off the hill and hollered for the sheriff. So the sheriff met up with him just down the road from this residence, and the two of them went back up to the residence to arrest this guy.

Well, this guy was waiting for them, so he ambushed them. When they pulled up to the residence, he was behind them. He shot the sheriff in the back and was shooting at the deputy. He killed both of them right there. That was a pretty bad thing.

The fellow that shot them was arrested and got the death penalty. However, right now he is still alive trying to get appealed. He is in prison at Eddyville, and I think he has just about relinquished all of his appeals as to what he can do. Hopefully, soon or later his sentence will be carried out.

Danny Rogers, Powell County, March 27, 2010

Chapter 10

COLLEAGUES

Stories in this chapter relate to sheriffs' colleagues, both employees (such as deputies and secretaries) and associates (such as magistrates and attorneys). Along with tributes to fallen officers are a number of lighthearted tales, including those describing a constable who always sneaked up on teenagers parked at the local lovers' lane, a one-hundred-year-old honorary deputy sheriff, and the mysterious case of a terrible odor in the office.

MISAPPROPRIATION OF FUNDS

As sheriff, I've been fortunate to knock on wood. Way back in time, I caught one of my girl workers who went to work here. We kind of didn't check her out, and she had bought one of the Louis Vuitton purses; had been unemployed about two years. We thought, "Something ain't right here" when we come up with about $200 short and didn't know where it went.

Jerry "Peanuts" Gaines, Warren County, July 20, 2009

MAGISTRATES AND CONSTABLES

My magistrates are good, so I want to say something good about them. My daddy was a constable and he was also a deputy sheriff. They try to not let constables do a lot in Warren County, because they're not trained. So they work ballgames and things like that, and that's about the extent of their jobs.

Jerry "Peanuts" Gaines, Warren County, July 20, 2009

Constable Cracks Down on Kissing

This story is about a constable, but I never was captured by him! We had a constable in Johnson County back during my teenage days, and even prior to me becoming a teenager, who was known to go where young people would find a place to park. That was back in the early 1960s. He would always try to sneak up on them and try to arrest them for maybe getting out and having a kiss or two. I don't know how to phrase that! But he was notorious in the area for doing that.

William D. Witten, Johnson County, August 7, 2009

Death of a Deputy

One of my two deputies that were killed died accidentally in the line of duty, May 8, 1993. He ended his shift and was on his way home, driving south on U.S. 23. A fellow that had driven three to five miles north on U.S. 23 was seen by the deputy coming up toward him in the wrong lane of traffic. The deputy, whose name was Poster Keene, activated his push lights but couldn't get out of the way of the forthcoming car. The fellow that hit the deputy was driving drunk, and the test showed that he was three times the legal limit. The crash killed the man instantly, as well as my deputy.

Deputy Keene made a humanitarian run for us one time. A few years before he passed away I received a call in the late evening. The caller, who was a friend of mine, told me that he had a friend that was on the kidney transplant list in a hospital in Cincinnati. They had planned to fly him to Cincinnati, but the weather was so bad that the plane couldn't get in, nor get out. They had just a few hours to get him there, so they asked me if I could get him there quickly.

I called Deputy Keene and asked him to take the trip for me, and he was glad to do so. Snow covered the highway, but he got him there within an hour before he was to go through operation. The fellow is living today and getting along fine.

Charles E. "Fuzzy" Keesee, Pike County, August 7, 2009

Laughter at Work

I've got a deputy whose name is Scott Daniels, and he is a very good deputy. I also have two other deputies, Randy Abernathy and Mark

Cromwell. I've got one secretary, Sarah Huckleby, who is in the office and she keeps us all straight. She's a very good secretary, and she's kept me out of jail a lot! [*Laughter*]

Of course, Scott gets out here and gets into some of the funniest things that happen. For example, he had stopped this car one night, then called to tell us where he was at. Of course, we always call and tell where we are at in the county when we call in regarding a traffic stop. When Scott called he said there were two or three in the car with him, so I headed in that direction.

When we got there Scott and this other guy were rolling across the blacktop road. Scott yelled, "Help me, help me, I can't get him to stop!"

Of course, this guy was really drunk and Scott was trying to get him in the car. They started wrestling around, and we got to laughing at Scott over that.

We've had a few things to happen that we can laugh about.

James Pruitt, Cumberland County, August 10, 2009

SECRET SOURCE OF AWFUL SMELL

We had a terrible smell in the courthouse, especially in the sheriff's office. We couldn't figure what in the world it was, and it got worse and got to getting up in the courtroom. You could smell it everywhere. That smell went on for at least a week, but nobody would say a word. Every day in the rest of that courthouse you could smell it, but nobody said a word.

Well, one day I told them there is something wrong here somewhere. So I got a spud bar, a big long steel bar, out of our iron shop here and took it. Our counter was built into that floor, so I got that spud bar and took it with another fellow and raised that counter up. Believe it or not, there were two or three dead rats in a plastic sack under that counter.

Those rats were smelling, and there was a paperclip on the bag. We took that bag out and then used some cans of that perfume stuff you use to get rid of smells. We really put that perfume stuff around in that building, but it took three or four days to get rid of that awful smell.

I know who put that bag of rats under the counter, but I won't say who it was. When some things like that happen, you can figure out who did it. So I knew, but didn't say anything. That was their game, not mine! That was really funny, so I never did get mad about it. I'd already done what I set out to do.

Harold E. Tingle, Shelby County, August 14, 2009

COMMUNITY POLICEMEN

After I became sheriff I don't know what I would have done if it hadn't been for Chuck Reed, a state policeman. He taught me many a trick—how it operated, you know; how to get along with people. Man, I learned a lot from him when I was a deputy. Also a state detective from Spencer County, Claude Owens, worked a lot with me when I was a deputy. Both of them probably kept me out of a lot of trouble.

Anybody can be a policeman, but not everybody can be a deputy sheriff. Of course, the deputy sheriff job is changing a little bit, especially from what it was in my day. You have got to be kind of community organized in order to be a deputy sheriff. About 50 percent of the job is on the criminal side, and if you think it's not being done right, you go to the person to help straighten their act up. A deputy sheriff could always do that pretty easy, especially because they knew what was going on. They always talked to individuals in the community and found out about things.

This didn't always work, but I tried to get deputies when they went home and come to work to go on different routes. They'd get in the car and drive over the county and see people working along the road. It doesn't bother the public when you stop to talk with them. That way they are community policemen. It is getting away a little from that now.

When I was sheriff I tried to preach that to them. Some of them would want to wear those camouflage things and all that kind of stuff. I said, "If you are going to be a deputy sheriff, wear your uniform regardless, so as to look professional."

Harold E. Tingle, Shelby County, August 14, 2009

TIMING

We had one constable when I was deputy sheriff. One day I was in a place in the southern portion of the county and was talking to a lady. After talking to her I left the house through the front door and went to my vehicle. Then she hollered for me, so I went back to the door. That took about two minutes going from the door, to the car, then back to the door.

I got back to the jail, and when I walked up the ramp this guy had broke out of jail and shot and killed that constable. I've always said if that lady hadn't called me back to her house to ask me a little question, I'd have walked right in on that shooting there at the jail.

That fellow who killed the constable took off, but they finally caught him at Ft. Knox. I don't know what they did to him for killing the constable.

I've always said, "I was lucky on that deal."

Harold E. Tingle, Shelby County, August 14, 2009

Honorary Deputy Sheriff

When I took office I did some research, and also invited the public to share some of their sheriff ancestry with me, and get their pictures put up on the wall. That goes back many, many years with former sheriffs, and also in honor of one of the deputy sheriffs/constables, Earl Johnson. Since becoming sheriff, I made him an honorary deputy sheriff to the Todd County Sheriff's Department on his ninety-ninth birthday, December 4, 2007, and gave him the honorary badge number of 7-99. On December 4, 2008, I took him a plaque in honor of his hundredth birthday and changed his badge number to 7-100.

I'm looking forward to December 4 of 2009. He is suffering from health problems, but he's still got his wits! Earl Johnson could truly tell some wonderful stories.

W. D. "Billy" Stokes, Todd County, September 17, 2009

Mean "Trooper"

This is about a trooper that was here for years. He was a good guy and was afraid of nothing. However, he would let the persons he was arresting get by more than anybody else, unless they really pushed him. His name was Joe Webb, and he's dead now.

One time he arrested this drunk man, and the drunk wanted to ride in the front seat for some reason, and back then they didn't have screens, or cages, as I called them.

Well, on the way in this guy was all over the road, and Joe had to stop and check him out. He was DUI, so Joe put him in the back seat. So the guy started fussing on the trooper coming in. Well, the other drunk that was in the front seat with Joe had Joe's trooper hat on the drunk. Joe reached around and smacked him, then the guy said, "You don't talk to us this way."

When we got over there, this guy said to the jailer, "This is the meanest trooper I ever saw in my life."

The jailer said, "You don't have to worry about it. He'll be up there with you in just a few minutes." [*Laughter*]

Kenneth Lee Morris, Butler County, October 11, 2009

DEPUTIES ON NATIONAL AND KENTUCKY LAW ENFORCEMENT MEMORIAL

In the fall of 2002 a lady at Eastern Kentucky who was working with the Kentucky Memorial for Fallen Officers contacted me. She informed me she had a brief article where a Lewis County deputy had been killed by gunfire in 1878 and would forward it to me.

I initiated the arduous task of researching the death of this deputy from long ago. Along the way we discovered that three other deputies had been killed in the line of duty while serving with the Lewis County Sheriff's Office. So I assigned Crystal Dyer, who works in my office, as the lead researcher of this project. The following information outlines the process of having deputies' names that were killed in the line of duty placed on the National and Kentucky Law Enforcement Memorial:

1. All documents pertaining to the fallen officer must be accumulated. The first step required several hours spent at the Lewis County Historical Society and the Lewis County Clerk's Office. Those documents obtained included newspaper articles that included obituary, death certificate (if available), court transcripts, letters from family members, and appointment of deputy sheriff in the court's record book.
2. Contact and review any living relatives.
3. Complete the National Law Enforcement Officers Memorial Fund Application to request an officer's name be added to the memorial. If the fallen officer's name is placed on the national memorial in Washington, DC, the name is automatically placed on the state memorial.
4. Submit all documentation along with the application to the National Law Enforcement Officers Memorial Fund.
5. If at all possible, locate the grave of the fallen officer.

Out of the four officers that were killed in the line of duty, Deputy John R. Ruggles was the most difficult. I could not obtain much information regarding his life. He died at a very young age and had no living relatives to interview. Here are the stories of our four fallen officers:

Deputy Sheriff John R. Ruggles

Deputy Sheriff John R. Ruggles was born October 31, 1854, to the late B. B. and M. J. Ruggles. On January 7, 1878, the Lewis County Sheriff Department and a posse were attempting to arrest the notorious Jesse Underwood Gang in Concord, Kentucky. That gang was known as horse thieves and was wanted in several jurisdictions. Jesse Underwood shot Deputy Sheriff John R. Ruggles in the chest with a handgun. Ruggles was killed instantly. He was twenty-four years old. The reporter of a newspaper article in the *Weekly Maysville Eagle* stated the following: "The deceased was well known to your correspondent as a most worthy young man. He was a native of Vanceburg, single and the main support of a widowed mother."

Deputy John R. Ruggles is buried in the Clarksburg Cemetery off of Ky. 9, near Twelve Trees subdivision. His headstone is very worn, almost to the point of being illegible. His name was placed on the National Law Enforcement Memorial in 2003.

Deputy Sheriff James Owens

Sue Chafin from Daleville, Indiana, contacted me via letter in April 2006. Her grandfather James Owens was a deputy sheriff in Lewis County and killed while on duty. She had several unanswered questions regarding her grandfather's untimely death, but most importantly she wanted him recognized and honored as an officer who was killed in the line of duty. Between her research and mine, we were able to compile all the necessary information to have her grandfather James Owens added to the national and state Law Enforcement Officers Memorial.

Our research revealed that he was born May 16, 1882, in Carter County. He had been working for the Lewis County Sheriff Department for two years and eleven months under the administration of Sheriff J. Smith McGill. Sheriff McGill deputized James Owens to assist in "breaking up" moonshine stills in the county.

Deputy Owens was on duty at the Raccoon School in Emerson, Kentucky, on Election Day, November 6, 1928. The school was utilized as an election poll for voters out in that area. A fight broke out between two teenage boys. Deputy Owens broke up the fight and was escorting one of the boys off the premises when the boy's father came from behind and struck Owens in the back of the head with a wagon iron. Before Owens fell to his death, he turned and fired his pistol at the man who shot him, hitting him in the mouth. Another man allegedly picked up Deputy Owens's weapon and shot Owens in the back.

Deputy James "Jim" Owens was forty-six years old when he passed away. He left behind a wife and seven children. He is buried in the Owens-Lawhorn Cemetery in Smokey Valley, Carter County. His name was placed on the National Law Enforcement Memorial in 2007.

Deputy Sheriff Oza B. Moore

Oza B. Moore was born August 11, 1903, to the late J. M. and Ella Moore. On December 25, 1924, he married Iona Rice, and they had two children, Marcella and Mary. Oza was sworn in as a deputy sheriff with the Lewis County Sheriff's Office, December 16, 1929, under the administration of Sheriff J. Smith McGill.

On August 15, 1931, Deputy Moore was en route from the sheriff's office on his motorcycle to serve papers in Ironton, Ohio. A bus owned by Employees Bus Co. was traveling in front of Oza when it made a sudden stop. Deputy Moore's motorcycle collided with the bus in a curve in the Hanging Rock area.

Oza suffered a fractured skull, and both jaws were also fractured. It is reported he died shortly after being transported to a nearby hospital. A 1930 Kentucky fishing license card found among his personal items identified him.

Marcella Moore Applegate, daughter of Oza Moore, lives in Tollesboro, Kentucky. She did not know much about the details of her father's death. However, she did provide me with a photo of her father. Marcella was three years old, and her sister, Mary, was two when Oza passed away. Marcella instructed me as to the whereabouts of her father's grave. He is buried in the Webster Cemetery, located in Clarksburg.

Oza's name was added to the national and state Law Enforcement Memorial in 2004.

Deputy Sheriff Creed J. Johnson

Creed J. Johnson was born in Letcher County, Kentucky, April 11, 1891. He was the son of Joseph and Susan Potters Johnson. Creed was sworn in as a deputy sheriff under the administration of Sheriff Ray E.

Cooper. He had only held the position for three years when he was shot and killed on Salt Lick Road (Ky. 989), October 31, 1952.

Sheriff Ray Cooper and Deputy Johnson were attempting to take a mentally ill person into custody. The mentally ill subject threatened to kill the first person that tried to take him. Deputy Johnson approached the house to throw a tear gas bomb through the window when he was shot (and killed) with a shotgun blast in the chest.

Creed J. Johnson left behind a wife, Mary Martin Johnson, five sisters, and two brothers. His body was laid to rest in the Waring Cemetery, Garrison, Kentucky. His name was placed on the National Law Enforcement Memorial in 2003.

William D. Lewis, Lewis County, January 13, 2010

Moral: "Keep Your Cruiser Door Shut"

In 2000 my office received a call from a person in Cincinnati, Ohio, stating they had a relative who lived in Lewis County and had not heard from them for several weeks. They requested my office make a welfare visit to see if the relative, who was a criminal, was okay. The area the deputy had to go to was in an extreme rural area of Lewis County.

When the deputy arrived he exited his cruiser, leaving his driver's door open. He knocked on the front door of the residence, which was a single-wide mobile home, with no response. The deputy went around the trailer beating on the exterior walls and could hear a dog barking and running inside the trailer. The deputy contacted me on the radio, and I informed him to make forced entry to check inside the residence. The deputy made entrance and observed a small black dog under a curtain that was hanging from the window onto the floor. The little black dog ran out of the mobile home into the deputy's cruiser and onto the front seat.

The deputy located the person, who had been dead for at least a week, and found a detached arm under the curtain where the dog had been eating on the arm. The deputy could not lure the dog from the front seat of the cruiser, and eventually had to summon the dog warden to remove the animal.

The brother of the victim walked into my office a week later to get some information regarding his brother. Under his right arm he was carrying a little black dog. I think this is where the *Psycho* music starts, i.e., mental processing.

The moral of this story is to keep your cruiser door shut.

William D. Lewis, Lewis County, January 13, 2010

CHANGING TIMES

There's a lot of things that sheriffs deal with that are dangerous if you do your job. When I was sheriff I usually took care of things myself, or maybe one deputy, but nowadays sheriffs take two or three others with them. The only time I ever called a state police officer to help me was when I really needed them. But now they call them on lots of little things, but they seldom come anymore.

What money I made [was used] to buy my cars and pay for them—I had to personally buy three cars. The state didn't furnish them then, and the county didn't furnish them. I paid for them out of arrest fees and tax money I collected. I also had one deputy that I paid for out of the fees I took in. My wife worked free. That's one reason why we had to work day and night. But now the sheriffs get new cars and new trucks and everything.

My deputies paid their own wages, but they really worked. I had one deputy that worked day and night on weekends, and he worked for no extra money. He liked it, and it was in his blood, as his grandpa had been a lawman. But in contemporary times, if they have to work more than eight hours, they have to have overtime, or most do.

Glynn Mann, Clinton County, February 8, 2010

"OLD FLAMES"

I didn't know too much about the law business, so I rode around with the state police. If people they were after tried to run off and leave us, I was like the old troopers so I'd want to shoot their tires down. The state policemen I was with would beg me not to do that.

Well, sometimes we'd be together after a four-wheeler or something and I'd be off the road. When that happened, and that four-wheeler would be trying to run off and leave me, I never did want to shoot anyone, but I'd shoot up in the air.

Many times state trooper George Cravens called my old .357 Magnum Old Flames. I didn't know this, but he told my wife, said, "Glynn would pull out Old Flames, fire it, and there would be a streak of fire about eighteen inches wide come out of that weapon!"

But I was shooting up in the air. He thought I was shooting at the person I was chasing.

Selbert Byers, an old-time deputy, didn't know I had a bulletproof vest. He advised me to do like he did. He told me that when he went after a bad person, he would put a steel plow point over his heart.

Glynn Mann, Clinton County, February 8, 2010

Rowdy Teens

I got along really good with the state police officers, and Judge Larry Hatfield also got along well with them. Virtually every night the state police would come to get me to ride with them a little while. We would go out on Highway 90 and write three or four speeding tickets, then patrol the county. There were posted signs that had messages intended for rowdy teenagers, such as "No Trespassing." I got me a ladder one time and put a "No Trespassing" sign up in a tree, and these teenagers climbed up there and tore it down! They were primarily teenage boys.

I gave them permission to go around the fields with their four-wheelers, but they'd go right down through the middle and would tear up a man's hay and everything. That's the reason we ran them out. I didn't hold it against them. Actually, some of the most rowdy boys went on to become outstanding citizens.

Glynn Mann, Clinton County, February 8, 2010

Colleagues and Friends

While I was sheriff many state police officers and others working "undercover" would call me on the police radio and ask me to ride with them. After I was out of office I visited the State Fair and one of the largest air shows. The state officers and families had front-row seats on the belvedere overlooking the Ohio River.

As I walked by them a state police sergeant with the Bowling Green Drug Task Force saw me and recognized me. When that happened he yelled out to the gateman, "Let that fellow in here." He knew me from many months past.

I was friends with defense and prosecuting attorneys. One day prosecuting attorney David Cross said to me, "Upstairs in the courtroom we were enemies, but back downstairs we were friends!"

Glynn Mann, Clinton County, February 8, 2010

Deputy Baldy a Character

I remember things about deputies more than I do about other sheriffs. Three years after I became a Kentucky State Police officer I came to Letcher County from Knott County in 1975. The sheriff at that time had a deputy sheriff, and we called him Baldy, but his real name was George Davis, if I remember correctly. He was a character. When he arrested somebody, he'd say, "Now, you are under arrest. I told you, so get in that car." He'd always say, "I told you!"

We all got to know him, and at that time you didn't have to have any training. You could just take anybody and make them a deputy, and they'd go out and work. So a lot of them didn't have the training, the expertise, and didn't know the law. They would arrest somebody and it was not even against the law what that person had done.

Baldy was just a character, and one day he arrested this guy and he hit him with his pistol on the side of the head. He didn't shoot him, just hit him with his pistol. The guy he hit filed a civil rights violation against him in civil court. The FBI had to investigate that case. I knew the FBI agent, and I was working on the road sitting there when the FBI agent pulled up beside me. He asked me, "Do you know this George Davis?"

At first I didn't recognize the name, because I always called him Baldy. But after I realized who it was I said, "Oh, yeah, he is a deputy."

The FBI agent then said, "I've got this complaint from a guy that said he hit him with his gun. What kind of fellow is he?"

I said, "He is just a character, but he will tell you the truth."

Well, the FBI agent went over to Whitesburg. A few hours later I was back up there at the edge of the county when the FBI agent come by and was shaking his head. He said, "I went down there and talked to that deputy. I asked him, 'Why did you hit him with your gun?'

"He said, 'Because that's the only damn thing I had to hit him with.'" [*Laughter*]

Danny R. Webb, Letcher County, February 27, 2010

Good and Bad Times

When I first started as sheriff in 1999 I had two cars, three deputies, one dispatcher, and one bookkeeper. Now I have nineteen deputies, seven dispatchers who work twenty-four hours, seven days a week, and now I have thirteen cars, some of which are on grants. I received my first grant from the federal Grant Administration Division in 1999 or 2000 to employ school resource officers, and I was allowed one at the high school and one at the middle school. The resource officers' job was to protect the schools by keeping strangers and drug dealers away, break up fights, control the hallways and parking lots, and things like that. The school furnished the car and I furnished the equipment like radios, lights, and things like that.

I applied for a second grant in three years and received $157,000. The schools had to pay for the rotation year, which was the fourth year. I then applied again and got the same grant again. The schools were pleased in getting another grant, so they decided to include more schools. I had a middle school and high school, and also Joe Harrison Elementary School and one at Gamaliel. The Tompkinsville Elementary and Joe Harrison Carter Elementary split their days up.

Things worked out pretty good, but at times it got hard when money got tight with the schools, as well as my office and other offices. So I'm now down to only one resource officer because of the financial situation in the sheriff's office and the department of schools.

Jerry "Slick" Gee, Monroe County, March 18, 2010

BIOGRAPHIES OF STORYTELLERS

Wayne Agent

Wayne Agent was born in Marion, Crittenden County, in 1966. He graduated from Crittenden County High School in 1984. He and his wife, Melissa, have one daughter, Leana (Agent) Riley. Wayne graduated from the Police Academy in Richmond, Kentucky, in 1993, and was elected as Crittenden County Sheriff in November 1998. He served as sheriff for eleven years.

Mike Armstrong

Mike Armstrong took office in 1990, and is a highly respected public servant still actively pursuing his job. Many years before Mike became sheriff, his father was a deputy sheriff in Shelby County.

Larry L. Bennett

Larry L. Bennett was born in Russell County, December 1, 1950, to Robert L. and Irene Shearer Bennett. He has one sister, Sue Ann Collins, and three brothers, Darris, Bruce, and Robert. Larry has lived in Russell County all his life except for four years he served as a Kentucky state trooper in Monroe County. He was first elected as sheriff of Russell County in November 1989 and took office on January 1, 1990. At the end of his present term, he will have served twenty-one years as sheriff.

Patrick Boggs

Patrick Boggs was a deputy sheriff in Mason County for nine years before being elected sheriff in 2006, an office through which he provides devoted service to residents of Mason County. He attended Kentucky Wesleyan College. His wife is a pharmacist.

Charles L. Boston

Charles L. Boston, known as Charlie, was born in the Mill Springs community, Wayne County, December 3, 1946. His parents were Ola Jackson Boston and Thelma (Lovell) Boston, who had seven sons and six daughters. Charlie graduated from Wayne County High School in 1965. Four years later he married Phyllis Baird, a native of Jellico, Tennessee. Their daughter, Charlene, married Robert E. Ellis, a police officer for ten years, and they have a son, age thirteen.

Charlie was hired in 1975 as a deputy to Sheriff Hershel Henniger, and remained in this position for two and a half years. He also served as a deputy under sheriffs Joe

Conn (early 1980s) and Jim Hill (late 1980s). He was elected sheriff in 2006 and is currently serving the fourth year of his term. As a devoted servant of Wayne County citizens, he was reelected in 2010.

Across the years Sheriff Boston has served on the Monticello/Wayne County Fair Board of Directors; as president of the Wayne County Saddle Club; as a board member of Lake Cumberland Drug Task Force; and as a member of Monticello/Wayne County 911 Board. He is a current member of the Sheriffs' Association.

Keith Cain

Keith Cain, son of Laymond and Lottie Cain, was born in 1952. He is a military veteran with service in the USMC, which included a tour of duty in Vietnam. He has served continuously with the Daviess County Sheriff's Office since 1974. His past duties include patrol, investigations, narcotics, and chief deputy. He was elected sheriff in 1999 and is currently serving his third term.

Sheriff Cain received a bachelor of arts degree in criminal justice from Kentucky Wesleyan College and a master of arts degree in education from Western Kentucky University. He is a graduate both of the FBI National Academy (156th session) and the National Sheriffs' Institute. He also serves on the board of directors of the National Sheriffs' Association, where he chairs the association's Drug Enforcement Committee. Sheriff Cain is an adjunct faculty member of the Owensboro Community and Technical College, and is a Kentucky Law Enforcement Council–certified law enforcement instructor. He also serves as chair of the council, a body responsible for all police training in Kentucky. He has twice been the recipient of the Governor's Award for Outstanding Contribution to Kentucky Law Enforcement, in 2004 and 2008.

Joseph Conn

Joseph Conn is a former sheriff of Wayne County. His service ended during the early 1980s.

James Ralph Curry

James Ralph Curry was born March 3, 1945, to Lester and Hazel (Burton) Curry. He grew up in Columbia in Adair County. He has been married for forty-six years to the former Treva Polston. They have one child, Jada, who married Eric Coomer, and they have one child, Ethan. He presently lives on a farm in Adair County, and enjoys farming, fishing, and activities at Bethany Baptist Church. He served as a deputy for eight years and as sheriff for thirteen years. He is looking forward to retiring this year and spending more time with his grandson.

Qulin K. Escue

Qulin K. Escue was born February 22, 1950, to James L. and Annie Escue, Jackson, Madison County, Tennessee. Qulin and six of his seven brothers and two sisters were all born at home. The Escue family moved to Grayson County, Kentucky, and Qulin graduated from Caneyville High School in 1970. He and his first wife were the parents of sons Darrin and Jamie and daughter Kimberly K., who died January 18, 1993, as the result of a vehicle accident. Qulin and his current wife, Charlotte, are the parents of Keith. They have nine grandchildren, four girls and five boys.

He was elected sheriff in 1981 and served in this capacity until 1999. After taking office he attended Kentucky State Police Training for two weeks. In 1999 he was employed by Grayson County as an assistant road foreman and presently works for the City of Leitchfield.

Jerry "Peanuts" Gaines
Jerry Gaines, known nationally as Peanuts, is a Warren County native, born June 28, 1937. A military veteran, he served as a magistrate before being elected sheriff for the first time in 1977. He has been elected as sheriff seven times, and is known as a hands-on sheriff making a beneficial difference in Warren County. Sheriff Gaines has served in numerous state, regional, and nationwide organizations—as president, treasurer, sergeant at arms, and chairman. He also created the Sheriff's Prevention Partnership, which focuses on antidrug and antiviolence initiatives.

Sheriff Peanuts Gaines received the Buford Pusser Law Enforcement Officer of the Year Award in 2006, was recognized as Kentucky's Sheriff of the Year in 1987, and was the first sheriff in Kentucky to be presented the Samuel McDowell Jr. Award by the U.S. Marshal Service. He was selected by the National Sheriffs' Association as winner of the 2010 Ferris E. Lucas Award for Sheriff of the Year, thanks to his outstanding contributions to the office of sheriff on the local, state, and national levels. He was the National Sheriffs' Association president in 2000–2001.

Jerry "Slick" Gee
Slick Gee served as a Tompkinsville police officer for twenty-four years, then served as assistant commonwealth detective until 1997, at which time he decided to run for sheriff of Monroe County. He was elected and began service as sheriff in 1998, and was reelected two times. He retired at the end on 2010. His wife, Paula B. Gee, is a teacher.

LeeRoy Hardin
LeeRoy Hardin attended the academy at Eastern Kentucky University, graduating in 1989. He began service as a deputy on January 16, 1990, and continued in that capacity for thirteen years. He was elected as Boyle County sheriff in the fall of 2003, then again four years later. He decided to leave the sheriff's office on January 1, 2010. Numerous county residents are trying to persuade him to run for the office again, but he declines. LeeRoy and his wife own and operate a store in Junction City.

Boston B. Hensley Jr.
Boston B. Hensley Jr., a lifelong resident of Hart County, Kentucky, was born on March 15, 1955. He began serving as Hart County sheriff in 2005. Prior to becoming sheriff Boston was a Kentucky state trooper for twenty years. Before that he was a police officer for the City of Horse Cave. He received a bachelor of science degree in police administration from Eastern Kentucky University in 1978.

Sheriff Hensley has been dedicated to protecting the citizens of Hart County by providing qualified, well-trained personnel. His focus has been on waging an effective battle against illegal drugs, securing over one hundred drug arrests during his first year in office.

Barney Jones

Barney Jones was born at home on June 24, 1942, in a little farmhouse in Warren County. He is the fifth-generation owner of the farm and house. He is the only child of Beatrice (Dossey) Jones and Virgil Barney Jones. He married Betty Sue Johnson, and they have three children, six grandchildren, and one great-grandchild.

Barney attended North Warren Elementary School and High School in Smiths Grove, graduating from the latter in 1960. He worked as a farmer and in an industry, then served as deputy sheriff from 1984 to 1988, when Gale Wood was sheriff. He was elected sheriff in 1989 and served in that capacity through 2006.

Charles E. "Fuzzy" Keesee

Presently the longest-serving sheriff in the history of the commonwealth, Charles E. "Fuzzy" Keesee was born on September 9, 1927, in Belfry, Kentucky. His parents, Della Mae Myers, a housewife, and Moss Keesee, a businessman, had nine children including Fuzzy.

Fuzzy's dedication to hard work began at the age of eleven, when he worked in the family grocery store. After graduating from Belfry High School, where he was on the basketball team, in 1946, he worked different jobs, including hauling coal and working a bread route. It was during this time that Fuzzy met his first wife, Evelyn Hatfield, whom he married in December 1947; they became the parents of one daughter, Mildred. Fuzzy was drafted into the army in May 1953, serving two years in the Medical Corps. He was stationed in El Paso, Texas, for a short period and was then sent overseas to Paris. After being discharged in May 1955, Fuzzy moved to Louisville, Kentucky, and worked for B. F. Goodrich Chemical.

The sheriff's department became a part of Fuzzy's history when his father was elected in January 1958. When the call came from his father asking him to work at the Pike County Sheriff's Department, Fuzzy was eager to return to his roots and serve the people he knew best. After his father, Moss, served his first term, Fuzzy ran for office and succeeded him, taking office in January 1962.

In earlier years sheriffs could not succeed themselves in office. Thus Fuzzy held various jobs between terms. It wasn't until a new law was passed in 1984 that he was able to run for an unlimited amount of terms. Since then Fuzzy has been working hard to keep the Pike County Sheriff's Department at a professional level of law enforcement.

In 1992, after over forty years of marriage, Fuzzy's wife, Evelyn, passed away. Fuzzy is now married to Edith Dotson Maness and they share two daughters from Edith's previous marriage.

Currently serving his ninth term as Pike County sheriff, Fuzzy has brought many improvements and advancements to the department, such as requiring all paid deputies to receive training at the Police Academy and to undergo forty hours of continuing training each year. Fuzzy also brought professionalism to the department through providing official uniforms for his officers. He implemented a communication system that includes radios, in-car cameras, and laptops, which were not previously available in the police cars.

Fuzzy has also taken part in many activities, both statewide and nationally. He has served on the Kentucky Sheriffs' Association Board of Directors many times, and held the title of president for one term. He also served on the Rules and Regulations Committee for the National Sheriffs' Association.

Fuzzy and his wife now reside in Phelps, Kentucky.

Charles Lee "Chuck" Korzenborn

Sheriff Charles Lee "Chuck" Korzenborn was born December 11, 1938. He and his wife, Ruth Green, have two children, Chuck J. and Rebecca Agner, and four grandchildren. After graduating from Beechwood High School in Fort Mitchell, he served in the U.S. Army, then attended the University of Kentucky Northern Extension Center. He was elected Kenton County sheriff in 1999. Since taking office Sheriff Korzenborn has worked devotedly to help various county offices, departments, and innovative programs, and has made the sheriff's department more visible to Kenton County's cities and communities. Across the years he completed various professional training programs, and received leadership and service awards from the FBI and U.S. Marshal Service. Sheriff Korzenborn's professional training and associations include the FBI Joint Terrorism Task Force, U.S. Attorney's Antiterrorism Task Force, Kentucky Sheriffs' Association (presently he is secretary and treasurer), National Sheriffs' Association, F.O.P. Kenton County Lodge #20, and the Northern Kentucky Police Chiefs' Association. He has received awards from numerous U.S. and Kentucky law enforcement agencies, is a member of numerous local clubs and organizations, and has received many letters of appreciation from various law enforcement agencies in Kentucky.

Chuck is now running for his fourth term as Kenton County sheriff.

William D. Lewis

Sheriff William D. Lewis is a native of Carter County but moved to Lewis County in 1971 when assigned there as a Kentucky State Police trooper. He earned a bachelor's degree in police administration at Eastern Kentucky University in 1977, and a master's degree in criminal justice, also from Eastern, in 1985. Before that, he served in the U.S. Army as a paratrooper, Eighty-second Airborne Division, and in combat duty in the Dominican Republic and in Vietnam, 1966–67.

He worked for the Kentucky State Police for numerous years, serving as trooper, detective, sergeant, lieutenant, captain (post commander), and as lieutenant colonel (director of field operations). Upon retirement from these significant duties, he was elected sheriff in 1998, began service in 1999, and continues in this capacity. A Republican, he was Lewis County campaign chairman for George W. Bush in 2000.

Sheriff Lewis is a graduate of the FBI National Academy, Quantico, Virginia; the Southern Police Institute, Louisville; and the Kentucky State Police Academy, Frankfort. He was given the KSP's Meritorious Service Award in 1981, and has served as an instructor at both Marshall University, Huntington, West Virginia, and Maysville Community College, Maysville, Kentucky.

A resident of Tollesboro, Lewis County, Bill Lewis is married and has four children and nine grandchildren.

It is worthy of mention that most of the personal stories Sheriff Lewis provided for inclusion in this book were also described in news articles published in the *Lewis County Herald*. Sheriff Lewis is well known for his masterful services in caring for and helping local people.

Glynn Mann

Glynn Mann was born during the Great Depression, on November 3, 1929, at Creelsboro, Kentucky, which is in Russell County, to Leo R. Mann and Ethyl Summers, both Russell Countians. His family was poor during his early childhood, though his father was a stock trader, a farmer, and also a constable. Glynn graduated from Clinton County High School in 1945. He enrolled in Travecca Nazarene College in Nashville, Tennessee, when he was only fifteen, staying there for a year and a half. During that time he got a job with Western Union Telegraph Company delivering telegrams—the bicycle he rode for the job was the first he had ever owned

Glynn subsequently worked for various companies in Indiana, then in a line crew for Western Union Telegraph Company out of Atlanta, Georgia, serving in nine states as a line and cable foreman for ten years. He also spent two years in the army as a line and cable instructor at Ft. Gordon, Georgia, and one year in Korea as an infantry wireman. He was discharged from military service as a sergeant. He then returned to Clinton County, where he worked full-time as a mail carrier for thirty years.

Glynn began service as sheriff in 1989. After his term as sheriff expired, he chose not to seek reelection.

He and his wife, Shirley, have three children, two grandchildren, and two great-grandchildren.

Carl E. Meece

Carl E. Meece was elected constable in 1969, serving in that capacity for three or four months before being hired as deputy. After four years of service as a deputy, he ran for sheriff and was elected, 1974. After his first term as sheriff, he ran for the county judge executive's office and won, becoming the first person in Casey County ever to hold that office. He was elected to serve three additional terms as sheriff.

Carl retired as sheriff in January 1994. All total, he served four years as constable and deputy, four terms as sheriff, and one term as judge, his service time amounting to twenty-four years.

Kenneth Lee Morris

The oldest of six sons born to Ellis "Bub" Morris and Mabel Smith Morris, Kenneth Lee Morris was born October 2, 1945, in Butler County. He earned his GED in Butler County, then completed training at the Kentucky Sheriffs' Academy in December 1989. Soon thereafter he attended the FBI Training Center, Quantico, Virginia, and received in-service training at the Kentucky Law Enforcement Training Center, Richmond, Kentucky. He also attended several classes with the National Sheriffs' Association, the Kentucky State Police, and the Kentucky Sheriffs' Association.

He served as a deputy sheriff from August 1, 1976, through August 10, 1979. After that, Kenneth was Butler County magistrate in District 5 from January 1, 1986, through December 29, 1989. Kenneth won the sheriff's office race in December 1989 and became sheriff January 1, 1990. He served in this capacity through December 31, 2006. Throughout his years of service Morris won several awards, including Deputy of the Year, Sheriff of the Year (1991), and two Meritorious Achievement awards.

Kenneth Lee Morris has one son, Steven L. Morris, who is currently a deputy sheriff in Warren County.

James Pruitt

Known as Goody, James Pruitt began serving as sheriff in Cumberland County in 1990, but prior to that he was a deputy sheriff for one year and a city police officer for three years. He was born in Cumberland County, February 24, 1950. His father was Richard Herman "Doc" Pruitt, and his mother was Robbie (Lee) Pruitt, both of whom are deceased.

He has four children, Jimmy, Angela, Chad, and Patrick, and nine grandchildren. He enjoys restoring old cars and trucks in his spare time.

Danny Rogers

Danny Rogers, Powell County native, was elected sheriff in 2006 and began service in 2007. Before becoming sheriff, he was a police officer for seventeen years.

John E. Shipp

John E. Shipp is a native of Campbellsville, Taylor County, born November 21, 1948. He is a military veteran, having served his country for eight years in Vietnam and other countries. He retired from the Kentucky State Police in 1995 after serving as a road trooper, detective, and in the governor security division. John was appointed Taylor County sheriff in June 1995, after the resignation of the sitting sheriff. Subsequently, he won a special election in November 1995, and has been sheriff to the present day.

John "Tuffy" Snedegar

John "Tuffy" Snedegar was born August 5, 1949, in Bath County, to Cynthia Robinson and Osbin "Hick" Snedegar. He went to school in Owingsville, Bath County, graduating from high school in 1969.

He explains his nickname thus: "When I was born my granddaddy called me Tuffy, before I even had a real name given to me by Mom and Dad. Granddaddy said, 'There lays Tuffy.' That name he gave me has stayed with me. My banking checks and other things use Tuffy as my real name. I'd say that more than three-fourths of Bath County residents don't know my real name. I'm just known as Tuffy. . . . [My granddaddy] was the city judge here in Owingsville, so that's probably why I wanted to get involved in law enforcement."

Tuffy was elected sheriff of Bath County in 2008.

W. D. "Billy" Stokes

At age twenty-one, Billy Stokes started serving in various law enforcement positions in Todd County, including special deputy, constable, city police officer, and in the sheriff's office in various capacities.

Harold E. Tingle

Harold E. Tingle was born in Finchville, Shelby County, went to grade school there, then graduated from high school in Simpsonville in 1955. He never went to college, although he did have some scholarship offers to play basketball, choosing instead to stay home and farm. His family moved from Finchville to Chestnut Grove in December 1954.

Harold served as deputy sheriff for seven years. First elected sheriff in 1989, he served in that capacity for thirteen years.

Danny R. Webb

Danny R. Webb was born September 16, 1948, at the home of his parents in the Letcher County community of Whitco. He lived in Whitco until 1998, when he purchased an old house in Whitesburg that he is still renovating. Danny graduated from Whitesburg High School in 1966, then earned a bachelor of science degree from Eastern Kentucky University during his adult years, graduating in 1998. Much of his college work was done while serving as a state trooper.

Sheriff Webb's wife is Sharon (Necessary) Webb, and they have three sons: Danny, an English teacher at the Whitesburg Community College; Justin, who works for an advertising firm in Lexington; and Jody, who works at Whitaker Bank in Whitesburg. Danny and Sharon have two grandchildren, Maggie and Daniel.

Danny worked as a state trooper and in related positions for thirty years, then was elected sheriff and began his dedicated service in that capacity in 2003.

William D. Witten

William D. Witten was born in Paintsville, grew up in Johnson County, and graduated from Flat Gap High School in 1966. His family has always been involved in politics, starting with an uncle who served as commissioner from 1962 until 1970. His father became county judge in 1976. William credits this family history with playing a major part in his interest in becoming a public servant.

He was elected sheriff in 1998, then began service in 1999. In 2001, while still in his first term, he was honored by the Kentucky Sheriffs' Association as Kentucky's Sheriff of the Year.

He and his wife, Sharon, have one son and two grandchildren. He is a member of the local Masonic Lodge and also a Shriner.

Wayne "Tiny" Wright

Wayne "Tiny" Wright is a lifelong resident of Woodford County and graduated from Woodford County High School. The oldest child of Billy and Wanda McDonald Wright, he has a brother, David, and a sister-in-law, Tai. He has been married to Tracie Reynolds Wright for twenty-four years. They have a daughter, Brittany, who is nineteen and a sophomore at Midway College.

He began his law enforcement career in 1985 as a police officer with the Versailles Police Department under Chief Robert Y. Brown. He graduated from the police academy at Eastern Kentucky University in August 1985. He was designated as a field training officer while with the Versailles Police Department, working with young recruits.

In 1995 Tiny accepted a position with the Woodford County Sheriff's Office, and in 2006 he was elected sheriff of Woodford County, beginning his term in January 2007. He ran for a second term in 2010 and was reelected. Tiny explains: "After I began working at the sheriff's office, I knew that this was my future path; a dream of a young boy playing cops and robbers has truly turned into a love for this badge pinned to my shirt."